John James Lias

The second epistle to the Corinthians

with notes, map and introduction

John James Lias

The second epistle to the Corinthians
with notes, map and introduction

ISBN/EAN: 9783337728977

Printed in Europe, USA, Canada, Australia, Japan

Cover: Foto ©Lupo / pixelio.de

More available books at **www.hansebooks.com**

The Cambridge Bible for Schools and Colleges.

GENERAL EDITOR:—J. J. S. PEROWNE, D.D.,
DEAN OF PETERBOROUGH.

THE SECOND EPISTLE TO THE

CORINTHIANS,

WITH NOTES, MAP AND INTRODUCTION

BY

THE REV. J. J. LIAS, M.A.,
VICAR OF ST EDWARD, CAMBRIDGE.

EDITED FOR THE SYNDICS OF THE UNIVERSITY PRESS.

Cambridge:
AT THE UNIVERSITY PRESS.
1890

PREFACE
BY THE GENERAL EDITOR.

THE General Editor of *The Cambridge Bible for Schools* thinks it right to say that he does not hold himself responsible either for the interpretation of particular passages which the Editors of the several Books have adopted, or for any opinion on points of doctrine that they may have expressed. In the New Testament more especially questions arise of the deepest theological import, on which the ablest and most conscientious interpreters have differed and always will differ. His aim has been in all such cases to leave each Contributor to the unfettered exercise of his own judgment, only taking care that mere controversy should as far as possible be avoided. He has contented himself chiefly with a careful revision of the notes, with pointing out omissions, with

PREFACE.

suggesting occasionally a reconsideration of some question, or a fuller treatment of difficult passages, and the like.

Beyond this he has not attempted to interfere, feeling it better that each Commentary should have its own individual character, and being convinced that freshness and variety of treatment are more than a compensation for any lack of uniformity in the Series.

Deanery, Peterborough.

CONTENTS.

I. INTRODUCTION.   PAGES

   Chapter I. Date, Place of Writing, Character and Genuineness of the Epistle .. ..   7—11

   NOTE A. On the Undesigned Coincidences between the Acts of the Apostles, the First and Second Epistles to the Corinthians.................   11—13

   NOTE B. On the Thorn in the Flesh ....   13—18

   NOTE C. On the English Versions of the New Testament   18

   Chapter II. Analysis of the Epistle.

   PART I. St Paul's Principles of Action ....   19—21

   PART II. The Collection for the poor Saints at Jerusalem   21

   PART III. St Paul's Vindication of his Apostolic authority..   21—23

II. TEXT AND NOTES ....   25—138

III. General Index   139

IV. Index of Words and Phrases explained   140

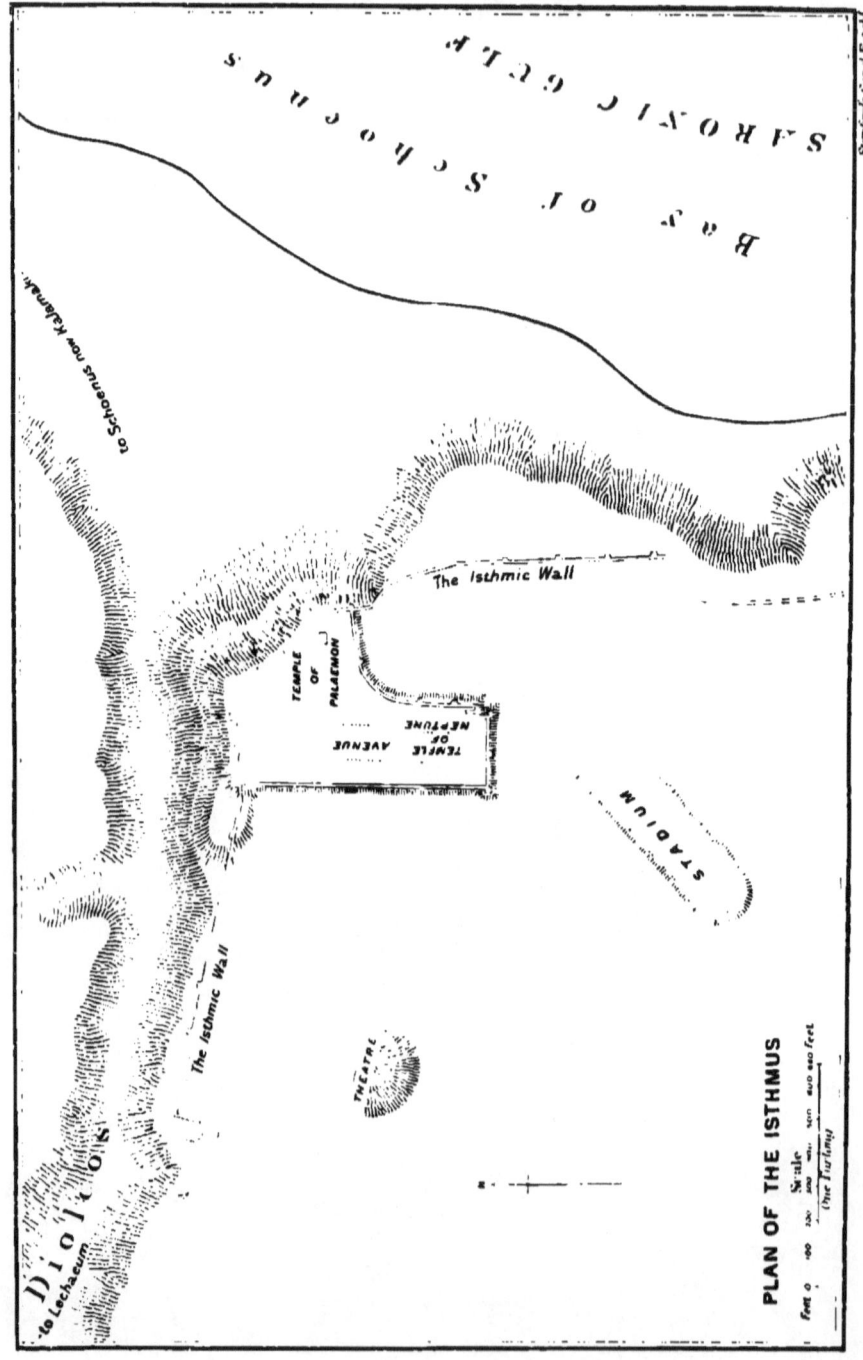

INTRODUCTION.

CHAPTER I.

DATE, PLACE OF WRITING, CHARACTER AND GENUINENESS
OF THE EPISTLE.

1. *Date and place of writing.* The Second Epistle to the Corinthians was written not long after the First. We read that St Paul had resolved to visit Macedonia and Achaia, but that he delayed the fulfilment of his purpose for a while, sending two of his disciples, Timotheus and Erastus, to announce his intention and to prepare for his arrival[1]. Directly after the tumult at Ephesus, and possibly to a certain extent in consequence of it, he set out on his journey. He arrived at Troas, and expected there to have met Titus, who had probably been sent to Corinth in charge of the first Epistle[2]. The non-arrival of Titus filled him with anxiety[3]. He found it impossible to take advantage of the opportunity there afforded him of preaching the Gospel with success, and hurried on to Philippi, where it seems probable the long-expected tidings at last reached him, and filled his heart with conflicting feelings of joy and disappointment. The nature of Titus' report was such that, although much encouraged by what he heard, he felt it necessary to send at once another letter of expostulation, that all might be peace and concord at his arrival[4]. This letter was probably written at Thessalonica, in the summer of the year 57. It is not

[1] Acts xix. 21, 22; 1 Cor. xvi. 8.
[2] See Introduction to First Epistle, p. 14.
[3] Ch. ii. 12, 13.   [4] Ch. x. 2, xii. 20, 21, xiii. 2, 10.

probable that it was written at Philippi, as some have supposed, because St Paul speaks of the liberality of the *Churches* of Macedonia[1], as though he had visited more than one of them, whereas Philippi would be the first in his way from Asia.

2. *Character and contents of the Epistle.* It has been universally remarked that the individuality of the Apostle is more vividly displayed in this Epistle than in any other. Human weakness, spiritual strength, the deepest tenderness of affection, wounded feeling, sternness, irony, rebuke, impassioned self-vindication, humility, a just self-respect, zeal for the welfare of the weak and suffering, as well as for the progress of the Church of Christ, and for the spiritual advancement of its members, are all displayed by turns in the course of his appeal, and are bound together by the golden cord of an absolute self-renunciation dictated by love to God and man. The Epistle may be divided into three main portions. The first, consisting of the first seven chapters, is devoted to an exposition of St Paul's principles of action in his dealings with his converts. The second, contained in chapters viii. and ix., treats of the collection for the poor saints at Jerusalem. The third, which embraces the whole of the rest of the Epistle, is an animated vindication of his Apostolic authority. There is no particular system in this outpouring of the Apostle's heart. The variety of feelings described above display themselves in the most rapid alternation. But its one object is to place himself on such terms with the Corinthian Church before his arrival, that he might be spared the necessity of exercising discipline when he came.

The unsystematic character of the Epistle is due to the fact that the opposition to St Paul was to so large an extent personal. A large portion of the Corinthian community had been completely won over by his first Epistle[2]. The question at least of the incestuous person had been settled according to his desires by the decisive action of the majority[3]. But there still remained an uneasy feeling of distrust, aggravated by the taunts and insinuations of St Paul's opponents, which it seemed necessary

---

[1] Ch. viii. 1. Ch. ix. 2.   [2] Ch. ii. 14, vii. 6, 7.
[3] Ch. ii. 6.

to dissipate. The Apostle's disposition was represented as changeable and his conduct based upon no settled principles[1]. He was inclined to unnecessary self-laudation[2]. He was assuming an authority to which he had no right[3]. He was a traitor to his country and a renegade from his faith[4]. He was no true minister of Christ at all[5], although he ventured to place himself on a level with those who were[6]. The violence of these accusations and the immense effect they produced, is shewn by the fact that two centuries afterwards they were repeated by the Judaizing party, which by that time had severed itself from the Church. In the Ebionitish writings which have come down to us we find similar imputations cast upon St Paul, and even when professedly assailing Simon Magus, occasional covert attacks are made upon the Apostle's person and doctrine[7].

There can be no question therefore of the necessity of making some reply, and the present Epistle proved so much to the purpose that we find no trace of any subsequent serious resistance to St Paul's claims, at least within the pale of the Christian community. The Corinthian Church, as we learn from the Epistle of Clement, written shortly after the Apostle's death, was still given to faction, but the memory of its founder was held in affectionate and unquestioning veneration. It is therefore most important to notice the way in which St Paul stilled the clamours of his adversaries. He begins by enlisting their sympathies with him in the sufferings he had undergone on behalf of the faith at Ephesus[8]. He proceeds to clear himself from the charge of fickleness[9]. He next explains the object he had in view in delaying his visit, and appeals to facts to shew the deep interest he took in the Corinthian Church[10]

---

[1] Ch. i. 15—20.
[2] Ch. iii. 1, v. 12, x. 8.
[3] Ch. x. 14.
[4] Ch. xi. 22.
[5] Ch. x. 7, xi. 23.
[6] Ch. xi. 5, xii. 11.
[7] The Clementine Recognitions, and still more the Clementine Homilies, purporting to be written by Clement, the first Bishop of Rome (see Phil. iv. 3), repeat all these accusations and reflect very strongly, although indirectly, upon the presumption of St Paul in venturing to place himself on a level with St Peter.
[8] Ch. i. 3—14.
[9] Ch. i. 15—22.
[10] Ch. ii.

Then, after a full and profound exposition of the principles on which a minister of Christ was bound to act[1], he winds up this portion of his Epistle by an earnest and affectionate entreaty that they will open their hearts as freely and frankly to him as he has done to them[2]. He next turns to the collection for the poor saints at Jerusalem, which was one of the objects he had in view in writing. He exhibits great anxiety lest the Corinthians should come short in any way of the character he has given them among other Churches, and urges them to be prepared beforehand, lest they should be taken by surprise when he comes[3]. And lastly he enters into an elaborate vindication of his claims to the obedience of the Corinthian Church. Desirous as he is of appealing to a higher standard, he feels that to many of those whom he is addressing such an appeal would be thrown away. There is nothing left to him but to descend to their level, and to shew that even from their own point of view they had no right to withhold their allegiance from him. He first remarks, not without a touch of sarcasm, that he at least does not build upon another man's foundation, nor intrude into any other man's sphere of labour to take credit to himself for what that man has done[4]. With many apologies for boasting 'according to the flesh,' he shews that whether in Hebrew extraction and patriotism, or in genuine labours for Christ's sake, he has as much right, if not more, to describe himself as a minister of Christ, as any other teacher can possibly have[5]. He distantly hints at the sublime visions of things unseen which God has vouchsafed to him[6], and then condescends to defend himself from the coarse charges of deceit and roguery[7]. And after a final assertion of his Apostolic authority, and of the power he has received from Christ to carry it out, he concludes with a brief and touching exhortation and benediction, and thus brings to a close the most remarkable revelation of an Apostle's mind and an Apostle's work which is handed down to us in the New Testament.

3. *Genuineness of the Epistle.* The contents of this Epistle

---

[1] Ch. iii.—vi.   [2] Ch. vii.   [3] Ch. viii., ix.
[4] Ch. x.   [5] Ch. xi.   [6] Ch. xii. 1—12.
[7] Ch. xii. 13—18.

are the best guarantee of its genuineness. Not only do they fall in with what we know from other sources concerning the history of St Paul[1], but the animation of the style, the earnestness of the appeals, the variety and minuteness of the personal details with which the Epistle abounds, place it beyond the reach of a forger. But external testimonies are not wanting. Beside several quotations made from the Epistle, without naming it, by Ignatius[2] and the author of the Epistle to Diognetus[3] in times immediately succeeding those of the Apostles, we have the distinct authority of Irenaeus, who not only attributes it to an Apostle, and that Apostle St Paul[4], but refers in two different places[5] to the 'visions and revelations' spoken of in ch. xii. as well as to the thorn in the flesh spoken of in the same chapter[6]. From the time when Tertullian (about the year 208 A.D.) introduced an elaborate analysis of the Epistle into his treatise against Marcion, its genuineness has never been doubted in the Church[7].

NOTE A. ON THE UNDESIGNED COINCIDENCES BETWEEN THE ACTS OF THE APOSTLES, THE FIRST AND SECOND EPISTLES TO THE CORINTHIANS.

The subject of the coincidences between the Acts of the Apostles and the two Epistles to the Corinthians, which cannot by any possibility be attributed to design, is treated of exhaustively by Paley in his *Horae Paulinae*, and they are among the most decisive arguments for the genuineness of all these three books of Holy Scripture, though they are

---

[1] See Note A.   [2] See Ep. to Trallians, c. 3.
[3] The Epistle to Diognetus is usually supposed to have been written by some anonymous author in the early part of the second century. It has been lately attacked in the *Church Quarterly Review* as a forgery of the 16th century, but the arguments in favour of the theory are not conclusive. It is, however, regarded with suspicion by many scholars.
[4] *Adv. Haer.* IV. 26, 28.   [5] II. 30, and V. 5.   [6] V. 3.
[7] Tertullian also makes copious extracts from this Epistle in his Treatise on the Resurrection, and enters into a minute investigation of the case of the incestuous person as recorded in both Epistles, in his *De Pudicitia*, while it is continually quoted as the work of St Paul in the rest of Tertullian's writings.

too often overlooked by student and critic alike. A brief summary is here given of the more important of Paley's arguments, for the sake of those who have not the opportunity of consulting the book itself. The rest will be found touched upon in the notes.

1. St Paul refers at the opening of this Epistle to some great trouble and danger which had befallen him, though he does not mention what it is. On consulting the Acts of the Apostles, a book by a different author, and written at a different time, we find[1] that he is referring to the violent tumult stirred up at Ephesus by Demetrius and the craftsmen.

2. St Paul says in his first Epistle[2], that he purposes passing through Macedonia. In the Acts, we find[3] that St Paul does leave Ephesus for Macedonia. In the Second Epistle[4], we find him in Macedonia.

3. In the Second Epistle St Paul refers to a change of purpose on his part. He had originally intended to go to Corinth first, and to return to Asia Minor by way of Macedonia[5]. But the Acts of the Apostles leads us to believe that when he sent Timothy to Greece he had intended to visit Macedonia first[6]. Consequently we draw the conclusion that his purpose had been already changed *before* the mission of Timothy. It is in remarkable, but most undesigned agreement with this conclusion, that not only is there no mention of the former plan in the First Epistle, which was sent off soon after Timothy's departure[7], but we learn from 1 Cor. xvi. 5, that the change of purpose had already taken place.

4. In the fifth chapter of the First Epistle mention is made of a private wrong inflicted by one member of the community upon another. In the Second Epistle[8] there is *another* mention of a private wrong to which St Paul had formerly referred. In the First Epistle he bids the community inflict punishment upon the offender. In the Second[9] he bids them restore him upon repentance. None of these things lie upon the surface. They were clearly not put in to lend a plausible colour to the idea that the Epistles were by St Paul. This strengthens materially the evidence we have that St Paul himself, and none other, was their author.

5. In 1 Cor. xvi. 1, St Paul gives directions to the Corinthian

---

[1] Ch. xix.
[2] Ch. xvi. 5.
[3] Ch xx. 1.
[4] Ch. ix. 1—4.
[5] 2 Cor. i. 15, 16.
[6] Acts xix. 21.
[7] 1 Cor. iv. 17.
[8] Ch. vii. 12.
[9] Ch. vii.

Church to be prepared to supply him with contributions for the poor saints at Jerusalem. But he gives his directions in such terms as to make it clear that they had been already informed that it was to take place. Accordingly we read in the Second Epistle, written a few months after the former, that Achaia was 'ready' and 'forward' *in the previous year*[1]. Again, the amount, as we find from the Second Epistle, had *still to be collected*[2]. On turning to the First Epistle, we find that this was because the Corinthians had been exhorted to lay by at *home* every week[3], so that the sums they had at their disposal might be handed over when St Paul arrived. Such minute instances of agreement could not possibly be intentional; they therefore afford the surest proofs of the genuineness of the Epistles.

6. Paley thinks that there is another instance of this kind of coincidence in the fact that St Paul does not disclose the reason of the change of purpose mentioned above until his first Epistle had produced its effect[4]. His object, he declares[5], was to make proof of their fidelity to him, as well as to avoid the necessity of harsh measures when he came. Nothing could be in more entire harmony with this express declaration than his entire silence in the First Epistle about the *reasons* of his change of plan, as well as the brief sentence in which he announces the change of plan itself[6].

NOTE B. ON THE THORN IN THE FLESH.

The interpretations of 2 Cor. xii. 7 are so numerous that it demands more space than an ordinary note. The 'thorn in the flesh' of which the Apostle speaks has been supposed to be every possible infirmity or temptation to which man is liable. We can but remark on the most probable suggestions that have been offered.

1. It is to be remarked that the word translated 'thorn' in the A. V. has also the meaning 'stake.' The latter is more common in Classical Greek, the former seems to be more usual in the Alexandrian Greek of the LXX. It is obvious that the latter word suggests the idea of a more grievous affliction than the former, speaking as it does of an actual impalement of the body by a stake thrust through it, while the former gives the idea rather of irritation and annoyance, of a visitation painful indeed, but not serious in its nature. It is obvious that our view of the

[1] Ch. viii. 10, ix. 2. [2] Ch. ix. 5. [3] Ch. xvi. 2.
[4] Ch. vii. 6, 7, 11. [5] Ch. ii. 9. [6] 1 Cor. xvi. 5.

nature of the affliction must depend largely upon which of these two translations we decide to adopt. The Vulgate, as well as the ancient Latin translator of Irenaeus, who is supposed to have done his work at the beginning of the third century, translates by *stimulus*, a prick or goad, but Tertullian renders by *sudes*, 'stake.'

2. We find from the New Testament as well as the Old, that Satan was supposed to be permitted to exercise considerable power over the bodies of men. Not only was he called the 'prince,' or 'ruler' of this world[1], but we find him, in the book of Job, inflicting, with God's permission, the most grievous calamities on Job and his family[2]. We also find our Lord Himself giving His sanction to the view that all temporal evil, including pain and disease, has Satan for its author, in the case of the woman whom 'Satan had bound[3]'. A similar idea meets us in Rev. ix. 2—10.

3. This power, however, was sometimes permitted to be exercised for the amendment of the offender, as we find from 1 Cor. v. 5 (where see note) and 1 Tim. i. 20. Tertullian[4] enlarges much on the remedial aspect of Satan's visitations as evidenced by these three passages. Not that it was imagined that Satan could in any way be intentionally an instrument of good, but since all evil, physical as well as moral, was attributed to his agency, as the enemy of mankind, the physical evil was sometimes permitted to exist, that the graver moral evil might be prevented. In the present instance the object of the punishment is distinctly specified. It was lest the Apostle might be uplifted with pride, in consequence of the many signal tokens of God's favour he had received.

4. We now proceed to consider the nature of the temptation. The first point to remark is that the words 'in the flesh' cannot be restricted to the idea of bodily suffering. The word 'flesh,' as used by St Paul, refers to man's unregenerate nature as a whole[5], and not to the bodily organization alone. It may therefore fitly be interpreted of that "infection of nature" which, we are told[6], "doth remain, yea, even in them that are regenerated." An infirmity of that kind is far more likely

---

[1] St John xii. 31, xiv. 30, xvi. 11; 2 Cor. iv. 4; Eph. vi. 12.
[2] Job, Chapters i. and ii. [3] St Luke xiii. 16.
[4] *De Pudicitia*, 13, *De Fuga in Persecutione*, 2. Cf. Irenaeus, *Adv. Haer.* v. 3.
[5] See for instance Rom. vii. and viii. 1—13, and especially Gal. v. 19—21. Cf. also 1 Cor. iii. 3, 4.
[6] Art. IX. on Original Sin.

to have proved a serious trouble to the Apostle than any mere physical ailment, and it is probable that a solution of the difficulty may be looked for in that direction rather than any other. We will, however, review the interpretations which have found most favour with interpreters, and having placed the evidence before him, will leave the student to decide for himself.

a. The idea of temptations in the flesh of the nature of suggestions to impurity, which has found great favour with Roman Catholic writers, need only be noticed to be rejected. There is not the slightest hint in any of St Paul's writings that he ever experienced such temptations. There is one passage in which he appears to assert the contrary[1]. The idea finds no support in early tradition. Tertullian, for instance, in his remarks on this passage[2], enlarges on the contrast between the incestuous person, and the soul of the Apostle, entirely unstained by such suggestions, and only uplifted on account of his superior sanctity and innocence. The idea that the Apostle refers to struggles with such sins in the seventh chapter of the Romans can only arise from the contracted notion of the word 'flesh,' which has just been shewn to be incorrect. In fact this interpretation is entirely the growth of an age which, by the exaggerated regard paid in it to celibacy, brought such struggles into special prominence, and made them almost the sole test of saintliness [3].

b. We have no tradition on which we can depend for the nature of the affliction. The earliest writers, Clement, Ignatius, Justin Martyr, and others of that date, are silent concerning it. Irenaeus, to the special nature of whose information we have referred in the notes on ch. xii. 2, 4, contents himself with speaking of St Paul's infirmity as a proof that God does not despise the flesh of man, as the heretics supposed. The first writer who goes so far as to specify the nature of the complaint is Tertullian, in the passage cited above, who supposes it to be "a pain in the ear or head." He speaks of this, however, only as a matter of common report. Nearly every possible kind of pain or disease has been suggested as well as these. It seems hardly probable, however, that the Apostle should speak of ailments so slight in terms so strong. Other writers, therefore, have suggested that the Apostle was subject to epileptic fits. And if we are to suppose that the passage refers to bodily

---

[1] 1 Cor. vii. 7. Cf. *v.* 9 and ch. ix. 5.   [2] *De Pudicitia*, 13.
[3] The passages cited by Estius from St Jerome as favourable to this view will not bear examination, and one of them, that from his letter to Eustochium, explains the passage quite differently. It was in a still later age that this view seems to have originated.

ailments at all, we must suppose something of this sort, or at least some kind of bodily infirmity sufficiently serious to prove an actual hindrance to the Apostle in his work of evangelizing the world. Dean Stanley mentions several instances of great men, such as Alfred the Great and William III., struggling against severe physical infirmities while discharging the most onerous duties of public life, and it is by no means impossible that St Paul's thorn in the flesh may have been of this kind. See also 1 Cor. ii. 3, 2 Cor. x. 10, xi. 30, Gal. iv. 13, 14, vi. 17.

c. There is one kind of bodily infirmity, however, which is made so much more probable than all others by certain passages in the Acts of the Apostles and in St Paul's Epistles, that it deserves special consideration. Many have thought that a defect of sight, consequent on the dazzling light which shone upon him at his conversion, resulting in a three days blindness, was the physical defect under which he laboured, and have seen in such passages as Gal. iv. 14, 15 and vi. 11 (the latter passage being supposed to imply that St Paul's defective vision obliged him to write with characters unusually large)[1] a confirmation of this view. This opinion is deserving of consideration, but when it is sought to confirm it by such passages as Acts xiii. 9, xxiii. 1, it must be remembered that the same word precisely is used of the council in Acts vi. 15, of St Stephen in Acts vii. 55, and would seem to imply an intent and piercing gaze, the very opposite of that caused by defective vision[2]. Such a gaze we might well suppose the Apostle to have possessed, capable of riveting the attention of his hearers, in spite of a weak voice, an unstudied manner, and considerable personal disadvantages.

d. It is very characteristic of Martin Luther, with his terrible mental struggles and temptations to suicide, that he should have imagined in the mental history of a man in some respects not unlike himself, the direct suggestions of the enemy to blasphemous and unbelieving thoughts and acts. But it is hardly possible to suppose that one whose leading characteristic, both before and after his conversion, was an ardent and undoubting faith, should have been troubled with misgivings like these. Nor is there in any of St Paul's writings, whatever cares and anxieties (as in ch. xi. of this Epistle) he describes as weighing upon him, the slightest hint at even the most transient shadow of doubt concerning Him to the ministering of Whom he had devoted his whole life.

[1] St Paul says 'with how large letters,' not 'how large a letter,' as in A. V.
[2] Cf. St Luke iv. 20; Acts i. 10, iii. 4, 12, &c., where the same Greek word is used.

e. Many of the Greek commentators suppose St Paul to be referring to the opponents of his Apostolic authority, supposing that there was one of these antagonists specially prominent[1]. But this seems hardly reconcileable with the manner in which St Paul speaks of the visitation.

f. Our last alternative must be some defect of character, calculated to interfere with St Paul's success as a minister of Jesus Christ. And the defect which falls in best with what we know of St Paul is an infirmity of temper. There seems little doubt that he gave way to an outbreak of this kind when before the Sanhedrim, though he set himself right at once by a prompt apology[2]. A similar idea is suggested by St Paul's unwillingness to go to Corinth until the points in dispute between him and a considerable portion of the Corinthian Church were in a fair way of being settled. His conduct was precisely the reverse of that of a person who felt himself endowed with great tact, persuasiveness, and command of temper. Such a man would trust little to messages and letters, much to his own presence and personal influence. St Paul, on the contrary, feared to visit Corinth until there was a reasonable prospect of avoiding all altercation. In fact, he could not trust himself there. He 'feared that God would humble him among them[3].' He desired above all things to avoid the necessity of 'using sharpness,' very possibly because he feared that when once compelled to assume a tone of severity, his language might exceed the bounds of Christian love. The supposition falls in with what we know of the Apostle before his conversion[4]. It is confirmed by his stern language to Elymas the sorcerer[5], with which we may compare the much milder language used by St Peter on a far more awful occasion[6]. The quarrel between St Paul and St Barnabas makes the supposition infinitely more probable. The passage above cited from the Epistle to the Galatians may be interpreted of the deep personal affection which the Apostle felt he had inspired in spite of his occasional irritability of manner. The expression that he 'desired to be present with them and to change his voice[7],' would seem to point in the same direction. And if we add to these considerations the fact, which the experience of God's saints in all ages has conclusively established, of the difficulty of subduing an infirmity of temper, as well as the pain, remorse, and humiliation such an

---

[1] The ὁ ἐρχόμενος of ch. xi. 4.
[2] Acts xxiii. 2—5.
[3] 2 Cor. xii. 21.
[4] Acts vii. 58, ix. 1.
[5] Acts xiii. 10.
[6] Acts v. 3, 9.
[7] Gal. iv. 20.

infirmity is wont to cause to those who groan under it, we may be inclined to believe that not the least probable hypothesis concerning the 'thorn' or 'stake' in the flesh is that the loving heart of the Apostle bewailed as his sorest trial the misfortune that by impatience in word he had often wounded those for whom he would willingly have given his life[1].

NOTE C. ON THE ENGLISH VERSIONS OF THE NEW TESTAMENT.

The six most important versions of the New Testament in English, to which frequent reference is made in these pages, are as follows:

1. Wiclif's Translation, made by John Wiclif about 1380.
2. Tyndale's Translation, made by William Tyndale in 1526.
3. Cranmer's Translation, issued by Archbishop Cranmer in 1539.
4. The Geneva Bible, undertaken by the refugees during the Marian persecution, at Geneva. It appeared in the reign of Elizabeth, in 1569.
5. The Rhemish Version, made at Rheims in 1582. It is generally known as the Douay Bible, because it is usually bound up with the version of the Old Testament made at Douay in 1609—10. It was brought out by the authorities of the Roman Catholic Church to counteract the influence of the versions made by the Reformers.
6. The Authorized Version (quoted as the A.V. in this volume) made under the auspices of King James I. in 1611.

---

[1] When this note was written, the Bishop of Durham's note on this subject in his "Epistle to the Galatians" had not been consulted. It confirms what has been written above, except on the last head, but adds from Pauli's *Life of Alfred* a striking parallel between the expressions used of the great English king and those used by St Paul, expressions the more remarkable in that there seems no ground to suppose that the former were suggested by the latter.

CHAPTER II.

ANALYSIS OF THE EPISTLE.

PART I. ST PAUL'S PRINCIPLES OF ACTION.

CH. I.—VII.

Section 1. Salutation, i. 1, 2.

Section 2. The mutual interdependence of St Paul and the Corinthian Church, i. 3—14.

- (α) Suffering a dispensation of God, bringing with it (1) Divine consolation for oneself, (2) the power to comfort others .... 3—7.
- (β) St Paul's trouble in Asia and the mode of his deliverance from it, namely God's mercy and the sympathy of the Church of Corinth .... 8—11.
- (γ) St Paul had deserved this sympathy .... 12—14.

Section 3. St Paul's reason for putting off his visit, i. 15—24.

- (α) St Paul's former resolution .... 15, 16.
- (β) The accusation of fickleness brought against him in consequence .... 17.
- (γ) Assertion of his consistency............................. 18—22.
- (δ) Reason for his delay....................................... 23, 24.

Section 4. St Paul's only object the spiritual advancement of his converts, ch. ii.

- (α) His object not to pain the Corinthians, but to display his love for them .... 1—4.
- (β) For the offender had not only pained St Paul, but the Corinthian Church itself .... 5.
- (γ) It was now time to forgive him .... 6—9.
- (δ) Beside manifesting his love, he wished also to test their obedience .... 9.
- (ε) He desires to be associated with them in the work of forgiveness.. 10, 11.
- (ζ) He loved the Corinthians so deeply that he could not rest till he had heard how they received his rebukes .... 12, 13.
- (η) Outburst of praise at the thought of the good God had wrought by his hands .... 14.
- (θ) Christ's doctrine life to those who accept, death to those who reject it....................................... 15, 16.
- (ι) Insufficiency, yet sincerity of St Paul................. 17.

Section 5. St Paul's ministry no self-assumed task, but the communication of the Spirit, iii. 1—6.
- (α) St Paul and his companions had no need to be recommended to the Corinthians .... 1.
- (β) The Corinthian Church itself was their recommendation .... 2, 3.
- (γ) A power from God had fitted them for the communication, not of a command which brings death, but of a Spirit which gives life .... 4—6.

Section 6. The Ministration of the Spirit superior to that of the Law, iii. 7—18.
- (α) If the law, which ministers death, were glorious, how much more the Spirit, which gives life? ... 7—11.
- (β) Contrast between the reticence of Moses and the free utterance of the preachers of the Gospel ... 12, 13.
- (γ) This reticence has produced its natural, though temporary, effect on the Jews .... 14—16.
- (δ) The Spirit, which has superseded the law, is none other than the Spirit of Christ Himself, and is a Spirit of liberty and spiritual progress .... 17, 18.

Section 7. The power of this ministry demonstrated by the weakness of the ministers, iv. 1—15.
- (α) St Paul's ministry a true and genuine one .... 1, 2.
- (β) If the light of truth be any longer hidden from any, it is in consequence of no reserve on the part of those who proclaim it, but is the fault of those who reject it .... 3—6.
- (γ) The weakness of the minister does but set off the efficacy of his doctrine .... 7—15.

Section 8. They are sustained by the hope of a future life, iv. 16—v. 10.
- (α) The minister in his weakness is animated by the hope of eternal life .... 16—18.
- (β) In which they hope to add to their present life in Christ, the possession of a body as suited, as their present one is unsuited, to the needs of that life v. 1—5.
- (γ) Yet though as yet absent from the Lord, they are never out of His sight .... 6—9.
- (δ) But He will one day pass judgment on all their deeds .... 10.

Section 9. The Christian ministry one of reconciliation, v. 11—21.
- (α) The fact of the coming judgment being admitted, St Paul strives to win men to the life of the Spirit, not for his own sake, but for theirs .... 11—13.
- (β) The love of Christ, who died as our representative, that we might partake of His life, is the motive which animates the true ministers of the Gospel 14, 15.

(γ) They take a new and higher view of humanity than men have hitherto taken	16, 17.
(δ) God is henceforth reconciled to the world in Christ, and has bidden His ministers proclaim the fact, and urge mankind to accept it	18—21.

Section 10. How God's ministers carry on the work of reconciliation, vi. 1—10.

(α) The ministers of God's purpose urge men not to let God's offers of favour be thrown away, but to close with them at once	1, 2.
(β) Their self-abnegation when engaged in the work...	3—10.

Section 11. Such a ministry demands a suitable response from those on whose behalf it is exercised, vi. 11—vii. 1.

(α) Appeal to the Corinthians to receive such a ministry in a spirit of affection	11—13.
(β) Advice to withdraw from society with the impure	14—18.
(γ) And to preserve real inward holiness	vii. 1.

Section 12. Exhortation to set aside suspicion and to trust St Paul, vii. 2—16.

(α) St Paul's conduct free from reproach	2.
(β) His language not of bitterness but of affection	3, 4.
(γ) This proved by his anxiety while waiting for the tidings from Corinth, his joy when it reached him	5—7.
(δ) The First Epistle written, not to give pain, but to produce reformation	8—12.
(ε) His delight that he had gained his end	13—16.

PART II. THE COLLECTION FOR THE POOR SAINTS AT JERUSALEM. CH. VIII., IX.

(α) Conduct of the Macedonian Churches............viii.	1—5.
(β) Mission of Titus to Corinth, to urge on the work there	6—15.
(γ) Character of Titus and his companions	16—23.
(δ) Exhortation to liberality	24—ix. 11.
(ε) Result of deeds of love	12—15.

PART III. ST PAUL'S VINDICATION OF HIS APOSTOLIC AUTHORITY. CH. X.—XIII.

Section 1. St Paul's intention of overcoming all opposition, x. 1—6.

(α) St Paul meek and gentle in conduct	1.
(β) But possessed of supernatural power	2—6.

Section 2. Caution not to trust in external appearance, x. 7—18.

(α) The Corinthians would be deceived if they imagined from St Paul's absence of self-assertion that he possessed no authority derived from Christ	7, 8.

- (β) He means to exert that authority when present, and not by letter only .... 9—11.
- (γ) He keeps within his own limits, and does not challenge comparison by intruding himself within the sphere of other men's labours .... 12—18.

Section 3. St Paul's defence against his accusers, xi. 1—17.
- (α) Appeal to bear with him if he descend for a moment to the level of unspiritual men .... 1.
- (β) On account of his anxiety for the purity of his converts' faith .... 2, 3.
- (γ) It is no question of a new Gospel, in which case to abandon St Paul might be reasonable, but of his authority to preach the Gospel he had preached, about which there ought to be no doubt .... 4—6.
- (δ) His desire not to cast the burden of his maintenance upon them could hardly be regarded as an offence 7—11.
- (ε) For he only acted thus to prevent the Corinthians from being misled by the affected disinterestedness of dishonest men .... 12—15.
- (ζ) St Paul does not wish to be thought willingly to abandon the high standpoint of the Gospel ...... 16, 17.

Section 4. St Paul permits himself to enumerate his labours on behalf of the Gospel, xi. 18—33.
- (α) St Paul will take the purely human view of things, since it is the only one recognized by some ...... 18.
- (β) For the Corinthians have so large a toleration for the folly of others that they may be expected to bear with his .... 19, 20.
- (γ) And he has actually been reproached with weakness for not imitating this folly, to which he will now, to a certain extent, condescend for the moment .... 21.
- (δ) His equality with his opponents on the score of race and nationality .... 22.
- (ε) His vast superiority to them in the true qualifications of the minister of Christ (a) in labours, (b) in care and sympathy .... 23—29.
- (ζ) These boasts are not unbecoming, for his qualifications are not what he has done, but what he has undergone .... 30.
- (η) His escape from the hands of Aretas................. 31—33.

Section 5. St Paul's Visions and Revelations, xii. 1—6.
- (α) Lest he should be altogether despised, he will hint at higher qualifications for his task................ 1.
- (β) His being caught up to the third heaven and Paradise .... 2—4.
- (γ) Yet though he might glory in this, he prefers not to dwell on it... 5, 6.

INTRODUCTION. 23

Section 6. The Thorn in the Flesh, xii. 7—10.
- (a) It was sent him to preserve him from self-exaltation .... 7.
- (β) He besought that it might be removed .... 8.
- (γ) But he was told that God's power was most manifested in the weakness of his ministers .... 9.
- (δ) And this is why he boasts of his infirmities .... 10.

Section 7. Continuation of the Defence, xii. 11—21.
- (a) St Paul's folly rendered necessary by that of the Corinthians.. 11.
- (β) They had had every needful proof of his Apostolic authority, save his casting his maintenance upon them .... 12, 13.
- (γ) He intends to persist in refusing all support at their hands, in order to demonstrate the disinterestedness of his affection .... 14, 15.
- (δ) He meets a possible accusation of duplicity .... 16—18.
- (ε) And another that he is admitting his want of authority by condescending to enter upon a defence 19.
- (ζ) His object is not to establish his own authority, but to put an end to the disorders among his disciples .... 19—21.

Section 8. The Apostle's intention on his arrival, xiii. 1—10.
- (a) St Paul will thoroughly and fairly investigate the condition of the Church .... 1.
- (β) He will use severity if necessary........................ 2.
- (γ) They seek a proof of Christ's power in him, such as they have experienced in themselves, and they shall have it .... 3, 4.
- (δ) They can learn by their own experience that Christ's power is manifested in its influence upon the life .... 5.
- (ε) They shall know that the same power can be manifested through the ministry of St Paul .... 6.
- (ζ) Though it is not their high opinion he seeks, but the purity of their lives................................. 7.
- (η) The only power he has in Christ is a power to promote righteousness .... 8.
- (θ) He has no ambition for himself, but only desires their perfection .... 9.
- (ι) His only object in writing thus was to avoid the necessity of severity .... 10.

Section 9. Conclusion, xiii. 11—14.

II. CORINTHIANS.

CH. I. 1, 2. *Salutation.*

PAUL, an apostle of Jesus Christ by the will of God, and 1 Timothy *our* brother, unto the church of God which is at Corinth, with all the saints which are in all Achaia: grace *be* to you and peace from God our Father, and *from* 2 the Lord Jesus Christ.

CH. I. 1, 2. SALUTATION.

1. *by the will of God*] See note on 1 Cor. i.
and Timothy our *brother*] Literally, **Timothy** *the* **brother.** Wiclif, Tyndale, and Cranmer render 'brother Timotheus.' He is called sometimes Timothy and sometimes more fully Timotheus in the A. V. So we have Luke and Lucas, Mark and Marcus. He had therefore rejoined the Apostle after his mission to Macedonia, and possibly to Corinth. See Acts xix. 22 and 1 Cor. iv. 17, xvi. 10, and notes. Timothy's name is also found associated with that of the Apostle in the Epistles to the Philippians, Colossians, in both those to the Thessalonians, and in that to Philemon.

with all the saints which are in all Achaia] Chrysostom remarks that it is not St Paul's custom to address the Churches thus in circular letters, and that the two Epistles to the Corinthians, that to the Galatians (which however was addressed, see chap. i. 2, to a *region*, not to a city), and that to the Hebrews (if it be St Paul's) were the only exceptions. But this statement is not exactly accurate. If the Epistle to the Ephesians be identical with the Epistle to Laodicæa (and there are many reasons for supposing it to be so—see Col. iv. 16) the Epistles to the Colossians and Ephesians must be added to the list. It is probable that Corinth was the only Christian Church of any note in Achaia, and that the few scattered Christians to be found elsewhere in that province were regarded as a part of that community. See notes on 1 Cor. i. 2.

Achaia] We are to understand by this Hellas and the Peloponnesus, which, with Macedonia, made up the whole of Greece. Macedonia, however, was scarcely recognized by the Greeks in their best days as forming a part of their land. See Articles *Achaia* and *Hellas* in Smith's *Dictionary of Geography*.

2. *Grace*] See note on 1 Cor. i. 3, and below, *v.* 12.
be to you and peace from God our Father, and from the Lord Jesus

3—14. *The mutual interdependence of St Paul and the Corinthian Church.*

3   Blessed *be* God, even the Father of our Lord Jesus Christ,
4 the Father of mercies, and the God of all comfort; who comforteth us in all our tribulation, that we may be able to

Christ] Here, as in 1 Cor. i. 3 (see note there), Jesus Christ is associated with the Father as the source of grace and peace.

3—14. THE MUTUAL INTERDEPENDENCE OF ST PAUL AND THE CORINTHIAN CHURCH.

3. *Blessed be God, even the Father of our Lord Jesus Christ*] Two feelings rise at once in the Apostle's mind. The first is an overwhelming gratitude for his deliverance from his distress, the second the keen sense of his entire unity of heart and soul with the Corinthian Church, and his desire to impart to them whatever blessings he had received from God. Our version follows Wiclif here, substituting, however, *even* for *and*. The other English versions have *God the Father of our Lord Jesus Christ*, save the Rhemish, which renders accurately by *the God and Father*, &c. See St John xx. 17; 1 Pet. i. 3 and note on 1 Cor. xv. 24.

the Father of mercies] Either (1), with Chrysostom, the God Whose most inherent attribute is mercy, or (2) the source from whence all mercies proceed. But perhaps the former involves the latter, a sense, however, of which the fact that 'mercies' is in the plural forbids us to lose sight. Cf. Eph. i. 17; James i. 17. Even if we regard the phrase 'Father of mercies' as a Hebraism, it is stronger than the expression 'merciful Father.' So Estius, "valde multumque misericordem et beneficum."

and the God of all comfort] Why does St Paul say 'the *Father* of mercies and the *God* of comfort?' Because the term 'Father' implies mercy, suggesting as it does the close and affectionate relation between God and man. See the O. T. *passim*, and especially Ps. ciii. 13. Compare also 'Our Father which art in heaven.' God is called 'the God of comfort' (see next note) because it comes from Him.

comfort] This word, or the verb compounded from it, occurs *ten* times in this and the next four verses. In our version, which here follows Tyndale, they are rendered indifferently by *comfort* and *consolation*, a rendering which considerably lessens the force of the passage. For *consolation* the Rhemish substitutes *exhortation*, and Wiclif *monestynge* (i. e. *admonishing*) and *monestid*, after the Vulgate, which renders indifferently by *exhortatio* and *consolatio* here. Perhaps the best words which can be found to express the double meaning of consolation and exhortation conveyed by the Greek are *encourage* and *encouragement*. *Cheer* would be more appropriate still had not the noun become almost obsolete. The original sense of the English word (late Latin *confortare*) denotes *strengthening*.

4. *tribulation*] *Tribulatio*, Vulgate. The word thus translated is rendered *trouble* in the next clause, and in the Vulgate by *pressura*, and is

comfort them which are in any trouble, by the comfort wherewith we ourselves are comforted of God. For as the 5 sufferings of Christ abound in us, so our consolation also aboundeth by Christ. And whether we be afflicted, *it is* 6 for your consolation and salvation, which is effectual in the enduring of the same sufferings which we also suffer: or

derived from a verb signifying to *squeeze, press*. The English word tribulation is derived from the Latin *tribulo*, to *thresh*. See Trench, *Study of Words*, Lect. II.

that we may be able to comfort them which are in any trouble] St Paul represents affliction (1) as a school of sympathy, (2) as a school of comfort (or rather encouragement), *v.* 5, (3) as a school of assurance, *v.* 10.—Robertson.

by the comfort wherewith we ourselves are comforted of God] We may observe here, as elsewhere in Scripture, that no gift is bestowed upon any one to keep to himself. If St Paul is encouraged by God, it is not only for his own sake, but that he may be able to impart to others the encouragement which he has received. See notes on First Epistle, especially on ch. vi. 12, viii. 13, x. 23, xiv. 5, 12. Cf. also St John xv. 1—17; Rom. xiv; 1 Cor. iii. 9, iv. 7; Eph. iv. 16; Col. ii. 19.

5. *For as the sufferings of Christ abound in us*] Rather **super-abound unto us**. All the principal English versions render *in us*, and thus many commentators have been misled. The word translated *abound* means to *exceed, be over and above* (Matt. v. 20, xiv. 20). Thus the meaning of the passage is that the sufferings of Christ overflow to us and that thus we are made partakers of them. See Matt. xx. 22; Mark x. 38; Gal. ii. 20; Heb. xiii. 13. For (see notes on ch. iv. 11, 12) our sufferings for Christ's sake arise from the same cause as His, namely the opposition of darkness to light, of death to the life that is imparted by Him to His members. Such passages as ch. iv. 10; Col. i. 24, carry the idea a step further, and represent Christ as suffering *in* His members, by virtue of His union with them. So also Matt. xxv. 40, 45; Acts ix. 4; Gal. vi. 17; Phil. iii. 10.

6. *And whether we be afflicted, it is for your consolation and salvation*] The same may be said of every kind of suffering endured for the cause of God and of truth. It is not merely, as in Heb. xii. 6 (Cf. Deut. viii. 5), that 'whom the Lord loveth, He chasteneth' for his own sake, but that the sufferings one man endures for a good cause are the source of profit to others. Cf. chap. iv. 15, 16; Eph. iii. 13; 2 Tim. ii. 10.

which is effectual in the enduring of the same sufferings which we also suffer] *Is effectual* may either be translated passively (as Chrysostom and the margin of A. V.) *is wrought out*, or, with most commentators, as middle, *works actively in you*. That is either (1) consolation and safety from the power of evil are wrought in you by the endurance of suffering, or (2) that consolation (or rather encouragement) and safety from evil work themselves out by the endurance of suffering. The former gives the simpler meaning, the latter is more according to the *usus loquendi* of the N. T.

whether we be comforted, *it is* for your consolation and
7 salvation. And our hope of you *is* stedfast, knowing, that
as you are partakers of the sufferings, so *shall ye be* also of
8 the consolation. For we would not, brethren, have you
ignorant of our trouble which came to us in Asia, that we
were pressed out of measure, above strength, insomuch that

7. *And our hope of you is stedfast*] Most editors agree in placing these words *before* 'or whether we be comforted,' &c. It would seem to be their most natural place, for not only do they come awkwardly before the word 'knowing,' but the expression of the hope is more appropriate in reference to the endurance by the Corinthians of suffering than to their enjoyment of encouragement. The majority of the best MSS. are in favour of this arrangement of the sentence. The text is in great confusion here.

as you are partakers of the sufferings, so shall ye be also of the consolation] Literally, **sharers**. See 1 Cor. i. 9, and note. Christians 'had all things,' even sufferings, in 'common.' Cf. 1 Cor. xv. 46, 49. Also Rom. viii. 17—23, ch. iv. 17. The words 'shall ye be' are not in the original. It would be better to supply 'are,' the encouragement being not a promise for the future, but a present possession. Observe the way in which *ye* and *you* are used indiscriminately as the nominative in the edition of 1611. Cf. also *vv*. 13, 14. In the later editions *ye* has been substituted. The substitution commenced in 1661, and gradually made its way after that time. The rule that *ye* is used only "in questions, entreaties, and rhetorical appeals" (see Abbott's *Shaksperian Grammar*, 236) does not seem to hold good here.

8. *For we would not...have you ignorant*] A favourite expression with St Paul. Cf. Rom. i. 13; 1 Cor. x. 1, xii. 1; 1 Thess. iv. 13.

of our trouble which came to us in Asia] Some have referred these expressions (1) to the tumult at Ephesus, Acts xix. Others have supposed, in consequence of the very strong expressions here, that some other trouble, a grievous sickness perhaps, is referred to, especially as St Paul says in Asia, not in Ephesus. But Dean Stanley's remark that "here, as elsewhere, we may observe the under-statement of St Paul's sufferings in the Acts" (see also ch. xi. 24—27 and notes), suggests the inference that the tumult at Ephesus was far more serious than it would appear to be from St Luke's account. We can hardly suppose that the mere 'dismissal of the assembly' by the 'town-clerk' entirely appeased the multitude. And it is quite possible, since St Luke's object in the Acts was rather a vindication of St Paul's ministry than a glorification of his person, that he omits to mention a determined attempt upon St Paul's life made by Demetrius and the craftsmen, as afterwards (Acts xxiii. 12—15) by the Jews at Jerusalem. For the word translated *trouble* here and elsewhere, see note on *v*. 4.

Asia] By this is meant *Asia Minor*. So also Acts ii. 9. But it seems (see Acts xvi. 6) not to have included the whole peninsula usually known by that name.

pressed] Literally, **weighed down**. *Gravati*, Calvin; *greved*, Wiclif,

we despaired even of life: but we had the sentence of 9
death in ourselves, that we should not trust in ourselves, but
in God which raiseth the dead: who delivered us from so 10
great a death, and doth deliver: in whom we trust that he
will yet deliver *us;* you also helping together by prayer for 11
us, that for the gift *bestowed* upon us by the means of many

whom the other English versions followed till the Rhemish, from which the A. V. appears to have borrowed its *pressed.* The expression conveys the idea of anxiety, but is not irreconcileable with the notion of a prolonged effort to escape those who thirsted for his life.

out of measure] Cf. for the same *Greek* word (though it is variously rendered in English) Rom. vii. 13; 1 Cor. xii. 31; Gal. i. 13, and especially ch. iv. 17. Dr Plumptre remarks that the word occurs exclusively in the Epistles of this period of St Paul's life.

despaired] This expression confirms the idea of a plot to kill the Apostle. Literally, it means that he was *utterly* at a loss (*rathlos*, Meyer) to know what to do to protect his life. See ch. iv. 8, where the same word occurs.

9. *sentence*] The word thus translated occurs only here in the N. T. It is translated *answer* by Wiclif, Tyndale, and Cranmer: the word *sentence* having been adopted by our translators from the Geneva version. At that time, however, the word *sentence* had not quite the same meaning which it bears now, but had rather the force of the Latin *sententia, opinion.* See Acts xv. 19. The word signifies not the answer itself, but rather the *purport of the answer,* as though the result of the Apostle's self-questionings had been a rooted persuasion, implanted from above, that, as he says in ch. iv. 12, 'Death worketh in us, but life in you,' a rooted persuasion, that is, of the transitoriness of the natural life, of the permanence of the new life that comes from God. Cf. 1 Cor. iv. 9, especially in the Greek.

10. *from so great a death*] i.e. from so great peril of death. St Paul speaks of the liability to death as *death.* Cf. ch. iv. 11, 12. Some regard it as equivalent to 'so terrible a death.' Yet surely the *mode* of death was a matter of trifling consequence to one like St Paul. See Phil. i. 21—23. Also ch. xi. 23.

and doth deliver] These words are wanting in many MSS.

we trust] Literally, we have hoped, i. e. with Erasmus, *spem fixam habemus.* The word here translated 'trust' is not the same as that so translated in the preceding verse.

11. *You also helping...by prayer for us*] Cf. 1 Thess. v. 25; 2 Thess. iii. 1; Heb. xiii. 18; James v. 15, 16. "For the right understanding of this Epistle, the identity of feeling between the Apostle and his converts must be borne in mind throughout...It is the liveliest instance of the real community of feeling introduced by Christianity into the world."—Stanley. Cf. ch. iv. 15, ix. 12. Also Acts xii. 5, 11; Rom. xv. 30, 31; Phil. i. 19; 2 Thess. iii. 1, 2; Philemon 22.

the gift] χάρισμα. See 1 Cor. xii. 4 (note).

persons thanks may be given by many on our behalf.
12 For our rejoicing is this, the testimony of our conscience, that in simplicity and godly sincerity, not with fleshly wisdom, but by the grace of God, we have had our conversa-

persons] Literally, **faces.** The word originally, perhaps, signifies a *mask*. Hence it came (see note on ch. ii. 10) to mean 'face' or 'presence,' and thus, as in the present passage, it comes to mean 'person.' But the signification *face* occurs in Homer.

12. *For our rejoicing is this*] "It is this," says the Apostle, "which causes such a perennial flow of joy and consolation into my heart amid all my anxieties and distresses. I can feel in my conscience that what knits us together in sympathy is a Divine and not a human bond. On my part there is the inspiration from above, on yours the verifying faculty which enables you to recognize the truth of what I deliver to you." This seems to be the connection of thought in this and the two following verses. The connection with what precedes appears to be the conviction of the Apostle that the honesty and genuineness of his efforts to minister Christ to the Corinthians have fairly entitled him to hope for a share in their prayers.

the testimony of our conscience] Cf. 1 Cor. iv. 4. Also Acts xxiii. 1, xxiv. 16; Rom. ix. 1; 1 John iii. 21.

that in simplicity and godly sincerity] For *simplicity* the best MSS. and editors read *holiness;* but *simplicity*, i.e. *singleness of purpose*, seems to suit the context best. The word translated sincerity, *clenness*, Wiclif, *pureness*, Tyndale, originally signifies that which is *tested by the sun's rays*, and is therefore entirely transparent. See note on 1 Cor. v. 8. See also ch. ii. 7; Phil. i. 10; 2 Pet. iii. 1. The word *sincerity* was adopted by our translators from the Rhemish version. The words translated *godly sincerity* are in the original *sincerity of God*, i.e. either (1) *that which is His gift, comes from Him*, or, (2) *that which is befitting His service*, as in the A. V.

not with fleshly wisdom] Literally, **in.** Cf. 1 Cor. i. 17, ii. 1, 4, 13. These passages shew that there existed among the Corinthians a tendency to exalt the wisdom of this world, i.e. acquirements such as those of dialectic skill and rhetoric above the spiritual enlightenment obtained by the submission of the intellect and will to the direction of God.

but by the grace of God] Literally, **in** *the grace of God*, i.e. in possession of it. The word grace, like the Latin *gratia*, originally signified *favour, kindness*. St Paul here would say that his behaviour at Corinth, to which he appeals, was the result of the favour of God to him, enabling him to shape his life in obedience to God's commands.

we have had our conversation] This word, which is a nearly literal rendering of the Greek, is derived from two Latin words signifying *to turn together*, and hence from the idea of having *your attention turned* to a thing, being *versed* in it, it has the signification of a man's *ordinary conduct in life*. It has come to mean in modern English interchange

tion in the world, and more abundantly to you-wards. For 13
we write none other *things* unto you, than what you read
or acknowledge; and I trust you shall acknowledge even
to the end; as also you have acknowledged us in part, that 14
we are your rejoicing, even as ye also *are* ours in the day
of the Lord Jesus.

15—24. *St Paul's reason for putting off his coming.*

And in this confidence I was minded to come unto 15

of thought in speech. In the Epistle to the Philippians it is twice used as the translation of 'citizenship.'

and more abundantly to you-wards] This either refers (1) to the special proofs the Apostle had given the Corinthians of his singleness of purpose and avoidance of fleshly wisdom, or (2) to the fact that he had remained longer at Corinth, and so had additional opportunities of displaying those qualities; or it has reference perhaps (3) to his self-abnegation in refusing to receive his maintenance at the hands of his Corinthian converts. See 1 Cor. ix. and ch. xi. 8—10.

13. *For we write none other things unto you*] i.e. for we are not writing to you about anything with which you have not had the opportunity of being fully acquainted.

than what you read or acknowledge] It is impossible to give the full sense of this passage in English. In the first place there is the play upon ἀναγινώσκετε and ἐπιγινώσκετε, after a fashion usual with St Paul, and next there is the fact that ἀναγινώσκω has a double meaning, to *recognize*, *know accurately* (as in Xen. *Anab.* v. viii. 6), and to *read*. The word translated 'acknowledge' signifies to know thoroughly either (1) by examination, comparison, reasoning, or (2) by intuition. Here the former idea is predominant.

14. *As also*] St Paul connects "the future for which he *hopes*, with the past of which he *knows*."—Meyer.

in part] It is here delicately hinted that the *whole* Corinthian Church did not acknowledge St Paul.

we are your rejoicing] Rather, **ground of rejoicing**. The word here rendered 'rejoicing' is rendered indifferently 'boasting,' 'glorying,' 'rejoicing,' 'whereof to glory' in the A.V. See Rom. iv. 2; 1 Cor. v. 6, and ch. ix. 3.

even as ye also are ours] See note on *v*. 11. It was, moreover, the special object of the Apostle to remind the Corinthians of the identity of their interests before he proceeded to vindicate himself or to rebuke them. *Some* of them, he says, already recognized this truth. See also next verse. Chrysostom remarks on the humility of the Apostle in thus placing himself on a level with his converts.

in the day of the Lord Jesus] See 1 Cor. iii. 13, iv. 3, 5 and notes.

15—24. ST PAUL'S REASON FOR PUTTING OFF HIS COMING.

15. *And in this confidence*] It was the conviction of this community

16 you before, that you might have a second benefit; and to pass by you into Macedonia, and to come again out of Macedonia unto you, and of you to be brought on 17 *my* way toward Judæa. When I therefore was thus minded, did I use lightness? or *the things* that I purpose, do I purpose according to the flesh, that with me there should

of interest which made St Paul desire to visit Corinth. It was (see v. 23) the consciousness that all his converts did not realize it which made him anxious to try the effect of a letter first. See ch. ii. 3, vii. 8—12.

I was minded to come unto you before] i.e. before going to Macedonia. *that you might have a second benefit*] Lit. **grace**. These words would be more intelligible had they been placed at the end of the next verse. By the 'second benefit' is meant the effects of the visit which the Apostle hoped to have paid to the Corinthians after his return from Macedonia. It has been explained, (1) of the favour of the Apostle's presence, (2) of the outpouring of God's grace or favour which St Paul, as an Apostle of Christ, had the privilege of imparting. See Rom. i. 11. Tyndale, who is followed by Cranmer and the Geneva Version, renders *one pleasure more*. Wiclif, *the* (Rhemish *a*) *secunde grace*.

16. *to pass by you into Macedonia*] It was probably when this resolution (which may have been announced in the lost Epistle, see 1 Cor. v. 9) was given up, that the mission of Timothy referred to in 1 Cor. iv. 17, and in Acts xix. 22 was substituted, and as still more urgent necessity arose, that of Titus, ch. viii. 16—24, xii. 17, 18.

and of you to be brought on my way toward Judæa] The exact opposite of this was what actually took place. St Paul went through Macedonia on his way to Corinth, and returned through Macedonia, and was brought on his way toward Judæa by the Macedonian Churches. The word translated 'brought on my way' is used of the pecuniary and other assistance given by the Churches towards the journeys of the brethren. See Acts xv. 3, xx. 38, xxi. 15; Rom. xv. 24; 1 Cor. xvi. 6, 11; Tit. iii. 13; 3 John 6, and note on 1 Cor xvi. 6.

17. *did I use lightness?*] Literally, **the** *lightness*, i.e. either the lightness with which St Paul had been reproached, or perhaps merely the abstract quality. The reproach of fickleness was cast upon the Apostle for his change of purpose. It is to be remarked that *this* is the only charge he is attempting to meet in this and the next six verses. One of the special features of this Epistle, according to Robertson, is its exhibition of "the way in which a Christian may defend himself when maligned or misrepresented...An uncontradicted slander is believed readily, and often for long, and meanwhile influence is crippled or lost. Conceive what might have ensued, had St Paul not met the slander against his character with denial at once! For few persons take the trouble to sift a charge which is not denied."

according to the flesh] i.e. 'Are they the decisions of my human will, which is subject to change through caprice, or are they decisions made

be yea yea, and nay nay? But *as* God *is* true, our word 18 toward you was not yea and nay. For the Son of God, 19 Jesus Christ, who was preached among you by us, *even* by me and Silvanus and Timotheus, was not yea and nay,

according to the promptings of God's Spirit, and, as such, removed out of the region of human inconstancy of purpose?' Cf. Acts xix. 21. See also note on ch. v. 16, and ch. x. 2, 3.

that with me there should be yea yea, and nay nay] Some have rendered this (1) *that with me the yea should be yea and the nay nay*, as though in this last member of the sentence St Paul was shewing how impossible it was for him to be obstinate and to refuse to change his purpose for a reasonable cause. But the context is against this. Chrysostom, who adopts this view, lays the stress upon the words 'with me,' as though St Paul's private and individual will were contrasted with the dictates of the Spirit, which he was bound to follow, whether they laid him open to the charge of inconsistency or not. But the best way is (2) to interpret the passage in the usual manner, and to regard the Apostle as denying that he was infirm of purpose, and as reminding the Corinthians that he had but one definite end in view which he was resolutely bent upon attaining, namely, the ministering to them the Spirit of Jesus Christ. To this one purpose all minor plans and resolutions must give way.

18. *But as God is true, our word toward you was not yea and nay*] There was no more infirmity of purpose in the Apostle's preaching than there is untruth, or rather, *unfaithfulness* in God. 'Word' here means *speech, discourse*, as in 1 Cor. i. 5.

was not] Rather, **is** *not*, since the doctrine once preached remains ever the same. See Gal. i. 8, 9.

19. *For the Son of God, Jesus Christ*] St Paul now labours to impress the Corinthians with the weight of the commission with which he had been entrusted to them. It was nothing less than Jesus, the Promised and Anointed One, the Son of God, Whom he had preached.

was preached] Literally, **proclaimed**, as by a herald. The word has come usually to mean an exposition of God's Word in the Christian congregation.

Silvanus] Called Silas in the Acts. He was sent with Paul and Barnabas, as 'a chief man among the brethren,' to guarantee the authenticity of the Apostolic letter which the former brought back with them from Jerusalem to Antioch after the discussion recorded in Acts xv., since, had Paul and Barnabas returned alone, their opponents might not improbably have disputed its genuineness. See Acts xv. 22, 25, 27. He was a *prophet*, Acts xv. 32 (see 1 Cor. xiv.), and was chosen by St Paul, after his dispute with St Barnabas, as his fellow-traveller, by the advice of the Churches. Some have thought that he was the brother mentioned in ch. viii. 18, xii. 18. He is mentioned by St Paul with himself in the opening of each of the Epistles to the Thessalonians. He was with the Apostle at Philippi (Acts xvi. 19—40), at Thessalonica (xvii. 1, 4, 10), at Berea (xvii. 10), at Corinth (*not* at Athens, xvii. 15,

20 but in him was yea. For all the promises of God in him *are* yea, and in him Amen, unto the glory of God by

xviii. 5). He is not mentioned again in Scripture save by St Peter in his first Epistle (ch. v. 12), in which he speaks of him as one with whom he has little personal acquaintance, but much confidence. Silas is contracted from the fuller form Silvanus as Lucas from Lucanus. The similar signification of the two words *Lucas* and *Silvanus* have led some to suppose that St Luke and St Silas were the same person. But a perusal of the narrative in Acts xvi., xvii., especially ch. xvi. *vv.* 4—8, 10—17, 19, 20, will shew that they were two distinct persons. See Alford, *Prolegomena to Acts of the Apostles*, for a fuller investigation of this point. We may observe that not only does St Paul, in his humility, identify himself with the Corinthians (*v.* 14) but he takes care to associate his subordinates with him as fellow labourers in a common work. Paley, *Horae Paulinae*, remarks on the undesigned coincidence between this verse and Acts xxiii. 5. The two books are not written by the same person. There is no particular stress laid on the fact of Silas and Timotheus having been with the Apostle in either book, but the reference to them slips out quite accidentally. But *both* declare in this accidental way that Silas and Timotheus *were* with the Apostle at Corinth. Such minute agreement is beyond the power of the compiler of fictitious narrative. See a fuller discussion of this subject in the Introduction.

was not yea and nay, but in him was yea] The Son of God, the subject-matter of the Gospel, was no uncertain conception, sometimes affirmed and sometimes denied. The preaching of Him was the constant affirmation of a truth, an unchangeable blessing vouchsafed in Him to mankind. For '*in Him was* yea;' the original has the perfect, 'in Him i.e. in God, *v.* 18) *hath been* (or *become*) yea.' For in Him 'is no variableness, neither shadow of turning.' Numb. xxiii. 19; James i. 17. How then could the change of purpose in His minister be ascribed to the capricious infirmity of the mere human will? Cf. also Rom. xv. 8; Heb. xiii. 8.

20. *For all the promises of God in him are yea*] Literally, **for the promises of God, how many soever they be, in Him are yea.** The Apostle here, as elsewhere, reminds us that God's gifts depend upon His promise. Gal. iii. 14—29. And this promise is an affirmative utterance, never to be withdrawn or explained away. Whatever gifts are received by the ministration of His servants are the same in their character.

and in him Amen] This may refer either (1) actively, to the ratification by God of His own promises, see Heb. vi. 12—18, vii. 20, 21; Rev. iii. 14; or (2) passively, to the security *we* may feel that His Divine Word will never fail us. But our security is ever *in Him*. Some editors read (with the Vulgate) 'wherefore through him is the Amen,' in which case the meaning would be that *because* God's promises were unchangeable, they were to be depended upon.

unto the glory of God by us] i. e. through our instrumentality, because by the first preachers of the Gospel these glorious promises were made known.

us. Now he which stablisheth us with you in Christ, and 21 hath anointed us, *is* God; who hath also sealed us, and 22 given the earnest of the Spirit in our hearts. Moreover I 23

21. *Now he which stablisheth us with you in Christ*] Rather, and *He*, &c., as explaining the words 'by us.' 'Not as though we had any power in ourselves, to do anything of ourselves (cf. ch. iii. 5), but it is God who stablisheth us and Who anointed us for our great work.' The meaning of the Greek word translated *stablisheth*, as of the English one by which it is rendered (derived from the Latin *stabilio*), is to *make firm*, *immoveable*. For '*in Christ*,' the original has *unto* or *upon* Christ, i.e. by the faith and hope in Him which are 'as an anchor of the soul, both sure and steadfast,' Heb. vi. 19; cf. 1 Cor. iii. 11. Also Matt. xvi. 18; Eph. ii. 20.

and hath anointed us] Observe the change of tense here from the present to the past. The Greek however is not the perfect as in the A. V., but the aorist (so Wiclif, the perfect having been introduced by Tyndale, whom the other versions follow). That is, at some indefinite time in the past God 'anointed' St Paul and his fellow-labourers (see Acts x. 38; and 1 John ii. 20, 27, for the expression 'anointed'), i.e. when He commissioned them for their task (see Acts xiii. 2), which was to be 'ministers of Christ,' the Anointed One, 1 Cor. iv. 1.

is God] From no less than Him did their commission proceed, and in Him, and in none less, were their ministerial acts done.

22. *Who hath also sealed us*] Here again the Greek has the aorist. We must refer it here to the attestation God gave to his calling and anointing by the manifest signs of His presence with His ministers. See ch. iii. 1—3, xii. 12. Also Rom. xv. 15—19; 1 Cor. ix. 2. A *seal* (see note on 1 Cor. ix. 2; cf. Rom. xv. 28) is used to attest and confirm a legal document, which, according to our present legal custom, derived from the practice of past ages, when but few were able to write their names, must be 'sealed' as well as 'signed,' before it is 'delivered' to another person to act upon. For the expression 'sealed with the Spirit,' see Eph. i. 13, iv. 30, and also, for a similar expression, St John vi. 27.

and given the earnest of the Spirit] The Apostle here, as in ch. v. 5 and Eph. i. 14, uses the Hebrew word *arrhabon*, which, derived from a verb signifying to *plait* or *interweave*, and thence to *pledge* or be *security* for (as in Gen. xliii. 9), came to have the meaning of *earnest*. An *earnest* is to be distinguished, however, from a *pledge* (see Robertson *in loc.*), in that the latter is "something different in kind, given as assurance for something else," as in the case of the Sacraments, while the former is a *part of the thing to be given*, as when "a purchase is made, and part of the money paid down at once." Schleusner translates into German by *handgeld* or *angeld*. The Hebrew word however, has also the meaning of pledge, as in Gen. xxxviii. 17, 18. The word is found in the Greek and in a modified form in the Latin language, and exists to this day in the French "arrhes," and was no doubt derived by Greeks and Latins "from the language of Phoenician traders, as tariff, cargo, are derived in

call God for a record upon my soul, that to spare you I
24 came not as yet unto Corinth. Not for that we have
dominion over your faith, but are helpers of your joy: for
by faith ye stand.

English and other modern languages from Spanish traders."—Stanley.
See his whole note, and cf. Rom. viii. 23. Our own word *earnest* comes
from a root signifying to *run*, to *follow after eagerly*. The use of the
word in the text is due to the custom, common in all countries, of
giving some *pledge* of being in earnest. The words 'in earnest,' in
our sense of meaning what we say, occur early in our literature. See
Chaucer, *Legende of Good Women, Queen Dido*, line 1301. There is a
valuable note on this word in the Speaker's Commentary on Prov. vi. 1.

23. *I call God for a record upon my soul*] Literally, **to witness**, as
the Rhemish version. Tyndale, whom the other translators follow, has
recorde. Either (1) I call God to witness *against* my soul, i.e. to
avenge my perjury (so Calvin and Grotius; Wiclif, *agens*), or (2) *on
behalf of* my soul, as appealing to God as a witness of his sincerity.
See Rom. i. 9, and ix. 1; Gal. i. 20; Phil. i. 8; 1 Thess. ii. 5. Also
ch. xi. 31. In these passages, however, the form of the expression
is different. The word here translated 'call for a record' is not
used in Scripture in a bad sense. It signifies (1) to surname, as in
Matt. x. 3; (2) to appeal, as in Acts xxv. 11; and (3) to call upon, as
in Acts xxii. 16; 1 Cor. i. 2, &c. Augustine and other commentators
have remarked that it is lawful for a Christian to take an oath upon a
proper occasion. Cf. Matt. xxvi. 63.

that to spare you I came not as yet unto Corinth] Though St Paul
could 'use sharpness' if need so required he desired, as the minister of
the God of love, rather to come in the 'spirit of meekness.'

24. *Not for that we have dominion over your faith, but are helpers of
your joy*] *Ben lordis of* Wiclif, and so the other versions until the
Rhemish, which characteristically renders *overrule*. St Paul here
defines accurately his relation to his converts. What power he had—
and it was considerable (see 1 Cor. iv. 21; 2 Cor. ii. 9, vii. 15, x. 6,
xiii. 2, 10)—was simply *ministerial*, to assist the free growth of the
Christian life within them, one of whose foremost fruits (Gal. v. 22) was
joy, the joy of the man redeemed and sanctified in Christ, a joy which
could not be possessed by those who 'hold the truth in unrighteousness'
(Rom. i. 18). He had no right to place himself between their souls and
God, as a *necessary* channel in all cases of the Divine life.

for by faith ye stand] If they are enabled to stand firm against the
overrunning flood of ungodliness, it is not in dependence upon any
human being, however great and noble his mission (see *vv*. 21, 22;
Matt. x. 40; John xiii. 20, xx. 21; 1 Cor. vii. 25, 40; and 1 Thess. iv.
8), but by faith in a living Lord (cf. Rom. xi. 20; 1 Cor. xv. 1), Who
is able to save and to destroy.

CH. II. *St Paul's only Object the Spiritual Advancement of his Converts.*

But I determined this with myself, that *I* would not 2 come again to you in heaviness. For if I make you sorry, 3 who is he then that maketh me glad, but *the same* which is made sorry by me? And I wrote this same unto you, 3

CH. II. ST PAUL'S ONLY OBJECT THE SPIRITUAL ADVANCEMENT OF HIS CONVERTS.

1. *But I determined this with myself*] St Paul now further vindicates his consistency. Not only did he stay away from Corinth to spare the Corinthians the sharp rebukes which his immediate presence would have necessitated, but he hoped by means of the Epistle to work so salutary a reformation as to make his visit to Corinth a time of the deepest spiritual joy. The 'but' in the English version should be rendered *and*, thus carrying on the explanation from ch. i. 23. For '*with myself*' recent commentators prefer the rendering '*for* myself,' i.e. for the better carrying on of the work St Paul had in hand, which however (see 1 Cor. ix. 19—22, x. 33) was not his own profit, but the good of his converts. We may thus paraphrase his words, *I decided that the best course for me to pursue was not to come again to you in heaviness.*

that I would not come again to you in heaviness] There seems no need to suppose, with some commentators, that 'again' belongs to 'in heaviness,' and to explain it of some unrecorded visit which the Apostle paid in trouble of mind. The very contrary seems to be implied. St Paul's great anxiety was *not* to visit the Corinthian Church in such a frame of mind. It falls in best with the context to explain 'I determined that my *second* visit should not be paid while under the influence of painful feelings.' Olshausen remarks that the 'heaviness' here spoken of belongs as much to the Corinthians as to the Apostle. See next verse.

2. *For if I make you sorry*] So all the principal English translators. But the rendering gives a false impression to a modern ear. The best equivalent in modern English is 'if I *pain* you.' The idea of sorrow for the sin does not appear to have been introduced as yet. The '*I*' in this passage is emphatic; 'if I, whose sole delight is to see you happy, inflict pain, it is with the object of bringing about happiness in the end.' The connection of this verse with the preceding implied in the word 'for' seems to be as follows: "I *wrote* to cause pain, it is true, but it was in order that such pain should be removed before I came." Cf. ch. vii. 8.

who is he then that maketh me glad, but the same which is made sorry by me?] The apparent selfishness of this passage, in which St Paul appears to think that the grief he has caused is amply compensated for by the pleasure he receives from that grief, is explained by the words in the next verse, 'having confidence in you all, that my joy is the joy of you all.' See note there. The meaning would seem to be that St Paul

lest, when I came, I should have sorrow from *them of* whom I ought to rejoice; having confidence in you all, that my
4 joy is *the joy* of you all. For out of much affliction and anguish of heart I wrote unto you with many tears; not

wished not to come to Corinth in sorrow, but in joy, and that this end was attained by the result of the rebukes of his Epistle, which produced pain, and pain reformation, and reformation a pure and heavenly joy on the part of all, of St Paul, of the Corinthian community, and of the offender himself, conditions obviously the most favourable to an Apostolic visit. Cf. ch. vii. 11, 12, where the same idea is more fully expressed.

3. *And I wrote this same unto you*] Either (1) the announcement in 1 Cor. xvi. 7 of the Apostle's change of purpose, or (2) the rebukes in the former Epistle that grieved them, especially the passage in ch. v. of that Epistle which (cf. also *vv.* 2, 5—8 of this chapter) refers to a *single person*. The former agrees best with the context. In 2 Pet. i. 5, however, (3) the words here translated 'this same' are translated 'beside this.'

I should have sorrow from them of whom I ought to rejoice] St Paul hoped by his letter to produce such an effect that those who were blamed in it would abandon their sin. He *ought* to rejoice in such persons, for his rejoicing is to see them 'walk worthy of the vocation wherewith they were called' (Eph. iv. 1; cf. 1 Thess. iii. 8); and this, by virtue of their union with Christ, they might do if they would. Had he come, instead of writing, they must have caused him sorrow and not joy by the inconsistency of their Christian walk. Cf. ch. xii. 21.

having confidence in you all, that my joy is the joy of you all] Cf. ch. vii. 16. The Apostle still keeps in view that on which he had lately insisted, the identity of his feelings, hopes, aspirations with those of the Corinthians in virtue of their common life in Christ (see note on 1 Cor. i. 9). His joy and theirs is to see the members of the Corinthian community entirely led by the Spirit of Christ (Rom. viii. 14) and producing the fruit of the Spirit (Gal. v. 22) in all their actions. See John xv. 11.

4. *For out of much affliction and anguish of heart*] The word here translated anguish denotes a *drawing* or *holding together*, as we say, a *spasm*. It is only found here and in Luke xxi. 25. It was from no proud consciousness of superiority that St Paul wrote the rebukes of his former Epistle. He was no Pharisee who 'thanked God that he was not as other men are.' Neither did he take pleasure in grieving them, except so far as it tended to their profit. Therefore he wrote out of (i.e. they were the source from which his Epistle proceeded) much affliction and anguish of heart, not to distress them, but in order to shew his love, which took the shape of an anxious desire for their perfection. "It is the truest mark of affection," says Estius, "not to cloke the sins of those who are entrusted to your care, to rebuke them openly and plainly, even at the risk of causing considerable distress."

with many tears] "Which," says Calvin, "in the case of a brave and high-spirited man, are a token of intense grief."

that you should be grieved, but that ye might know the love which I have more abundantly unto you.

But if any have caused grief, he hath not grieved me, but 5 in part: that I may not overcharge you all. Sufficient to 6 such *a man is* this punishment, which *was inflicted* of many. So that contrariwise ye *ought* rather to forgive *him*, and 7

not that you should be grieved] Cf. ch. vii. 12.

5. *he hath not grieved me, but in part: that I may not overcharge you all*] According to the A. V. the meaning is that the Apostle, anxious not to lay too heavy a charge at the door of the Corinthian Church, to which (see 1 Cor. v. 2, 6) he considers the guilt to attach, declares that the offender has only pained him to a certain extent. But the words are capable of another rendering, 'But if any one hath caused pain, it is not *me* whom he has pained, but to a certain extent—not to press too heavily upon him—all of *you*.' This rendering is susceptible of two interpretations (1) he has caused pain to the whole community; but not to be too severe upon him, the Apostle is willing to admit that this pain is to a certain extent lessened by the mutual sympathy of the members of the Church. Or perhaps (2) there is a slight reproof here, implying, as in 1 Cor. v. 2, that the Corinthians had not sufficiently felt the disgrace brought on them all by such a crime. Cf. ch. i. 14. The Apostle thus, with no less adroitness than simple honesty, places the personal aspect of the question in the background, and deals with it as a matter of public principle, with which every member of the Church is as intimately concerned as himself. The whole passage refers to the offender mentioned in 1 Cor. v.

6. *Sufficient to such a man is this punishment*] See note on 1 Cor. v. 3—5. The discipline of the Apostolic Church, which had as its main object the restoration of the offender, was content when this object was attained. As soon as the offender renounced his sin, the end of the discipline was reached, and there was no further need of punishment. It was no desire of the Church in the Apostle's times, however much that important principle may have been lost sight of afterwards, that the offender should be 'swallowed up with overmuch sorrow.' "A plan diligently to be observed, for it teaches with what equity and clemency the discipline of the Church should be tempered, lest its rigour should exceed proper bounds." Calvin.

punishment] (*Blamynge*, Wiclif.) The word in the original signifies rebuke as well as punishment. Perhaps here it partakes of both senses. The public rebuke, coupled with separation from the Christian community and formal delivery over to Satan which St Paul prescribed (1 Cor. v. 5), was itself a severe punishment.

which was inflicted of many] Literally, **by the majority**. Some, perhaps, may have declined to take part in it, for there were many, as the latter part of the Epistle plainly shews, who still refused to acknowledge St Paul's authority.

7. *comfort him*] Better, perhaps, **encourage** him. See note on ch. i. 3.

comfort *him*, lest perhaps such a one should be swallowed
8 up with overmuch sorrow. Wherefore I beseech you that *you*
9 would confirm *your* love towards him. For to this end also
did I write, that I might know the proof of you, whether ye
10 be obedient in all *things*. To whom ye forgive any *thing*,

such a one] ὁ τοιοῦτος, the man of that description, the name by which St Paul always denotes the offender. See note on 1 Cor. v. 5. St Paul will not disgrace him to all future ages by mentioning his name.

swallowed up] Some commentators have supposed that St Paul here meant apostasy or suicide. But he designedly leaves the result indefinite. It is impossible to foresee what will become of a man overwhelmed with excessive sorrow.

with overmuch sorrow] Literally, **by the excess** of sorrow. "Nothing is more dangerous than to give Satan a handle whereby he may harass a sinner into despair." Calvin. Cf. also Gal. vi. 1 and Ecclus. viii. 5.

8. *Wherefore I beseech you, that you would confirm your love towards him*] The word 'your' is not in the original. It is not *their* love, but love *itself*, the fundamental principle (see 1 Cor. xiii. 1; 1 John iv. 8, 16) of the Christian covenant. The word here rendered *confirm* is used of the ratification, i.e. by some public act or token, of a covenant. See Gal. iii. 15, 17, where the same word is used in the original. The Vulgate, Calvin, Wiclif, the Geneva and Rhemish versions render *confirm*, Tyndale and Cranmer *that love may have strength*.

9. *For to this end also did I write*] St Paul here gives a third reason for writing the first Epistle. Not only was he anxious for the restoration of the offender, for a visit to Corinth which should have nothing of a painful character about it, but he wished to test the readiness of the Corinthians to submit to his authority (cf. ch. vii. 15, x. 6), a point on which (1 Cor. ix., 2 Cor. x.—xii.) at that moment there was considerable doubt. See also note on *v*. 6. Some commentators, however, contend that the word ἔγραψα, though an aorist, is, as what is called the Epistolary aorist, to be translated "I write" (as in 1 John ii. 14), and that it refers to the *present* letter, and that the test of obedience St Paul desired was the display of forgiveness. But this seems hardly consistent with 1 Cor. v. 2. See also Phil. ii. 12, and *v*. 3 of this chapter.

the proof] That which has been tested and has borne the test. The word is variously translated in our version. In Rom. v. 4 it is translated *experience*, in ch. viii. 2 of this Epistle, *trial*, in ix. 13, *experiment*, in xiii. 3 and in Phil. ii. 22, *proof*.

10. *To whom ye forgive any thing, I forgive also*] St Paul is here exercising the power of the keys (see Matt. xvi. 19, xviii. 18; St John xx. 23). He is not speaking of any private forgiveness of a personal injury, but of the public absolution of an offender lying under the censure of the church. See 1 Cor. v. 4, 5. We may observe (1) that St Paul acts upon the report of the Corinthian Church properly

I *forgive* also: for if I forgave any *thing*, to whom I forgave
it, for your sakes *forgave I it* in the person of Christ; lest 11
Satan should get an advantage of us: for we are not ignorant of his devices.

Furthermore, when I came to Troas to *preach* Christ's 12

authenticated by Titus, his representative there (ch. vii. 6—14), and (2) that he gives his official sanction to their act.

to whom I forgave it] Most modern Editors read *what* for *to whom*, and the verb stands in the perfect, implying that the affair is at an end. '*What I have forgiven, I have forgiven on your account.*' St Paul does not claim the right to ratify their act for the satisfaction of his own sense of importance, but because his Apostolic office is necessary for their edification and guidance.

in the person of Christ] Cranmer and the Geneva version render 'in the *sight*' (literally, in the **face**) of Christ. So also Calvin. The Vulgate which is followed by Wiclif, and of course the Rhemish, renders as in the text. Tyndale renders *roume*. As the Greek word signifies both *person* and *face*, the point must be left undecided. If the A. V. be correct, then St Paul acts in this matter as Christ's representative. If the other is the correct rendering, then he performs a solemn public act in the sight of Christ and the powers unseen. It should however, be added that in this Epistle we have the word here used in the sense of *person* in ch. i. 11, and in the sense of *face* in ch. iii. 7, 13, 18, and that the expression occurs again in ch. iv. 6, where see note.

11. *Lest Satan should get an advantage of us*] See note on 1 Cor. v. 10. The word signifies (1) to have more, (2) to be greedy, and hence (3) to overreach, to defraud.

devices] The word properly means *mental processes*, " the product of mind." Meyer. It is translated *minds* in ch. iii. 14, iv. 4, xi. 3; Phil. iv. 7, *thought* in ch. x. 5. In reference to Satan, all whose thoughts are evil, it may legitimately be translated devices, i.e. things which he *devised*. Luke xxii. 31. 1 Cor. vii. 5. Cf. 1 Pet. v. 8. Rev. xii. 12. St Paul's meaning here is that to refuse forgiveness when the time for it had come would be only to give Satan an advantage. The offender had been delivered over to him (see 1 Cor. v. 5 and notes). Not to release him from the bondage when he was truly repentant would be to afford the enemy of souls an opportunity of which he would not be slow to avail himself. Nothing is so likely to plunge a man into every kind of crime as despair. See notes on *v.* 7.

12. *Furthermore, when I came to Troas*] Another proof is now given of the Apostle's sincere desire for the well-being of his converts, his distress at the non-arrival of Titus at the time expected. In spite of the opportunity afforded him of preaching the gospel at Troas, his anxiety would not suffer him to rest, but he hurried on to Macedonia, where at length he found Titus, and heard from him the tidings for which he had scarcely dared to hope.

to Troas] Rather, to **the Troad**, the angle of territory to the south of the Hellespont on which Troy was situated. See Acts xvi. 8, 11,

13 gospel, and a door was opened unto me of the Lord, I had no rest in my spirit, because I found not Titus my brother:

xx. 5; 2 Tim. iv. 13. " Still, it must have been at the city that the Apostle stayed. It had been built" (upon the ruins of the ancient city, as Dr Schliemann's discoveries seem to prove) "by Antigonus (Alexander's lieutenant) under the name of Antigonia Troas, was afterwards called by Lysimachus, another of Alexander's generals, Alexandria Troas, and was at this time a Roman 'colonia Juris Italici' and regarded with great favour by the Roman emperors, as the representative of the ancient Troy, of which it has been supposed to occupy the site."—Stanley. It must be remembered that the Romans, as Virgil's *Aeneid* testifies, were under the belief that they were the descendants of the ancient Trojans. See Acts xvi. 8, xx. 5, 6 also Conybeare and Howson's *St Paul*, and Smith's *Dictionary of Geography*.

to preach Christ's gospel] Literally, **unto**, i.e. **for the furtherance of the good tidings of Christ.** The word *gospel*, as is well known, is derived from the Anglo-Saxon *god*, good, and *spell*, history or narrative. Some have supposed it to have been *God's* spell or history, but the former derivation accords best with the Greek. *Spell* is now used only to signify the naming the letters of which a word is composed, or of a magical incantation. But both these are derived from the same Anglo-Saxon root.

and a door was opened unto me of the Lord] Door, in New Testament phraseology, is equivalent to *opportunity*. See 1 Cor. xvi. 9; Rev. iii. 8. St Paul had come to Troas with the special purpose of preaching the Gospel, and not merely as a traveller. Unusual opportunities offered themselves, but his anxiety about the condition of the Corinthian Church caused him to forego them all. Calvin and Estius discuss the propriety of St Paul's leaving unused the opportunity offered to him at Troas. But he soon (Acts xx. 6) returned thither, and he evidently had good reason to believe the state of things at Corinth to be the more urgent of the two. It was of more importance to keep those who were called by the name of Christ from disgracing Him, than to bring fresh souls to the knowledge of Him.

13. *I had no rest in my spirit*] i.e. the higher and nobler part of his being, superior to the soul. Cf. 1 Cor. ii. 14, 15 and notes. Also 1 Cor. xv. 44—46.

because I found not Titus my brother] Titus (see ch. viii. 6, xii. 18) had been sent by the Apostle to superintend the 'collection for the saints' at Corinth (1 Cor. xvi. 1). He was most probably the bearer of the former Epistle, and was anxiously expected by the Apostle (ch. vii. 6) to bring information regarding the effect it had had upon the Corinthian Church. Though Titus is not mentioned in the Acts of the Apostles, he possessed in a high degree the confidence of the Apostle (ch. viii. 16), as is shewn by his taking the chief place—he seems even to have held a position of greater prominence than 'the brother whose praise is in the Gospel throughout all the Churches' (ch. viii. 18)—in this important mission. Before this, he, as a Gentile, had been the subject of some discussion between St Paul and the Judaizing party at Jerusalem. The

but taking my leave of them, I went from *thence* into Macedonia. Now thanks *be* unto God, which always causeth us 14 to triumph in Christ, and maketh manifest the savour of

latter maintained that Titus ought to be circumcised, the former that he ought not; but St Paul carried his point. His character seems to have been one of deep earnestness and zeal (ch. vii. 13, 15, viii. 16, 17) calculated to win the confidence of the great Apostle. He was afterwards placed in charge of the church in Crete, and in this capacity received from St Paul a letter of instruction known as the Epistle to Titus. The last mention of him in point of date is in 2 Tim. iv. 10, when he is said to have 'departed to Dalmatia,' doubtless on a mission. For the Apostle's feelings on this occasion (ch. vii. 5—13) compare a similar anxiety displayed at an earlier period of his Apostolic career in 1 Thess. iii. 2, 5—9.

I went from thence into Macedonia] Cf. Acts xx. 1.

14. *Now thanks be unto God*] This passage is an instance of the abrupt digressions peculiar to St Paul's style. See Introduction to the first Epistle, p. 16, and 1 Cor. iv. 8. Also Introduction to this Epistle. "As soon as St Paul came to the word Macedonia, memory presented to him what had greeted him there," i.e. the favourable intelligence brought by Titus (ch. vii. 6, 7) "and in his rapid way—thoughts succeeding each other like lightning—he says, without going through the form of explaining why he says it, 'Now thanks be to God.'" Robertson.

which always causeth us to triumph in Christ] The verb here rendered *causeth us to triumph* may also be rendered, *leadeth us in triumph*. It is used in the latter sense in Col. ii. 15, the only other place in which it occurs in the Bible, but the former sense is defended here by the analogy of other verbs used causatively. See Rom. viii. 37.

and maketh manifest the savour of his knowledge] The word *savour* (from the Latin *sapor*, flavour) is, with *one* exception (Matt. v. 13), used in the Scriptures to denote an odour. See Gen. viii. 21; Eccl. x. 1; Joel ii. 20, &c. The Apostle as yet does not refer to the 'sweet savour' of the sacrifices (Exod. xxix. 18; Lev. i. 9, 12, &c.). If we take the rendering of the A.V. in the former part of the verse, 'the savour of his knowledge' (i.e. the sweet scent of the knowledge of God), is the incense, either "rising from fixed altars or wafted from censers" (Dr Plumptre *in loc.*), which it was customary (see Smith's *Dictionary of Antiquities*, Art. *Triumphus*) to burn as the conqueror to whom a triumph was decreed passed along. This custom has been revived in our own day, on the occasion of the public entry of the Princess of Wales into London before her marriage. If the sense '*leadeth us* in triumph,' be adopted, it regards the ministers of Christ either, (*a*) as the partners in the triumph of their Master, or (*b*) as the captives of the enemy he has overcome, delivered by His victorious arm, or (*c*) as the enemies he has defeated and led captive. Either of these yields a good sense, while the 'savour' is still the incense which attends the victor's triumph. See Wordsworth *in loc.* Dr Plumptre notices the fact, one of great interest to the inhabitants of these Islands, that

15 his knowledge by us in every place. For we are unto God a sweet savour of Christ, in them that are saved, and in
16 them that perish: to the one *we are* the savour of death unto death; and to the other the savour of life unto life.

the last triumph which had taken place at Rome before these words were written, was in commemoration of the victories of Claudius in Britain, and that the British king Caractacus was then led in triumph through the streets of Rome.

by us] St Paul is either (1) the altar (Rom. xii. 1) from which the odour of God's knowledge arises, or more probably (2) the thurifer or incense-bearer who diffuses that odour abroad as he passes along.

in every place] The history of the church shews that the first ministers of the Gospel extended their operations over a wide area. It is hardly tradition which regards St Thomas and St Bartholomew as having preached in India, and St Andrew in Scythia. And the first Epistle of St Peter bears witness to a wide dissemination of the Gospel in Asia. See 1 Pet. i. 1, and v. 13.

15. *For we are unto God a sweet savour of Christ*] The form of the expression is here altered in two ways: (1) the Apostle himself now becomes the 'sweet savour,' while (2) the idea of sacrifice is first brought in. The Apostle now uses the phrase used in the LXX. for a sacrificial odour (see note on last verse). The ministers of Christ are a sweet savour of Him, the great Atoning Sacrifice, not only because they make Him known, but because they are imbued and interpenetrated with the spirit of His Sacrifice, 'always bearing about in the body the dying of the Lord Jesus.' And this not only in themselves but in those to whom they minister the Spirit of the Lord (cf. ch. iii. 3) as soon as they in their turn begin to display the same spirit, or even in a certain sense (see next note) when they do not. See Eph. v. 2; Phil. iv. 18.

in them that are saved, and in them that perish] The tense in the original speaks of no *completed* work, but is strictly present: those who are *in process* of being saved or of perishing. Cf. Luke xiii. 23; Acts ii. 47; 1 Cor. i. 18; ch. iv. 3. The imagery of the triumphal procession is still before the Apostle. *Some* of those who took part in it were destined to rewards and honours, others were doomed to perpetual imprisonment or death. Christ and His servants are a savour of life unto them who are in the way of salvation, because through conformity to the spirit of Christ's sacrifice arises conformity to His life, a savour of death unto those who are not in the way of salvation, because a deliverance refused does but make destruction inevitable. Cf. Matt. xxi. 44; Luke ii. 34; John iii. 18—20, ix. 39, xii. 48, xv. 22.

16. *To the one we are the savour of death unto death; and to the other the savour of life unto life*] The reading accepted by most recent editors is 'a savour arising from death and resulting in death,' and 'a savour arising from life and resulting in life,' according to a construction common to St Paul, of which the most remarkable instance, perhaps, is Rom. i. 17. The Gospel is a savour arising from death, because it proclaims the Death of Christ as the foundation of all reconciliation.

And who *is* sufficient for these *things?* For we are not as 17 many, which corrupt the word of God: but as of sincerity, but as of God, in the sight of God speak we in Christ.

Cf. John ix. 39; 1 Cor. i. 23, 24, xv. 14—18; 1 Pet. ii. 7, 8. To those only who believe in a risen, ascended, living Christ, is the Gospel a savour arising from, and tending to life. Dr Plumptre remarks on the way in which the figure of the triumphal procession is kept before the reader. To some of those who were being led in procession the odour of the incense "would seem as a breath from Paradise, giving life and health; to others its sweetness would seem sickly and pestilential, coming as from a charnel house."

And who is sufficient for these things?] The thought occurs to the Apostle that the wondrous effects consequent on the first proclamation of Christ's Gospel are far above unassisted human powers. Cf. 1 Cor. ii. 12—16. But he defers the consideration of this topic to ch. iii. 5, confining himself at present (see next verse) to assigning the reason for his exclamation, namely, that he can fearlessly appeal to what was above man's natural ability, the transparent honesty, and thorough faithfulness to God, of his preaching. Perhaps also the Apostle intends to convey the idea that what may be an easy task for those who proclaim a spurious Gospel, is one that demands the utmost watchfulness on the part of the genuine minister of Christ.

17. *For we are not as many, which corrupt the word of God*] The original makes 'many' definite with the article, thus clearly pointing out the false teachers, against whom so much of this and the former Epistle is directed. The word of God may be corrupted (1) by the admixture of foreign doctrines, e. g. those of the Judaizers, who grafted on Christianity the alien doctrine of the universal obligation of the Jewish law, (2) by degrading the doctrine of Christ into a system of argument and disputation (1 Cor. i. 17—31, ii. 1, 4, 5, 14), and (3) by the introduction of personal objects, such as influence, authority, the praise of men (1 Cor. iv. 6; 2 Cor. x. 12, xi. 18; Gal. iv. 17). The word here translated *corrupt* occurs nowhere else in the New Testament. It is derived from a substantive equivalent in meaning to our *higgler* or *huckster*, especially a dealer in wine (See the LXX. of Is. i. 22. The word is not in the Hebrew), and hence from the dishonest practices of these small dealers it has come, by a process somewhat similar to that of our reproachful terms 'higgling' or 'huckstering,' to mean *adulterate*, i. e. to mix what should be pure with worthless or even deleterious substances.

but as of sincerity, but as of God] See note on i. 12. The word is here opposed to the idea of corrupting by admixture. The Apostle does not lose sight even here of the truth to which he returns in ch. iii. 5, that his purity of heart is a supernatural gift. If he preaches Christ of sincerity, it is because the power to do so comes from God, Who gave the mission.

in the sight of God] A task imposed by God, and performed with the consciousness that His All-seeing Eye is upon those whom He has sent.

CH. III. 1—6. *St Paul's Ministry no self-assumed task, but the communication of the Spirit.*

3 Do we begin again to commend ourselves? or need we, as some *others*, epistles of commendation to you, or *letters* 2 of commendation from you? Ye are our epistle written in

speak we in Christ] St Paul, throughout the whole of this chapter, has had in view the vindication of himself from any ulterior motives or lower principles of action in preaching Christ. His sole object is to minister Him. He desires nothing for himself. If he rebukes, it is for the offender's sake. If he tests the obedience of the Church, it is because he is set over it for its benefit, not for his. If he preaches the word of God, it is by virtue of an inspiration from Him, whereby he preaches simply and faithfully the words put in his mouth by Christ. His doctrine is *of* God, delivered as in His sight, and spoken *in Christ*.

CH. III. 1—6. ST PAUL'S MINISTRY NO SELF-ASSUMED TASK, BUT THE COMMUNICATION OF THE SPIRIT.

1. *Do we begin again to commend ourselves?*] A charge had been apparently brought against St Paul that he had before (probably in 1 Cor. ii. 16, iii. 10, iv. 11—14, ix. 20—27, xiv. 18) indulged in unseemly self-laudation. He supposes that the same charge will be brought against him for his language in ch. ii. 14—17.

as some others] The opponents of St Paul had no doubt come armed with letters of commendation from some Apostle (as the Judaizers in Gal. ii. 12) or Church, and some of them had received similar letters from the Corinthian Churches on their departure, with a view to their reception by some other Church. St Paul appeals to the nature of his work among them as rendering such a proceeding on his part not only unnecessary but absurd.

epistles of commendation] Tyndale and Cranmer, better, **letters of recommendation**, the word from its derivation signifying rather *introduction* than what we now understand by *commendation*, i.e. praise, though it would seem to have come to this meaning in New Testament Greek. See last note but one. Instances of such letters commendatory are to be found in Acts xv. 25—27, xviii. 27; Rom. xvi. 1; Col. iv. 10. They became a common, almost a necessary, feature in the life of the early Church, and were known as *literae formatae*.

2. *Ye are our epistle*] See note on last verse.

written in our hearts] 'Others bear their letters of commendation in their hands, we in our consciences, being fully aware that the existence of the Church of Corinth, due, under God, to us, is a sufficient authentication of the genuineness of our ministry.' See 1 Cor. ix. 2. Olshausen, however, regards the words as referring to St Paul's intercession for the Corinthians, just as the High Priest (Exod. xxviii. 15—30) bore the names of the tribes of Israel on his breast when he went into the holy place to intercede with God. "The regenerate," he adds, "are

our hearts, known and read of all men: forasmuch as ye 3 are manifestly declared to be the epistle of Christ ministered by us, written not with ink, but with the Spirit of the living God; not in tables of stone, but in fleshy tables of

linked to the heart of their spiritual father by a spiritual bond." See notes above, ch. i. 9, ii. 3.

known and read of all men] See note on ch. i. 13. The play upon words so characteristic of the Apostle cannot be rendered into English.

3. *Forasmuch as ye are manifestly declared*] The Corinthians 'fell short in no gift,' but were 'enriched by Christ in all utterance and in all knowledge,' 1 Cor. i. 7. These were notorious facts that could not be gainsaid, capable of being 'known of all men.'

to be the epistle of Christ ministered by us] i.e. brought into existence through our instrumentality. It can hardly be said that St Paul has varied the figure of speech here. The Corinthians are an epistle. Of that epistle Christ is the author; the thoughts and sentiments are His. St Paul (cf. 1 Cor. iii. 5, 7, 9, iv. 1; 2 Cor. vi. 1) is the instrument by which the epistle was written. Its characters were preserved by no visible or perishable medium, but by the invisible operation of the Spirit. It was graven, not on stone, but on human hearts. And it was recognized wherever St Paul went as the attestation of his claim to be regarded as a true minister of Christ, and this equally in his own consciousness (see last verse) and in that of all Churches which he visited. Dean Stanley remarks on the number and variety of the similes with which this chapter is crowded.

ink] A black pigment of some kind was used by the ancients for all writings of any length. For shorter writings recourse was frequently had to waxen tablets. See Jer. xxxvi. 18; 2 John 12; 3 John 13, and articles Atramentum, Tabulae, Stilus, Liber, in Smith's *Dictionary of Antiquities*.

the Spirit of the living God] St Paul never seems to lose sight of the fact that Christianity is a communication of life,—the life of Him who alone is the fountain of life. See note on 1 Cor. xv. 1, and Rom. viii. 2, 10. Cf. also John i. 4, v. 26, 40, xiv. 6; 2 Tim. i. 10; 1 Pet. ii. 5.

not in tables of stone] See Exod. xxiv. 12, xxxiv. 1; Deut. ix. 9—11, x. 1. Here the Apostle first hints at what is to be the subject of the next section of the Epistle, the inferiority of the law to the Gospel. There is a slight incongruity thus introduced into the simile. One does not write with *ink* on tables of *stone*. But the Apostle, in the pregnant suggestiveness of his style, neglects such minor considerations when he has a great lesson to convey. Dean Stanley refers us to Ezek. xi. 19, xxxvi. 26, 27 and also suggests that the form of the expression 'tables of the heart,' may be derived from Prov. iii. 3, and vii. 3, not however from the LXX., which there has a different translation of the Hebrew word.

of the heart] Most recent editors read 'in *fleshy tables*, namely, *hearts*.' All the old English versions, however, follow the Vulgate here. It is extremely difficult to decide between the two readings, which depend

4 the heart. And such trust have we through Christ to God-
5 ward: not that we are sufficient of ourselves to think any
6 *thing* as of ourselves; but our sufficiency *is* of God; who
also hath made us able ministers of the new testament; not

upon the absence or presence of a single letter in the Greek. It should be noted here that the word translated *fleshy* does not mean *carnal*, i.e. *governed* by the flesh, but *made of flesh*.

4. *such trust*] Better, perhaps, with the Rhemish version, **confidence** (Vulgate and Calvin *fiducia*), i.e. the confidence which St Paul had above expressed (ch. ii. 14—17) in the reality of his mission and work, or in the fact that the Corinthian Church is in itself a sufficient guarantee of his Apostolic mission (*vv*. 2, 3). See also 1 Cor. xv. 10.

through Christ to God-ward] So Tyndale and Cranmer. Calvin and Erasmus *erga Deum*. The Vulgate, which is followed by Wiclif, the Genevan and the Rhemish version, has, more literally, *ad Deum*. The words have been interpreted to mean (1) which will stand the test of God's trial. (2) Which will be proved and rewarded in the judgment of God. (3) In our relation to God. Or the analogy of John i. 1 ("has His face continually directed towards the Eternal Father," Liddon, *Bampton Lectures*) may lead us to conclude (4) that our eyes are directed towards God, the source of our confidence, and that it is through Jesus Christ alone that we possess the right thus to rely on Him. This interpretation is strengthened by a reference to Matt. xix. 8, where the preposition is equivalent to *in regard to*.

5. *Not that we are sufficient*] We here return to the idea touched upon in ch. ii. 16, but then passed over on account of St Paul's eagerness to assert the purity of his motives.

of ourselves to think any thing as of ourselves] The two prepositions translated 'of' here are not the same in the Greek. The former signifies '*from*' simply, but not excluding the idea of origination in some source outside us. The latter signifies '*out of*' as from an original source.

but our sufficiency is of God] Cf. 1 Cor. iii. 9.

6. *Who also hath made us able ministers*] None of the old English versions have given the threefold repetition of the word by St Paul, who writes, 'Who hath made us *sufficient* ministers.' The word St Paul uses signifies the having *reached a certain standard* of ability.

of the new testament] We must dismiss all notions here of the book called the "New Testament." The word in the original (see note on 1 Cor. xi. 25) signifies both *testament* and *covenant*. The latter should be the rendering here. St Paul is contrasting the Mosaic with the Christian covenant. There is also no article. The Apostle's meaning may be thus paraphrased: 'Who hath endowed us with qualifications sufficient for us to become the ministers of a new covenant.' It is not to the covenant, but to its *newness*, that the Apostle would here ask our attention.

not of the letter, but of the spirit] See Jer. xxxi. 31—34, and Ezek. xi. 19, before cited. There is an obvious reference to these passages in the text. The difference between the old covenant and the new was

of the letter, but of the spirit: for the letter killeth, but the spirit giveth life.

7—18. *The Ministration of the Spirit superior to that of the Law.*

But if the ministration of death, written *and* engraven 7

that the former *prescribed*, the latter *inspired;* the former gave written precepts, the latter the power to fulfil them; the former laid down the rules, the latter brought man's heart into the condition in which such rules became a part of his nature. "The old form was superseded by the *principle.* Instead of saying, 'Thou shalt not say Fool, or Raca,' Christ gave the principle of Love." Robertson. The words 'of the letter,' and 'of the spirit,' however, depend not on the word *covenant,* but on the word *ministers.* See also Rom. i. 16; 1 Cor. i. 18, 24 and notes. Also, for the expression, Rom. ii. 27, vii. 6. "What then, was not that law spiritual? How then did he say, 'We know that the law is spiritual?' Spiritual indeed, for it came from God, *but it bestowed not a spirit.*" Chrysostom.

for the letter killeth, but the spirit giveth life] *Quykeneth,* Wiclif. Cf. 1 Cor. xv. 45. The formal enactment, whether positive or negative, can only *kill.* For while it makes no difference whatever in the condition of the man who fulfils it, it condemns him who disobeys or neglects to perform its precepts. See St John iii. 17, 18; Rom. iii. 20, iv. 20, v. 13, vii. 10. The *spirit,* the breath or influence proceeding from God, can only *give life,* since it comes from Him who *is life,* and by breathing into man a new heart, enables him to perform naturally, without the aid of any enactments, the things that are pleasing to God. "The law, if it lay hold of a murderer, putteth him to death; the Gospel, if it lay hold of a murderer, enlighteneth and giveth him life." Chrysostom. Cf. John vi. 63; Rom. viii. 11; 1 Cor. xv. 45; Gal. vi. 8; 1 Pet. iii. 18. Calvin remarks on a singular misconception of the meaning of this passage by Origen and others, who supposed that the reading of Scripture would be useless or even injurious, unless it were allegorically expounded. "Sensus ad Origenis damnata dogmata rejiciendus." Estius.

7—18. THE MINISTRATION OF THE SPIRIT SUPERIOR TO THAT OF THE LAW.

7. *But if the ministration of death*] He does not say 'which causeth,' but 'the ministration of death,' for that which *caused* death was sin, while the Law made the sin manifest, but did not cause it. Chrysostom. See Rom. vii. 7; 1 Cor. xv. 56; Gal. iii. 10, 21. As St Paul was the minister of Christ when he proclaimed the good tidings of salvation to mankind, so the law was the minister of death when it proclaimed the sentence of death to the soul that had sinned. See Ezek. xviii. 4.

written and engraven in stones] Wiclif, nearer to the original, *writun lettris in stones.* The reference is to the two tables of the law,

in stones, was glorious, so that the children of Israel could not stedfastly behold the face of Moses for the glory of his countenance; which *glory* was to be done 8 away: how shall not the ministration of the spirit be rather 9 glorious? For if the ministration of condemnation *be* glory, much more doth the ministration of righteousness exceed in

Exod. xxxi. 18. Some editors read 'the ministration of death *in the letter*, engraved in stones.'

was glorious] Perhaps rather, **was constituted, came into being**, in glory, i.e. accompanied by glory. Exod. xix. 16—20, xxiv. 6—11, xxxiv. 4—8.

so that the children of Israel could not stedfastly behold (literally, **gaze at**) *the face of Moses*] The brightness of God's glory was reflected upon the face of Moses (Exod. xxxiv. 29, 30) to such an extent that the children of Israel dared not approach him. See note on v. 13. The Hebrew word used for the rays of light emitted by Moses' face is derived from a word signifying *a horn*, according to a simile common among Eastern writers by which the first rays of the sun are called horns, and even the sun itself a gazelle by the Arabs. This the Vulgate renders by *cornuta*, a rendering which, as Dr Plumptre reminds us, has been the cause why the celebrated Moses of Michael Angelo, familiar to all who have visited Rome and to many who have not, is represented with beams of light in the shape of horns upon the head.

which glory was to be done away] Rather, **was being brought to nought.** The original meaning of the word rendered '*done away*,'—which (see note on 1 Cor. xiii. 8) is rendered in various ways in the A. V.—is *to make thoroughly useless or unprofitable*, and hence to *do away with, abolish, bring to nought.* The Apostle does not mean to say here that the brightness on Moses' face was destined to fade, but that it *was fading*.

8. *How shall not the ministration of the spirit be rather glorious?*] Literally, *how shall not the ministration of the spirit rather* **be in glory**, i.e. if the brightness which was actually fading was so glorious that the Israelites could not bear to look at it, how much more shall the ministration of the spirit, which is not destined to be transitory, be and remain glorious. The preposition *ἐν* denotes the permanency of the glory, the future tense of the verb indicates that whatever the glory of the Gospel dispensation now, there are greater glories in store. All this glory proceeds from the fact that it is the spirit of a Living God that the new dispensation ministers. See *v.* 3.

9. *For if the ministration of condemnation be glory*] *Dampnacioun*, Wiclif, and similarly the Rhemish version. The law must be understood to be a ministry of condemnation, "not in itself and in its own nature, but accidentally, in consequence of man's corruption," Turretin. So St Paul explains in Rom. vii. 12—14; Gal. iii. 23; and 1 Tim. i. 8—10. Cf. also Heb. xii. 18—21 and note on *v.* 7.

much more doth the ministration of righteousness exceed in glory] Or, **abound.** See last note but one. The Gospel was the ministration of

glory. For even that which was made glorious had no glory 10
in this respect, by reason of the glory that excelleth. For 11
if that which is done away *was* glorious, much more that
which remaineth *is* glorious. Seeing then that we have such 12
hope, we use great plainness of speech: and not as Moses, 13

righteousness because righteousness was imparted by the indwelling of
the Spirit of the Living God (*v.* 3). See notes on *v.* 6; also Rom. iii.
21, cf. ch. v. 21.

10. *For even that which was made glorious had no glory in this respect, by reason of the glory that excelleth*] Rather, **For even that which has been glorified** (i. e. the face of Moses, typical of the Law) **has not been glorified in this respect** (i. e. in comparison of the New Covenant. The Geneva Version renders 'in *this point*'—see ch. ix. 3, where the expression occurs again, also the received text in 1 Pet. iv. 16) **on account of the glory** (i.e. of the New Covenant) **which surpasses** (it). Other explanations of the passage have been given, but Bp. Wordsworth, who places this passage and the LXX. of Exod. xxxiv. in parallel columns, shews how St Paul throughout this chapter is using the very words of the LXX., which must therefore be the index to his meaning. He paraphrases thus: "that was *glorified*, but glorious as it was, it was not glorified in one respect—that is, it was not glorified relatively to and in comparison with the *Evangelical* Ministry, which far transcends its glory, and absorbs it."

11. *For if that which is done away*] Rather, is (or was) **being** done away. See note on *v.* 7.

was glorious] Literally, was **by means of**, or **through** glory, i. e. was accompanied with, or seen through a haze of glory. See note on *v.* 7.

much more that which remaineth is glorious] Literally, is **in glory**, i.e. as a *permanent* attribute. Some, however, think that the Apostle often uses different prepositions (see last note) to express the same meaning. The passages, however, to which they refer, though they render this view probable, do not establish it as a fact beyond the reach of doubt.

12. *Seeing then that we have such hope*] i.e. the hope that the Christian covenant is one of which the glory is permanent.

we use great plainness of speech] *Trist* (i.e. trust) Wiclif. *Boldness*, Tyndale and Cranmer. The translation *boldness of speech* we owe to the Geneva version. The word means originally (1) fulness or frankness of *speech*. Hence it comes to mean (2) openness, frankness generally, and hence (3) boldness, intrepidity. The former is the meaning here. St Paul contrasts the fulness and frankness of the Gospel on all matters relating to the future of man with the mysterious silence of the Law (i. e. the books of Moses), which hardly in the most distant manner allude to a future life. It may be remarked that even Jesus Christ himself used much reserve (Matt. viii. 4, ix. 30, xii. 16, xiii. 10—13, xvi. 20, xvii. 9) until His work on earth was finished. Then (Matt. xxviii. 19; Mark xvi. 15) He decreed that this reserve should cease for ever. "We speak everywhere with freedom, keeping back nothing, concealing nothing, suspecting nothing, but speaking plainly."

which put a vail over his face, that the children of Israel could not stedfastly look to the end of that which is abo-
14 lished: but their minds were blinded: for until this day

Chrysostom. "A ministry whose very life is outspokenness and free fearlessness—which scorns to take a *via media* because it is safe in the eyes of the world." Robertson.

13. *And not as Moses*] i.e. we do not act as Moses did, who put a veil on his face.

that the children of Israel could not stedfastly look to the end of that which is abolished] The Greek implies that Moses placed the veil on his face *after* speaking to the people that they might not see the glory on his face fading. The LXX. of *v.* 33 implies the same thing, and the Vulgate still more explicitly. The Hebrew is ambiguous, from the want of a pluperfect tense in that language. But the LXX. in *vv.* 34, 35, as well as the Hebrew, imply that Moses veiled his countenance *on account of the terror* with which its brightness inspired the Israelites. The latter says expressly that he kept his face unveiled *until he came forth* from speaking to God. So St Paul seems to imply himself in *v.* 7. The fact seems to be that St Paul, as is extremely common with him, and as occurs several times in this chapter (as in *v.* 3 and *v.* 18) gives the simile he is employing another direction. He has been contrasting the glory of the Mosaic with that of the Christian dispensation. He adduces the latter as a reason for the transparent sincerity of which he had boasted in ch. ii. 17. He proceeds to contrast that absence of reserve with the reticence of Moses in the law. The figure of the veil once more occurs to him as an illustration of the fact that the Jews were not, for reasons which are obvious enough, encouraged to look upon the Law as a transitory dispensation (though sometimes hints of this kind were vaguely thrown out, as in the celebrated passage in Deut. xviii. 15, 18, 19);—not allowed to see the gradual extinction of that glory which had seemed to them so great, and whose greatness was the surest guarantee of their obedience. Many commentators have supposed here an allusion to Christ as the end of the law (Rom. x. 4). But Olshausen pertinently asks, "How could St Paul say that Moses covered his countenance in order that the Israelites should not behold Christ?"

is abolished] Literally, **was being brought to nought.** See note on *v.* 7.

14. *But their minds were blinded*] They neither obeyed the Law when it was given, nor would cease to obey it when it was superseded. The word rendered *blinded* properly signifies hardened, and is so translated in Mark vi. 52, viii. 17; John xii. 40; and in the margin of Rom. xi. 7 (where the text gives the same translation as here). See also Eph. iv. 18. The rendering *blinded* is justified by the fact that many cases of what is called cataract are attributable to the hardening of the crystalline lens of the eye into a chalky substance, a process for which the Greek word here used is a proper equivalent. Our version here follows Tyndale. Wiclif has *but the wittis of hem ben astonied*, and

vv. 15—17.]   II. CORINTHIANS, III.   53

remaineth the same vail untaken away in the reading of the old testament; which *vail* is done away in Christ. But *even* 15 unto this day, when Moses is read, the vail is upon their heart. Nevertheless when *it* shall turn to the Lord, the 16 vail shall be taken away. Now the Lord is *that* Spirit: and 17

the Rhemish *but their senses were dulled*. For the word translated *minds* see note on ch. ii. 11. Cf. Is. vi. 9, 10; Matt. xiii. 14, &c., and ch. iv. 4. The word *but* implies that in consequence of the condition of the Israelites the Apostle's plainness of speech was, to them at least, of no avail.

remaineth the same vail untaken away] Most modern commentators, and some ancient ones, e.g. Chrysostom, take the words rendered *untaken away* with what follows, and translate *the same veil remaineth at the reading of the old covenant, it not being discovered that it is done away in Christ*. The reasons for this rendering are (1) that it is not the *veil* but the *old covenant* with its glories which is 'done away in Christ,' (2) that St Paul uses *another* word in the original to signify the taking away of the veil, and (3) that the hardness of the hearts of the Israelites, and not the doing away of the veil in Christ, is the reason the veil is not removed. This hardness of heart prevented them (1) from seeing that the Mosaic was a temporary covenant, and (2) that it was rendered unnecessary by the coming of Christ. See Acts vi. 11, 13, vii. 57, xiii. 45, xiv. 2, xxi. 20, 21, &c.; 1 Thess. ii. 14—16. The word here translated 'untaken away' is translated ' open,' i.e. 'unveiled' in *v*. 18.

in the reading of the old testament] The words *old covenant* (see note on *v*. 6) refer, as *v*. 15 shews, not to the books we now include in the Old Testament, but to the books of Moses. It could hardly be said that to the prophets the abrogation of the Old Testament in Christ was a thing unknown. See Jer. xxxi. 31 above cited. For the regular reading of the books of the Law in the synagogue, see Acts xiii. 15, xv. 21. The prophets were also read, as we learn from the former passage (and also *v*. 27) and St Luke iv. 17.

15. *the vail is upon their heart*] Literally, **a veil lieth on their heart.** Not upon their head. It was moral, not intellectual blindness which caused their unbelief. See Acts vi. 13, 14, vii. 51, xxii. 18, 21, 22. We may remark on the change of figure here (see note on *v*. 13). The veil is no longer upon Moses' face, but upon the Jewish heart.

16. *when it shall turn to the Lord*] The A. V. makes (1) *Israel's heart* the nominative to the verb in this sentence. Wiclif and the other Protestant translators (2) make *Israel itself* the nominative, while (3) the Rhemish version makes *Moses* the nominative, referring to the fact that in the narrative in Exod. xxxiv. he is said in almost the same words as here, to remove the veil when he turns to God. Origen (4) would supply *any one*. Each rendering is defended by commentators of note, but the first seems preferable. Cf. Rom. xi. 23, 26, 32.

the vail shall be taken away] The tense in the original is present, not future, and may be interpreted, (1) with Bp. Wordsworth, 'is in process of removal,' or perhaps better, (2) with Dean Alford, **is there and then**

18 where the Spirit of the Lord *is*, there *is* liberty. But we all, with open face beholding as in a glass the glory of the Lord,

removed, i.e. at the moment when the heart turns to the Lord, just as Moses took off the veil when he turned to speak to God. See also Is. xxv. 7. It is to be observed that these words are a quotation of the LXX. of Exod. xxxiv. 34, substituting, however, the *present* for the *past* tense.

17. *Now the Lord is that Spirit*] Literally **the** *spirit*, i.e. the spirit which was to replace the letter. The sense is as follows: 'The Lord (of whom I have just spoken—see last verse) is the spirit of which I have said (*v.* 6) that it should be substituted for the letter.' For the Lord, even Jesus Christ, is Himself that new power—that higher inspiration—through which man finds what he ought to do written, no longer in precepts external to himself, but in his own regenerate heart. The new birth of the Spirit is but the implanting in man the humanity of Jesus Christ. 'The last Adam was made a life-giving spirit.' 1 Cor. xv. 45. This expression like John iv. 24, refers, not to the *person*, but to the *essential nature* of God, just as in John vi. 63, the expression is applied even to the words of God, when they communicate to man essential principles of God's spiritual kingdom. Cf. also John i. 13, iii. 3, 5; Rom. viii. 2, 4. Other explanations of this most difficult passage have been given. (1) 'The Spirit is the Lord,' (Chrysostom); and he remarks on the order of the words in the Greek of St John iv. 24 in support of his translation. (2) 'The Lord is identical with the Holy Spirit.' (3) 'The Lord with Whom Moses spoke is the Holy Spirit.' (4) 'The Lord is the Holy Ghost in so far as the Holy Ghost is the living principle of the indwelling of Christ.' (5) 'The Lord no dout is a sprete,' Tyndale, whom Cranmer follows. It seems on the whole best to interpret the words as above. St Paul now boldly declares that the 'spirit' of which he has spoken is nothing less than Christ Himself.

and where the Spirit of the Lord is] Hitherto St Paul has been speaking of the *Divine Nature* of Him who transforms the heart of man. He now speaks of the *personal agency* through Whom that work is achieved. Christ does these things by His Spirit, who is also the Spirit of the Father. Rom. viii. 9. Cf. also Gal. iv. 6; Phil. i. 19; 1 Pet. i. 11, with St John xiv. 16, 17, 26, xv. 26; 1 Cor. ii. 10—12, &c. This interpretation involves no incongruity with the rest of the passage. The Three Persons in the Blessed Trinity are one in essence, and that essence is Spirit. But the personal agency whereby God works His purpose in man's heart is the Holy Spirit, as Scripture everywhere declares. See the passages cited above.

there is liberty] Liberty not only to speak openly (*v.* 12), but (*v.* 18) to gaze with unveiled face upon the glory of God, and thus to learn how to fulfil the law of man's being. This liberty is the special privilege assured to man by the Gospel. See John viii. 32; Rom. vi. 18, 22, viii. 2; James i. 25, ii. 12; 1 Pet. ii. 16.

18. *But we all*] i.e. we Christians, in contradistinction to the Jews. *with open face*] i.e. unveiled. Cf. 1 Cor. xi. 7.

are changed *into* the same image from glory to glory, even as by the Spirit of the Lord.

beholding as in a glass] Either (1), according to the more ordinary meaning of the word, '*beholding* as in a mirror,' or (2) with Chrysostom, '*reflecting* as in a mirror.' The latter rendering makes the rest of the verse more intelligible, and has the additional recommendation that the glory on Moses' face was a *reflected* glory, which we may suppose grew more and more intense the longer he gazed on God with unveiled face. The former interpretation sets Christ before us as the mirror of the Father's glory. See next note.

the glory of the Lord] i.e. of Christ, Who is the beaming forth (ἀπαύγασμα) of God's glory, Heb. i. 3, cf. John i. 14, and His image, ch. iv. 4 (and note) and Col. i. 15. Also John xvii. 24.

are changed into] This word is rendered *transfigured* in Matt. xvii. 2; Mark ix. 2, and no doubt the idea of the gradual beaming out of the inner glory which dwelt in Christ, producing a *metamorphosis* (this is the actual word used) which excited the wonder and awe of those that beheld it, was in St Paul's mind in this passage. He uses the word in another place, Rom. xii. 2, where the idea of the Transfiguration and that suggested in this passage are combined, in order to express the marvellous inward change which takes place in the man who offers his heart to the transforming influences which flow out from Christ.

the same image] These words are emphatic in the original. It seems impossible to interpret them of any other but Christ (ch. iv. 4), 'into the same image as Christ.' He, as man, beholding the glory of God, with infinitely more fulness than Moses under the Law, turns to speak with us. We behold Him, not, as the Jews, with veiled heart, but with unveiled face, and as we gaze, we reflect back more and more of His image (cf. 1 John iii. 2), until it be fully formed in us. Gal. iv. 19.

from glory to glory] i.e. *from one stage of glory to another*. Cf. Rom. i. 17, and note on ch. ii. 16.

even as by the Spirit of the Lord] Three renderings are given of this passage. The first, which is the Vulgate rendering and is given in the text, needs no explanation. It is open to the objection that it inverts the order of the words in the Greek. The second is the natural grammatical rendering, '*as by the Lord of the Spirit.*' The third, which is found in the margin of the A. V. and is adopted by St Chrysostom (who, however, interprets the passage of the Holy Spirit), '*as by* (*of*, A. V.) *the* (or *a*) *Lord, the* (or *a*) *spirit*,' seems to give the best sense. For it refers us back to *v.* 17 and to the former part of the chapter. The change that takes place in us is a spiritual change (see 1 Cor. ii., and notes on *v.* 6). It is not affected by formal enactments, which at best can but condemn, but it is the work of a Lord who works within, Who sends forth the beams of His light that they may transform, not the outer surface, but the heart, that so the man may reflect back undimmed thence the glorious Light that has shined on him. And so the man into whose heart the Light of Christ has entered progresses from one stage of spiritual glory to another, until

Ch. IV. 1—15. *Entrusted with so glorious a mission, the Ministers of the Gospel shrink from neither danger nor difficulty.*

4 Therefore seeing we have this ministry, as we have re-
2 ceived mercy, we faint not; but have renounced the hidden *things* of dishonesty, not walking in craftiness, nor handling the word of God deceitfully; but by manifestation of the

at last (Rom. viii. 29) he becomes fully conformed to the image of the Son of God.

Ch. IV. 1—15. Entrusted with so glorious a mission, the Ministers of the Gospel shrink from neither danger nor difficulty.

1. *Therefore*] The connection between this and what precedes is sufficiently obvious. Sustained by so great and glorious a mission, the Apostles of Christ are daunted by no trials.

as we have received mercy] St Paul not only bears in mind the glory of his commission, but the mercy, of which he never fails to feel himself undeserving (1 Cor. xv. 9; Eph. iii. 8; 1 Tim. i. 12—16). Thus there is a double reason for not sinking under the burden of his ministry.

we faint not] It is to be noted that in *both* these Epistles the Apostle now uses the singular and now the plural. He uses the first when his vindication is distinctly personal to himself, the second when he speaks of Christian ministers in general. This is clear from the two passages (ch. i. 19 and 1 Cor. ix. 6) in which he defines who 'we' are. The genuine Apostles of Christ, he would say, do not lose heart when all does not go smoothly with them. Nay, the very fact that they have sufferings to undergo stamps them the more unmistakeably as followers of Christ.

2. *But have renounced the hidden things of dishonesty*] Far from shrinking from the labour and suffering and opposition entailed by the preaching of the Gospel, and so inclining to suppress its utterance, the true ministers of Christ "even rejoice and speak boldly" (Chrysostom). Cf. ch. iii. 12. The word here rendered *dishonesty* (a word, however, which had three centuries ago a wider meaning than it has now, cf. *As you Like it*, Act III. Sc. 3) is rather **disgrace**. It is translated *shame* wherever else it occurs in the N. T., as, for instance, Luke xiv. 9; Phil. iii. 19; Rev. iii. 18. What the Apostle has renounced is all secret practices, which, when found out, cause shame. Cf. John iii. 20.

craftiness] The word means the conduct of a man who resorts to *all kinds of contrivances* to attain his end. An excellent illustration of the meaning of the word may be found in Luke xx. 20—23. See also ch. xi. 3, where it is rendered *subtilty*. St Paul was accused of this. See ch. xii. 16, note.

nor handling the word of God deceitfully] This word is the nearest translation of the Greek δολοῦντες. *Adulterantes*, Vulgate; *neither corrupte we*, Tyndale. Our translation is due to Cranmer. "It is done," says Meyer, "by alterations and strange admixtures." Cf. ch. ii. 17.

truth commending ourselves to every man's conscience in the sight of God. But if our gospel be hid, it is hid to 3 them that are lost: in whom the god of this world hath 4 blinded the minds of them which believe not, lest the light

but by manifestation of the truth] i.e. by bringing the truth clearly and plainly to light, without any attempt at concealment.

commending] The word *commend* has here obviously the same signification as *recommend*. This cannot be said of ch. iii. 1, where see note.

to every man's conscience] See note on ch. i. 24. The individual conscience is, and always must be, the ultimate tribunal to which all teaching must appeal, and St Paul assumes that in it there resides a faculty of appreciating and acknowledging truth.

3. *But if our gospel be hid*] Literally, **But if our gospel, too, be hidden** or **veiled** (see last chapter). The Apostle here refers to an objection: "You say that a vail lay upon the hearts of the Jews when Moses was read. But your Gospel is not clear and evident to all." For his answer see next note.

it is hid to them that are lost] Literally, **is hidden among the perishing.** Our Gospel *is* hid, too, in some cases, I grant. But it is hid only to perishing souls, who will not lay hold on the only hope of deliverance. Cf. John iii. 18; Acts iv. 12. This is not the language of logic, but of deep and strong conviction.

4. *in whom the god of this world*] i.e. the devil, who is called the *prince* or *ruler* of this world in John xii. 31, xiv. 30, xvi. 11. So also Matt. iv. 9; Luke iv. 6; Eph. ii. 2, vi. 12. He is so called because for the present he has power in it, Rev. xii. 12. The early fathers, in their zeal against the two gods (one good and one evil) of the Manichaeans and some sects of the Gnostics, repudiate this interpretation, and render, in defiance of the plain meaning, '*God hath blinded the understandings of the unbelievers of this world.*' On this Calvin makes some wise remarks: "We see what the heat of controversy does in such disputes. If all these men had read the words of Paul with a tranquil mind, it would never have come into their mind so to wrest his words into a forced sense. But because their adversaries bore hardly on them, they thought more of vanquishing them than of endeavouring to ascertain the mind of Paul."

hath blinded the minds of them which believe not] The meaning is either (1) that all were perishing alike (John iii. 18), but that some believed and Satan blinded the minds of the rest, or (2) that all were formerly unbelieving, but that some, by rejecting the good tidings of salvation through Christ, passed over into the category of the perishing. In support of (1) we may render 'in whom' by 'among whom.' The word here translated '*them which believe not*' is used in 1 Cor. vi. 6, vii. 12—15, x. 27, xiv. 22—24, of those who *do not believe in Christ.* For the word translated 'minds,' see note on ch. ii. 11. The word translated '*blinded*' is not the same as that used in ch. iii. 14.

of the glorious gospel of Christ, who is the image of God,
⁵ should shine unto them. For we preach not ourselves, but
Christ Jesus the Lord; and ourselves your servants for
⁶ Jesus' sake. For God, who commanded the light to shine
out of darkness, hath shined in our hearts, to give the light

lest the light of the glorious gospel of Christ] Rather, **lest the enlightenment** (Rhemish, *illumination*) **of the Gospel of the glory of Christ**. The word translated 'light' in the A. V. signifies rather the *result* of light than light itself. The words translated 'glorious gospel' are so translated in virtue of the constant occurrence of Hebraisms of this kind in the N. T. But it seems impossible to doubt that there is here a reference to the 'glory' so frequently mentioned in the last chapter, as in the word 'blinded' there is an obvious reference to the vail.

who is the image of God] Cf. ch. iii. 18, Col. i. 15. The word in the original is exactly equivalent to our word *likeness*. An image or likeness is a *visible representation* of an object. So Christ in His humanity (cf. Gen. i. 27; 1 Cor. xi. 7) is a visible representation of the unseen God. Cf. John i. 1—14 (especially the last verse), and Heb. i. 3. Also John xiv. 8, 9. No revelation of the wisdom and power of God that man has received can compare with that made in the Life, Death and Resurrection of the Incarnate Son. Also as the 'Mediator of the New Covenant' (Heb. xii. 24), glory, the glory of the Invisible God, streams from His Face, a glory far brighter than that with which Moses' face shone after communing with God.

5. *For we preach not ourselves*] A reason is here given for the foregoing statement. If St Paul's Gospel be hid, it is not because it is his own, and therefore destined to come to nought (see ch. iii. 7). No, it is the Gospel of Christ which he preaches, and if any refuse to listen to it, it is because he has suffered himself to be blinded by the devil. See note on *v.* 3.

but Christ Jesus the Lord] i. e. Christ Jesus as Lord, not ourselves.

and ourselves your servants] The original is stronger, *and ourselves your* **slaves**. "He does not say 'the slaves of Jesus,' but what is by far more humble and lowly, '*your* slaves.' Yet that he may not appear to speak or think in too abject a strain, he adds, 'for Jesus' sake.'" Estius.

6. *For God...shined*] Literally, **Because it is God Who shined**, and therefore, if the doctrine of the ministers of Christ were not received by any, it was not because they exercised any concealment or reserve (ch. iii. 13), much less on account of any adulteration of the pure word of God (*v.* 2), but because the soul of the unbeliever deliberately refused to receive the light of God's truth. Cf. John i. 5.

who commanded the light to shine out of darkness] First in the physical world (Gen. i. 3) and then in the moral and spiritual world, in the person of Jesus Christ. Cf. John i. 4, iii. 19, viii. 12, &c.

hath shined in our hearts] God makes use of human instrumentality in spreading the knowledge of His glory. Cf. ch. ii. 15, 16, iii. 3, 6.

of the knowledge of the glory of God in the face of Jesus Christ.

But we have this treasure in earthen vessels, that the 7 excellency of the power may be of God, and not of us. *We* 8 *are* troubled on every *side*, yet not distressed; *we are* perplexed, but not in despair; persecuted, but not forsaken; 9

to give the light of the knowledge of the glory of God] Literally, **in order to the enlightenment**: *illumination*, Rhemish. Knowledge is here spoken of rather as the effect of light than light itself. See note on *v.* 4.

in the face of Jesus Christ] The same word is used here as in ch. ii. 10. See note on the words 'image of God,' above. "A notable place, whence we learn that God is not to be investigated in His unsearchable height, for He inhabits the light unapproachable (1 Tim. vi. 16), but to be known as far as He reveals Himself in Christ...It is more useful for us to behold God as He appears in His Only-begotten Son, than to investigate His secret essence." Calvin. There is another interpretation of these words. We may translate them 'in the person of Christ,' and then the sense is that Christ was Himself the revealer of the glory of God. John i. 14, 18.

7. *But we have this treasure in earthen vessels*] 'I grant you that the exterior of the ministers of the Gospel is by no means in accordance with the description I have just given of the Gospel they preach. But why is this? but because, as I have said before, they desire not, they are not intended, to claim the glory and power as their own. It is stamped in their character, appearance, demeanour, sufferings, that they seek nothing for themselves, but are simply the servants of God, while the extraordinary results of their labours prove that it is He Whose messengers they are.' The metaphor of the glory is dropped, and the Apostles represented as the earthenware vessels in which treasures were frequently in those days kept, and often (see Wordsworth *in loc.*) carried in triumphal processions. Cf. ch. ii. 14. The treasure is Christ Himself, ministered by His disciples. See ch. iii. 3, and cf. Matt. xiii. 44.

excellency] This word has somewhat lost its force in modern English, its place has been taken by the word *superiority*. See *v.* 17, where the Greek is the same as here.

of us] The Greek implies *from ourselves as a source.*

8. *We are troubled on every side*] Perhaps '*in every way*.' For the word rendered 'troubled,' cf. ch. i. 4, vi. 4.

yet not distressed] This word, says Bengel, denotes *angustias tales e quibus non detur exitus*, "such straits as there are no escape from."

perplexed, but not in despair] The play upon words here (cf. ch. i. 13, iii. 2) has no exact equivalent in English. The nearest approach to it would be 'at our wits' end, but not out of our wits.' See also note on ch. i. 8.

9. *cast down, but not destroyed*] i.e. struck or thrown down, as in

10 cast down, but not destroyed; always bearing about in the body the dying of the Lord Jesus, that the life also of Jesus 11 might be made manifest in our body. For we which live are alway delivered unto death for Jesus' sake, that the life also 12 of Jesus might be made manifest in our mortal flesh. So 13 then death worketh in us, but life in you. We having the

warfare or wrestling, but not yet deprived of life, and therefore not unable to renew the conflict.

10. *always bearing about in the body the dying of the Lord Jesus*] Rather, *the* **slaying** (Vulg. *mortificatio*) *of the Lord Jesus*. So Wiclif. The word is only to be found in Rom. iv. 19, where it signifies the process by which a thing became dead, i. e. age. The same spirit of hostility to good which put Jesus to death is still at work in the world against His servants. Their sufferings, therefore, for His sake, are a kind of slaying Him anew. Cf. Col. i. 24.

that the life also of Jesus might be made manifest in our body] The life of Jesus dwelling in the hearts of His saints is shewn in the power they possess of enduring, in their often feeble frames, sufferings and toils such as might daunt the strongest men, as well as in the unselfishness which welcomes such sufferings and toils for the glory of God and the well-being of man. Meyer cites Ignatius *ad Magnes.* 6, "If we do not of our own accord accept death after the manner of His Passion, His Life is not in us."

11. *For we which live*] We, the possessors of the Divine life in Christ, the spiritual life which takes the place of the natural. Cf. ch. iii. 3, 6, 17, and 1 Cor. ii. 12, 16, and xv. 45, 46, and notes.

are alway delivered unto death] Literally, *are alway* **being delivered** *unto death*, i.e. while we are engaged in this ministry on behalf of Jesus Christ our Lord, calling on us as it does for a perpetual conflict with enemies without, and the weakness of our mortal flesh within.

that the life also of Jesus] Not only is what was stated in the last verse the fact, but it was God's purpose that it should be so. The labours and trials of the Apostles are due to the working of a principle of death which is ever hostile to life and God. But the operation of that principle in the mortal bodies of the Apostles is destined only to display the working of a still stronger principle, the life that comes from God. See next note.

12. *So then death worketh in us, but life in you*] See 1 Cor. iv. 9. The Apostle here enunciates a principle common to the material and the spiritual world. From death comes life, from decay regeneration. The death of Christ was the life of the world; the daily dying (1 Cor. xv. 31) of His disciples, by virtue of the same Spirit that lives in Him, is the means whereby that life spreads among mankind. Death may be said to be working in Christ's ministers, because of their visible sorrows, anxieties, persecutions (but see *v.* 16); life in their converts, because of the visible change in their character and acts. Cf. Plato, *Phaedo*, ch. 16;

same spirit of faith, according as it is written, I believed, *and* therefore have I spoken; we also believe, and therefore speak; knowing that he which raised up the Lord Jesus shall raise up us also by Jesus, and shall present *us* with you. For all *things are* for your sakes, that the abundant grace might through the thanksgiving of many redound to the glory of God.

"'What is that which is produced from life?' 'Death,' he said. 'What then,' replied he, 'from death?' 'It must be confessed that life is.'"

13. *We having the same spirit of faith*] The idea of boldness and outspokenness is still present with the Apostle. He speaks openly, because he has reason to believe what he says. And the thought is connected with the last verse by the fact that it is to his speaking that the Corinthians owe their life. The 'same spirit' means the spirit that dwelt in the Psalmist. See next note.

according as it is written] See Ps. cxvi. 10. The Psalmist was 'sore troubled,' but his faith enabled him to triumph over affliction and to declare the loving-kindness of the Lord. A similar faith enabled St Paul and his fellow-labourers to declare the good tidings of Christ, though encompassed by infirmity and trouble.

14. *knowing that he which raised up the Lord Jesus*] Here we have the source of the Apostle's faith and confidence. He knew that the Resurrection of Christ was an accomplished fact (see notes on 1 Cor. xv., and Introduction to First Epistle). Hence arose his persuasion that a life was given to him which should survive and overcome even death itself.

by Jesus] All recent editors substitute *with Jesus*, which, however, does not mean at the same time with, but by virtue of the operation of the same life and spirit. For the life that dwells in Jesus dwells also in His disciples, John vi. 54. We are the members, Christ the Head; we are the crop, Christ the firstfruits, 1 Cor. xv. 23. Cf. Rom. i. 4, as well as ch. iii. 17, 18, and Eph. ii. 5, 6; Col. ii. 13. Chrysostom omits the words altogether. Meyer remarks that though St Paul believed that he and the majority of his readers would live to see the actual coming of Christ in the flesh, the possibility that this might not be the case was ever before his eyes. See 1 Cor. xv. 51; 1 Thess. iv. 15.

and shall present us with you] i.e. shall place us in His own Presence. Cf. Rom. xiv. 10; Col. i. 22; Jude 24; ch. v. 10, and 1 Cor. viii. 8, and note.

15. *For all things are for your sakes*] Cf. 1 Cor. iii. 22, as well as the numerous passages in that Epistle where the well-being of mankind is represented as St Paul's (and indeed God's) only object, e.g. vi. 12, x. 23.

that the abundant grace] Literally, **that grace having abounded.** There is a very similar passage in ch. i. 11. And this passage, like that, is capable of being construed in various ways. We may either

IV. 16—V. 10.   *The Preachers of the Gospel are sustained
by the hope of a Future Life.*

16   For which cause we faint not; but though our outward man perish, yet the inward *man* is renewed day by
17 day.   For our light affliction, which is but for a moment,
worketh for us a far more exceeding *and* eternal weight

take it (1) *that grace, having abounded, might multiply on account of the
thanksgiving of the greater number*, or (2) *that grace, having abounded,
may by means of the greater number, multiply the thanksgiving to the
glory of God*, or (3) *that grace, having abounded through the greater
number, may multiply the thanksgiving to the glory of God.* The last
would seem the preferable rendering. For (1) God's grace or favour
abounds the more, the greater the number who are turned to Him,
(2) the larger the number of converts, the greater the thanksgiving
to God (for this use of 'the greater number,' see 1 Cor. ix. 19); and
(3) the word translated 'redound' in the A. V. has also the transitive
sense of 'make to abound,' as in Eph. i. 8; 1 Thess. iii. 12, and ch.
ix. 8. The Greek here, as in *v*. 11, indicates God's purpose, which
having its origin in His love, issues in beneficence. In the happiness
and gratitude of the beings He has created, He has thought fit to find
His own.

IV. 16—V. 10.   THE PREACHERS OF THE GOSPEL ARE SUSTAINED
BY THE HOPE OF A FUTURE LIFE.

16. *For which cause we faint not*] The Apostle now returns to the topic
he has already introduced (*v*. 1). But the digression, if indeed it be a
digression, only tends to strengthen the assertion he has made. 'We
faint not,' he says, 'not merely because we have a glorious ministry
(*v*. 1), not merely because we have the knowledge of God (*v*. 6), not
merely because, though oppressed and afflicted ourselves, we see the
blessed results of our ministry in others, but because (cf. *v*. 10, 11) our
sorrows and sufferings, the decay of our mortal body, are but external.
There is a spring of life within that can never fail, the new life, which
comes to us from God through Christ.'

17. *For our light affliction, which is but for a moment*] Literally,
For the momentary lightness of our affliction. The argument is advanced another step. Not only have we this inner fount of strength
and consolation, but we know that it is eternal, while our afflictions
endure but for a moment. Cf. Rom. viii. 18.

worketh for us] Literally, *worketh* **out, bringeth to perfection.** The
precise opposite of the word translated 'brought to nought,' 'done
away.' See ch. iii. 7.

a far more exceeding and eternal weight of glory] *Over measure an
everlasting birthun into higness of glorie*, Wiclif. Literally, **a weight
of glory in excess and unto excess**: the whole passage denoting that
the glory to come exceeds the power of words to tell. The Vulgate
renders 'supra modum in sublimitate.' Alford, 'in a surpassing and

of glory; while we look not at the *things* which are 13
seen, but at the *things* which are not seen: for the *things*
which are seen *are* temporal; but the *things* which are
not seen *are* eternal. For we know that if our earthly 5
house of *this* tabernacle were dissolved, we have a building

still more surpassing manner.' The old English versions, including the
A. V., follow Tyndale here. An expression very closely approaching
to this is the usual one in Hebrew for anything immeasurably great, as
for instance, in the original of Gen. vii. 19. The word *glory* in Hebrew
is derived from the original idea of *weight*. It is possible that this connection of ideas may have influenced St Paul in the choice of this
expression.

18. *while we look not*] Rather, **since** *we look not, do not fix our attention.*

at the things which are not seen] The Christian habitually views all
that comes before him from the standpoint of the invisible world,
which is revealed to him by the Spirit from within. See 1 Cor. ii. 9,
10, 13; 1 John iv. 5, 6. Also Heb. xi. 1.

for the things which are seen are temporal] Rather, **temporary**, i.e.
they last, and are intended to last, but a season.

but the things which are not seen are eternal] Here was the secret of
the Apostle's confidence. The invisible truths of which he was persuaded, which lay at the root of the Resurrection of Christ, and
therefore of the moral strength he felt within him and was enabled
to impart to others, rested upon no uncertain basis, but upon the unchangeable Will of the Eternal God. See notes on ch. i. 19, 20.

CH. V. 1. *For we know*] This verse gives the reason for what has
gone before. 'We are consoled in our present afflictions, sustained in our
hope of future glory, supported in our conviction that what is visible is
speedily to be replaced by what is eternal, by the knowledge, spiritually
acquired, that God has prepared a spiritual body (1 Cor. xv. 44) to
replace the present frail and temporary habitation of the soul.' Calvin
remarks that this with St Paul is not a matter of *opinion* or *belief*, but of
actual *knowledge*, a boast which no heathen dare have made.

our earthly house of this tabernacle] Earthly, not earthy. That which
exists *upon* the earth, not what is made of earth. Compare 1 Cor. xv.
40 and 47. See also John iii. 12; Phil. ii. 10. *House of this tabernacle* is better rendered **tabernacle-house**. The Hebraistic genitive is
"to define the nature of the house" (Stanley), i.e. as temporary, a *tent* or
tabernacle as opposed to a permanent dwelling. Stanley suggests our
English word *tenement* as best expressing the idea of the original, and
supposes the Greek word to have been suggested to St Paul by his
Cilician house, as well as by his occupation of tent-making, Acts xviii. 3.
A similar expression is found in 2 Pet. i. 13, and in Wisd. ix. 15.

were dissolved] or, perhaps, *were destroyed*. Cf. Matt. v. 17, xxiv. 2,
xxvi. 61; Gal. ii. 18, where the same Greek word is used.

we have a building of God] i.e. a building *originating* with God.
The present tense signifies either (1) that it awaits us "the moment our

of God, a house not made with hand, eternal in the heavens.
² For in this we groan, earnestly desiring to be clothed upon
³ with our house which is from heaven: if so be that being
⁴ clothed we shall not be found naked. For we that are in

present house is destroyed" (Stanley), or (2) that it *exists now* in the eternal purpose of God. See next note but one.

a house not made with hand] So the earlier copies of the Authorized Version. The later—the innovation seems to have been made about 1661—have 'hands,' which is less correct. "Not as contrasted with the earthly body, which is also 'not made with hand,' but with *other* houses which are made with hand." Alford. The expression is used to mark the Divine origin of the spiritual body.

in the heavens] These words should be joined with 'we have,' not as is usually done with 'eternal.' There is a difficulty here. The new body is said in 1 Cor. xv. 52; Phil. iii. 21; 1 Thess. iv. 15—17 to be given us at the coming of Christ. The condition of the believer between death and the judgment is represented as a sleep. The explanation is that we possess our future body already in the mind and will of God. So the Hebrew prophets frequently speak of a future event as past, because it is already decreed in the providence of God. We are said to 'have it in the heavens' because its organization and communication to us are not natural, but heavenly and spiritual.

2. *For in this*] i.e. this tabernacle.
we groan] Cf. Rom. viii. 23.
to be clothed upon] i.e. to put on in addition. See 1 Cor. xv. 53. "The flesh will not be annihilated, but spiritualized, glorified and beautified, as the human body of Christ was at the Transfiguration." St Jerome, cited by Bp Wordsworth. The Greek for the 'fisher's coat' spoken of in John xxi. 7 is, as Dean Stanley reminds us, derived from the word used here.

with our house] Rather, **dwelling-place.** The word house (οἰκία) is more absolute, dwelling-place (οἰκητήριον) has reference to the inhabitant. Bengel.

3. *if so be that being clothed we shall not be found naked*] Rather, with Tyndale, whom Cranmer follows, **yet if** (some recent editors, following another reading, would render *seeing*) **that we shall be found clothed, not naked.** This passage has been variously explained. Some regard it (1) as asserting that at the last day we are certain to receive a Resurrection-body, and not to be left as disembodied spirits. Others, as Bp Wordsworth, remembering that γυμνός does not mean literally *naked*, but (John xxi. 7; cf. Xen. *Anab.* IV. iv. 12) *destitute of the upper garment*, interpret it (2) 'if we shall be found in the Resurrection-body at the last day,' not in the frail mortal tenement which we must otherwise resume. The chief objection to these interpretations is that the word 'found' applies rather to the condition in which we *are*, than to that in which we *are to be* when Christ comes. It will therefore be best to follow the interpretation which regards the passage as referring to the possibility of St Paul and those to whom he is speaking being alive at the coming

this tabernacle do groan, being burdened: not for that we would be unclothed, but clothed upon, that mortality might be swallowed up of life. Now he that hath wrought us for 5 the selfsame *thing is* God, who also hath given unto us the earnest of the Spirit. Therefore *we are* always confident, 6

of Christ (see 1 Thess. iv. 17 and note on 1 Cor. xv. 51), and to translate *if* (in that day) *we shall be found clothed* (with the body), *not naked* (i.e. disembodied). The various readings which are found in this passage increase the difficulty of explaining it. For (1) the word translated *if so be* is found in two different forms in the early Greek copies of this Epistle, the one expressing a greater, the other a less degree of uncertainty. Then (2) some copies read 'unclothed' for 'clothed,' so that the passage then runs *if when unclothed* (of the body) *we shall not be found naked*. But this reading was probably introduced by some copyist who could not comprehend the passage as it stood.

4. *in this tabernacle*] Literally, in the tabernacle, i.e. the 'tenement,' of which we have already spoken (*v.* 1).

do groan, being burdened] "Not because we desire to be delivered from the body, for of it we do not wish to be unclothed, but we hasten to be delivered from the corruption that is in it." Chrysostom. This verse carries on the thought of *v.* 2 and explains it.

not for that we would be unclothed, but clothed upon] Better with Tyndale and Cranmer (also Wiclif), *for we wold not be unclothed, but wolde be clothed upon.* "It is quite possible that men might conceive (of the future state) as a disembodied state and suppose the Apostle to represent life in a visible form as a degradation." Robertson. Such was the view of Greek philosophers almost without exception (see note on 1 Cor. xv. 12). St Paul, affirming the old Jewish view that God had created all things, and made them very good, entirely repudiates this doctrine, and declares that he does not desire separation from the body, but only its spiritualization. "Paul regards it as an especial happiness not to taste death, not to be obliged to put off this body, but to be glorified living, like Elijah, drawing the heavenly body over the present mortal body as a garment, yet in such a manner that the mortal body is absorbed in the nature of the spiritual body." Olshausen. So Tertullian, "not as wishing to undergo death, but that death should be anticipated by life." The whole passage should be compared with 1 Cor. xv. 35—54. See also note on *v.* 2.

that mortality might be swallowed up of life] i.e. "covered over and arrayed in the vesture of immortality." Tertullian. 'Mortality' should rather be rendered **what is mortal.**

5. *wrought us*] Literally, **wrought us out,** i.e. fitted and prepared us by a course of training. See ch. iv. 17.

for the selfsame thing] The swallowing up of mortality by life.

the earnest of the Spirit] For earnest, see ch. i. 22, a very similar passage. Cf. also Rom. viii. 1—11. It is because the Spirit dwells in us by faith while we are here that we are raised hereafter. The body thus possessing a principle of life is as a seed planted in the ground

knowing that, whilst we are at home in the body, we are
7 absent from the Lord: (for we walk by faith, not by sight:)
8 we are confident, I say, and willing rather to be absent
9 from the body, and to be present with the Lord. Wherefore we labour, that, whether present or absent, we may
10 be accepted of him. For we must all appear before the

(1 Cor. xv. 36—38) to be raised again in God's good time. See Introduction to First Epistle and notes on ch. xv.

6. *Therefore we are always confident*] Because we always possess the inner life of the Spirit, and are therefore always, in a sense, with God.

at home in the body] The body (see note on *v.* 4) is really a *home*, though not a permanent one. "Quamdiu domi sumus in hoc corporis habitaculo." Erasmus.

we are absent from the Lord] "God is present with all mankind, because He sustains them by His power; He dwells in them, because 'in Him they live, and move, and have their being.' He is present with His faithful ones by the greater energy of His Spirit; He lives in them, dwells in their midst, and so within them. But in the meantime He is absent from us, in that He does not yet present Himself to be seen face to face; because as yet we are exiles from His kingdom, and lack the blessed immortality which the Angels, who are with Him, are privileged to enjoy." Calvin.

7. *for we walk by faith, not by sight*] Cf. ch. iv. 18 and John xx. 29. The word translated *sight* signifies not the *act of vision*, but *the thing seen*. Cf. Luke iii. 22, ix. 29; John v. 37, in two of which passages the word is translated *shape*, in the third *fashion*. This is the reason of the statement made in the last verse. We are absent from God, because we are not yet face to face with the heavenly realities, but dimly realize them afar off (1 Cor. xiii. 12; Heb. xi. 1).

8. *we are confident, I say, and willing rather to be absent from the body, and to be present with the Lord*] Our confidence is not even disturbed by death, though it is not (*v.* 4) death in itself that we seek. But even in death we 'sleep in Jesus' (1 Thess. iv. 14; cf. 1 Cor. xv. 18), and though removed from our earthly tenement we are still at home with God. Cf. also St Luke xxiii. 43. The word translated 'present' here is translated 'at home' in *v.* 6, a variation which commenced with Tyndale. He returns however to 'at home' in the next verse.

9. *we labour*] The word implies "*una ambitio legitima*," Bengel; a strife in which one's honour is concerned. See Rom. xv. 20, where the word is translated *strive*.

whether present or absent] *whether at home or from home*, Tyndale. The meaning is either (1) whether at home in the body, or absent from it, as in *v.* 6, or (2) at home with God or absent from Him, as in *v.* 8. The latter is preferable, as being in more immediate connection with what precedes. Cf. 1 Thess. v. 10.

10. *For we must all appear*] Literally, **be manifested**, the same Greek word being used as in the next verse. A reason for what goes

judgment seat of Christ; that every one may receive the *things done* in *his* body, according to that he hath done, whether *it be* good or bad.

11—21. *The Christian Ministry one of Reconciliation.*

Knowing therefore the terror of the Lord, we persuade 11 men; but we are made manifest unto God; and I trust

before. It is natural to try and please God when present with Him. But even when absent, Christians do not forget that He will judge them.

before the judgment seat of Christ] Cf. Matt. xxv. 31—46; Rom. xiv. 10. Observe that 'God' is the word used in the latter passage, as though "the two ideas were convertible." Stanley. The βῆμα, or 'judgment seat' (*trone*, Wiclif), is in Classical Greek the pulpit from which the orators addressed the assemblies. In the N. T. it is used of the judge's seat, which in the Roman basilica or judgment hall was "a lofty seat, raised on an elevated platform, so that the figure of the judge must have been seen towering above the crowd which thronged the long nave of the building." Stanley. This, he adds, was "the most august representation of justice which the world at that time, or perhaps ever, exhibited."

the things done in his body] Literally, **through the body**. Wiclif's translation is more literal, '*the propre thingis of the bodi, as he hath don.*' This is the reason why Christians are to strive during the present life to be pleasing to God. Their wages in the next world shall be according to their acts in this. Cf. Rom. ii. 5—10; 1 Thess. iv. 6; Jude 14, 15.

11—21. THE CHRISTIAN MINISTRY ONE OF RECONCILIATION.

11. *the terror of the Lord*] i.e. "His to-be-dreaded judgment." Beza. This translation is due to the Geneva Version, following Beza and Calvin (Wiclif, *drede*). Tyndale (whom Cranmer follows) renders more correctly '*how the Lorde is to be feared*' (literally 'the **fear** of the Lord,' *timorem Domini*, Vulg.). It is not the *terror* which God inspires, but the *fear* which man has of Him that is meant, 'knowing what it is to fear God.'

we persuade men] Rather, perhaps, we **win over** men. Compare the use of the Greek word here used in Acts xii. 20. The Apostle is still keeping in mind his object of clearing himself from the unjust accusations brought against him (cf. ch. ii. 17). That the digressions in ch. iii., iv., v. have not caused him to lose sight of his main object, the vindication of the purity of his motives from the aspersions cast upon them, may be seen by comparing *v.* 12 with ch. iii. 1. Having the fear of God's judgment continually before his eyes, he persuades men to obey the Gospel of Christ.

but we are made manifest unto God] Literally, we **have been** made manifest, i.e. we are and have been all along. He knows the purity of our motives, and will one day bear witness to them before all men. See note on last verse.

12 also are made manifest in your consciences. For we commend not ourselves again unto you, but give you occasion to glory on our behalf, that you may have *somewhat* to *answer* them which glory in appearance, and not 13 in heart. For whether we be besides ourselves, *it is* to 14 God: or whether we be sober, *it is* for your cause. For the love of Christ constraineth us; because we thus judge, that

and I trust also are made manifest in your consciences] Literally, **have been** made manifest, with the same meaning as above, either (1) 'by the change (see *v.* 17) which our ministry of Christ has produced in your hearts and lives,' or (2) 'in your conscientious conviction of our integrity.' Ch. iv. 2 makes the former the more probable interpretation. See also chap. xi. 6.

12. *For we commend not ourselves*] 'For' is omitted by the best editors, and its omission clears the sense. "We are not endeavouring once more to recommend ourselves to you by what we have said. (For 'again' see note on ch. iii. 1.) That is quite needless (ch. iii. 2, 3). We simply give you an opportunity of 'answering the fool according to his folly,' of shewing to those who judge by the appearance only, that *we*, too, have some fruits at least of our ministry to shew."

occasion to glory] The word here translated 'to glory' means, here as elsewhere in the N. T. (see note on ch. i. 14 and on 1 Cor. v. 6), *cause of glorying* or *boasting*. According to its strict meaning (which probably ought not to be pressed here) it should be rendered 'supplying you with a source whence you may find a cause of boasting on our behalf.'

in appearance] Literally, **in face**, i.e. in that which is visible. See ch. x. 7.

and not in heart] Who have no ground for boasting in the purity of their motives, because self-interest is the only spring of their actions. Cf. 1 Cor. iii. throughout, and ch. xi. 12, 13; Gal. iv. 17.

13. *For whether we be besides ourselves*] Literally, **were** beside ourselves, i.e. when we were with you. The reproach of madness was afterwards cast upon St Paul by Festus (Acts xxvi. 24), and may well have been cast upon him before this. Cf. Acts xvii.

it is to God] Better, **for** God, i.e. for His cause. See 'for your cause' below. Literally, **for you.**

or whether we be sober] The word here used signifies the quiet self-restraint characteristic of the Christian. Its original meaning is *to have one's thoughts safe*, and hence to be of sound, healthy mind (cf. the Latin *salvus* and our 'safe and sound'). Cf. Mark v. 15; Luke viii. 35 (where the word is opposed to the idea of madness). Also Rom. xii. 3; Tit. ii. 2, 4, 6, &c.

14. *For the love of Christ constraineth us*] i.e. the love which Christ has not only displayed, but imparted (De Wette). He refers to Rom. viii. 35; Eph. iii. 19 (which however must be read in the light of *vv.* 17, 18). The word translated *constrain* signifies to *coop up, keep within narrow bounds*. Cf. Luke xii. 50, where the same word occurs. It is also used by St Luke of diseases, as in Luke iv. 38; Acts xxviii. 8, and

if one died for all, then were all dead: and *that* he died for 15 all, that they which live should not henceforth live unto themselves, but unto him which died for them, and rose *again*. Wherefore henceforth know we no *man* after the 16 flesh: yea, though we have known Christ after the flesh,

of a multitude crowding, as in Luke viii. 45. Here it means 'prevents us from doing anything but serve you for Christ's sake.'

because we thus judge] Not merely equivalent to *think*, but strictly *judge*, i.e. form an opinion upon sufficient evidence.

that if one died for all, then were all dead] Most modern editors omit the 'if,' which is not contained in any of the best MSS. nor versions (except the Vulgate), and render thus, 'That one died for all: therefore all died,' not 'were dead' as in the A. V. The meaning of the Apostle would seem to be not that all men were dead in trespasses and sins, and therefore needed one to die for them, but that the death of Christ, Who had taken upon Himself to represent mankind before His Father's throne, was in a sense a death of *all mankind* (οἱ πάντες—all collectively. Wordsworth). "What Christ did *for* Humanity was done by Humanity." Robertson. Cf. Rom. vi. 6, 10, vii. 4, 6 (margin); Eph. ii. 13, 16; Col. i. 20—22; Heb. ix. 28, x. 10. Also Gal. ii. 19, 20, 'I through law died to law that I might live to God. I have been crucified with Christ.'

15. *that they which live should not...live unto themselves*] Cf. Rom. v. 8—11, vi. 10—13, xiv. 7; Gal. ii. 20, v. 24, 25, vi. 14; Col. iii. 1—4; 1 John v. 18. See also note on ch. iv. 10, 11. Christ's death is our life, because He thus made atonement for sin, reconciled us to the Father, shewed how He could be 'both just, and the justifier of him which believeth in Jesus,' and thus made obedience possible for us on the principle that we were 'reconciled to God,' and that henceforth there would be 'no condemnation' for our past sins or present sinfulness, provided we set ourselves to 'walk not after the flesh, but after the Spirit.' His death was the means of freeing us from our bondage to sin. His life was the enabling power which wrought our conversion.

16. *Wherefore henceforth know we no man after the flesh*] i.e. we regard no man from a purely fleshly point of view (see note on ch. i. 17), but look upon him as endowed with a new vital principle from above which has changed his heart. Cf. *v.* 17; Rom. viii. 1—11; 1 Cor. ii. 10—16. "Even in Christ a transition took place analogous to that which happened to man in regeneration. In the Resurrection the life according to the flesh passed over into a life according to the Spirit." Olshausen. "He who knows no man after the flesh has entirely lost sight in the case of a Jew, for example, of his Jewish origin, in the case of a rich man of his riches, in that of a learned man of his learning, in that of a slave of his slavery, and so on." Meyer. Cf. Matt. iii. 9; John viii. 39; Rom. ii. 28, 29, x. 12; 1 Cor. xii. 13; Gal. iii. 28; Col. iii. 11.

yea, though we have known Christ after the flesh] i.e. from a purely human point of view, as the Son of David simply (Rom. i. 3), not as the Incarnate Son of God, the Divine Word. See Bishop Wordsworth's note here. St Paul, and many others of the first preachers of

17 yet now henceforth know we *him* no more. Therefore if any *man be* in Christ, *he is* a new creature: old *things* are 18 past away; behold, all *things* are become new. And all *things are* of God, who hath reconciled us to himself by the faith (cf. Acts i. 6), had started with such carnal conceptions, but they had disappeared before the light of God's truth.

17. *Therefore*] i.e. as a conclusion from *vv.* 15, 16, in consequence of Christ's Death, His Life, His superhuman, Divine personality.

if any man be in Christ] The Vulgate puts no stop at Christ, and renders 'if there be any new creature in Christ' ('if ony newe creature is in Crist,' Wiclif). Tyndale translates as above. For 'in Christ,' see Rom. xvi. 7; Gal. i. 22; and chap. xii. 2.

he is a new creature] These words may be rendered *there is a new creation*, i.e. a new creation takes place within him. Whosoever is united to Christ by faith, possesses in himself the gift of a Divine, regenerated, spiritual humanity which Christ gives through his Spirit (cf. John v. 21, vi. 33, 39, 40, 54, 57; 1 Cor. xv. 45; 1 Pet. i. 3, ii. 2; and 2 Pet. i. 4. Also chap. i. 21, 22, iii. 18, iv. 11, v. 5). This life, which he possessed not before, is in fact a new creation of the whole man, "not to be distinguished from regeneration." Meyer. So also Chrysostom. Cf. John i. 13, iii. 3, 5; Tit. iii. 5. The margin of the A. V. renders *let him be*, which is grammatically admissible, but hardly suits the context.

old things] Literally, **the** old things. Cf. the 'old man,' Rom. vi. 6; Eph. iv. 22; Col. iii. 9; the 'former conversation' or manner of living, before the soul was dominated by the Spirit of Christ.

are past away] Literally, **passed away**, i.e. at the moment of conversion. But as the Dean of Peterborough has shewn in the *Expositor*, Vol. VII. pp. 261—263, this strict use of the aorist cannot be always pressed in Hebraistic Greek.

behold, all things are become new] Many MSS., versions and recent editors omit 'all things.' The passage then stands 'behold, they are become new.' If we accept this reading, the passage speaks more clearly of a conversion of the *whole man as he is*, thoughts, habits, feelings, desires, into the image of Christ. The old is not obliterated, it is renovated. As it stands in the A.V. it relates rather to a *substitution* of a new nature for the old. Isai. xliii. 18, 19; Rev. xxi. 5.

18. *all things are of God*] Whether natural or spiritual. He is the Creator of heaven and earth, Gen. i. 1, as well as of the work of redemption and of the new heart of man. Cf. chap. i. 21, v. 5; 1 Cor. iii. 23, xv. 28; also John iii. 16; Rom. v. 8, viii. 32. Christ came only to fulfil His Father's Will (John iv. 34, v. 30, vi. 39, 40). The Father and He were one in love to the human race as in everything else, John xvii. 21—23. "All the life of God is a flow of this Divine self-giving charity. Creation itself is sacrifice, the self-impartation of the Divine being." Robertson.

who hath reconciled us to himself by Jesus Christ] We have to observe here that not only was man estranged from God, but God from man. "We cannot imagine that God, Who is essentially just, should not

Jesus Christ, and hath given to us the ministry of reconciliation; to wit, that God was in Christ reconciling the world unto himself, not imputing their trespasses unto

abominate iniquity, yet there is no incongruity in this—that a father should be offended with that son which he loveth, and at that time offended with him when he loveth him." Bp Pearson. "God is angry with the wicked. For Christ was the representative of God under the name of Humanity. Now Christ was *angry*. That therefore which God feels"—or rather the relation in which He stands towards sin—"corresponds with that which in pure Humanity is the emotion of anger. No other word then will adequately represent God's feeling" (or rather attitude). Robertson. But the reconciliation was God's work of love, carried out by Jesus Christ, Who came to reveal His Nature and beneficial purposes to mankind, and to accomplish them by taking our mortal flesh, by His pure and stainless life, by His mysterious Death upon the Cross for our sakes, by His Resurrection from the dead, as well as by His sending His Spirit to work out His blessed Will in us. This is 'reconciliation by Jesus Christ.' The words *reconcile, reconciliation*, are deliberately preferred by the translators of the A.V. to the word *atone, atonement*, which is only to be found as an equivalent for the Greek word here used in Rom. v. 11. Cf. Rom. v. 10, xi. 15; 1 Cor. vii. 11, as well as a similar word occurring in Eph. ii. 16; Col. i. 20, 21. See also notes below.

the ministry of reconciliation] Literally, **the** reconciliation, i.e. that which has just been mentioned. Cf. ch. iii. 3, where St Paul describes the Corinthians as an Epistle of Christ ministered by him with the Spirit of the living God. The word ministry signifies service rendered freely, not of compulsion. It carries with it the idea of diligence, whatever derivation of the Greek word we take. It was the Apostles' task, voluntarily undertaken by themselves, to proclaim the good tidings of reconciliation through Christ throughout the world, and thus to put it in men's power to accept and act upon it. Tyndale, followed by Cranmer and the Geneva Version, render *and hath given unto us the office to preach the atonement*.

19. *to wit, that*] i.e. this is the tenor of our message.

God was in Christ reconciling] Or 'that God in Christ was reconciling.' Either translation is grammatically and theologically admissible. The former translation, preferred by the Latin expositors, lays most stress upon the indwelling of God in Christ (cf. John xiv. 10, xvii.). The latter, which has found most favour among the Greek commentators, indicates the fact, not merely that God reconciled the world, but that the process of reconciliation was carried on "in the Person and work of Christ." Meyer.

the world unto himself] It is frequently declared in Scripture that God's *purpose* embraces all mankind ("the whole world," Alford). Cf. John i. 29, iii. 16, iv. 42, vi. 33; 1 Tim. ii. 4, iv. 10; 1 John ii. 2, &c.

not imputing their trespasses unto them] παραπτώματα, *trespasses*, literally, **fallings aside from the path**. The English word is derived from an old French word *trespasser*, which, like *transgress*, has a

them; and hath committed unto us the word of reconcilia-
20 tion. *Now* then we are ambassadors for Christ, as though
God did beseech *you* by us: we pray *you* in Christ's stead,

similar meaning to the Greek, namely, to *pass over the boundary*. This passage explains the nature of the process of reconciliation. It is a very simple one. It consists in the fact that in consequence of Christ's mediatorial work, God no longer imputes sin to man, i.e. regards his sin as though it had not been committed. Cf. Rom. iii. 25, iv., viii. 1. *Why* this is so, and how it comes to pass that God is both 'just and the justifier of him that believeth in Jesus,' the Apostle does not explain, nor is any complete explanation given in Holy Scripture, which has concerned itself on this point less with theory than with fact. See however *v*. 15—18; also Rom. v. 8—11; Heb. ix. 12—14, 28, x. 10—14, &c. The word here translated *imputed* is translated indifferently by that word, and by *reckoned* and *accounted* in the A.V. It signifies (1) to *consider* (as in Rom. viii. 18), and hence (2) *to consider a thing as having been done*, to *reckon* or *impute*.

and hath committed unto us] Literally, **and placed in us** (*puttid in us*, Wiclif). It signifies more than a simple entrusting with, including (1) the reception of the reconciliation by the first preachers of the Gospel, and (2) their proclamation of it as well by their lives as by their teaching.

the word of reconciliation] So Wiclif and the Rhemish Version. Tyndale, Cranmer and the Geneva Version render *the preaching of the atonement*. The Greek, which is here rendered by 'word,' signifies (1) the abstract reason of a thing, (2) the discourse which is held about it, and (3) the word which expresses it. The use of three distinct tenses in the three members of this sentence is not a little remarkable. The imperfect, used of God's reconciling work in Christ, relates to the continuation of that work throughout the whole of His earthly ministry. The present, in the word 'imputing,' signifies that this work of non-imputation is still going on. The aorist, used in the word translated 'hath committed,' relates to the moment when God 'accounted' St Paul 'faithful, putting him into the ministry,' 1 Tim. i. 12.

20. *Now then we are ambassadors for Christ*] Literally, **we undertake an embassy** (*legatione fungimur*, Vulgate; *usen message*, Wiclif). Tyndale, followed by Cranmer and the Geneva Version, render, *are messengers in the roume of*. The Rhemish characteristically renders by *legates*. The signification 'in the room of,' for ὑπέρ, is doubtful. It is perhaps better to render 'for' with the A.V. (Vulgate, *pro*). Cf. Eph. vi. 20. An ambassador represents the monarch from whom he is sent, in all matters relating to his mission. What the nature of the mission was, and what the powers of the ambassadors, is stated in the remaining words of the verse.

as though God did beseech you by us] See notes on ch. i. 3. God may be said rather to *exhort* or *encourage* than to *beseech* (*as if God monestith bi us*, Wiclif). This, then, was the object for which the full powers of the ambassadors were given, an object still more clearly defined in what follows. Cf. Mal. ii. 7; Gal. iv. 14.

be ye reconciled to God. For he hath made him *to be* sin 21
for us, who knew no sin; that we might be made the righteousness of God in him.

1—10. *How God's Ministers carry on this Work of Reconciliation.*

We then, *as* workers together *with him*, beseech *you* also 6
that ye receive not the grace of God in vain. (For he saith, 2

we pray you in Christ's stead, be ye reconciled to God] Rather, **we intreat on behalf of Christ** (see above). First there was the encouraging tidings that there was 'henceforth no condemnation' to those who accepted the reconciliation offered through Christ (or perhaps the exhortation to accept it, see last note), and next there the still more urgent entreaty on Christ's behalf that they would accept it.

21. *For he hath made him to be sin for us*] Literally, **He made**, i.e. in the Sacrifice on the Cross. The word *sin* has been variously explained as a *sin-offering*, a *sinner*, and so on. But it is best to take the word in its literal acceptation. *He made Him to be sin*, i.e. appointed Him to be the representative of sin and sinners, treated Him as sin and sinners are treated (cf. *v.* 15). He took on Himself to be the representative of Humanity in its aspect of sinfulness (cf. Rom. viii. 3; Phil. ii. 7) and to bear the burden of sin in all its completeness. Hence He won the right to represent Humanity in all respects, and hence we are entitled to be regarded as God's righteousness (which He was) not in ourselves, but in Him as our representative in all things. See also *v.* 14.

who knew no sin] Cf. Heb. iv. 15; 1 Pet. ii. 22; 1 John iii. 5; also John viii. 46.

that we might be made the righteousness of God in him] We not only are regarded as God's righteousness, but become so, by virtue of the inward union effected between ourselves and Him by His Spirit, through faith. See *v.* 17 and note. "He did not say righteous, but righteousness, and that the righteousness of God." Chrysostom. See also Bp Wordsworth's note. Cf. Rom. i. 17, iii. 22, v. 19, x. 3; 1 Cor. i. 30.

CH. VI. 1—10. HOW GOD'S MINISTERS CARRY ON THIS
WORK OF RECONCILIATION.

1. *We then, as workers together with him*] Cf. 1 Cor. iii. 9, which, together with the context here, shews that our translators, following the Geneva Version, rightly supply 'with Him' here. The earlier translations render more literally. Wiclif, *helpinge*. Tyndale, *as helpers*.

beseech you] Better with the earlier versions **exhort** (*monesten*, Wiclif). See note on ch. i. 3, v. 20.

that ye receive not the grace of God in vain] i.e. that ye make not His kindness in being reconciled to you through Jesus Christ useless by neglecting to walk according to the new life He hath given you in Him (ch. v. 17). That even the new life itself may be so received as to make

I have heard thee in a time accepted, and in the day of salvation have I succoured thee: behold, now *is* the accepted time; behold, now *is* the day of salva-
3 tion.) Giving no offence in any *thing*, that the ministry be
4 not blamed: but in all *things* approving ourselves as the ministers of God, in much patience, in afflictions, in neces-

its reception useless is clear from the words 'Every branch *in Me* that beareth not fruit He taketh away.' John xv. 2. "For lest they should think that believing on Him that calleth is itself reconciliation, he adds these words, requiring the earnestness which respects the life." Chrysostom.

2. *For he saith*] In Isai. xlix. 8. The passage follows the LXX. translation.

I have heard thee in a time accepted] The words in the original refer to Christ. Here, however, they are applied to His Covenant people, united to Him by faith and the communication of His Nature, and therefore naturally entitled to expect the fulfilment of the promises made to Him. "We know," says Calvin, "what is the relation between the Head and the members."

behold, now is the accepted time] The word in the Greek is stronger than before; 'the time of *favourable* acceptance.' Our translation is due to Cranmer. Tyndale marks the distinction by translating *accepted* above, and *well accepted* in this place. The Vulgate renders by *accepto* and *acceptabile*. The life of the Christian is a continual acknowledgment in life and conduct of the 'word of reconciliation' he has received. The 'time of favourable acceptance,' therefore, the 'day of salvation,' is ever, not in the past, but in the present.

3. *Giving no offence in any thing*] This verse is closely connected in sense with *v*. 1. St Paul now enters upon a long passage in which he shews how the 'ministry of reconciliation' is practically carried on. The demeanour of the Apostles towards those among whom they preached the Gospel is as forcible a mode of proclaiming the reconciliation as their words. Yet he has not lost sight of the vindication of himself, which runs through the whole Epistle. You may judge for yourself, he is saying in effect, whether this be the conduct to expect from one charged with such a mission.

offence] The Greek word is derived from a verb signifying to *dash to the ground*, and signifies, therefore, anything which causes one to fall.

the ministry] i. e. of reconciliation. See above.

4. *approving*] The word is the same as is translated 'commend' in ch. iii. 1, and there is an obvious reference here to *v*. 1—3 of that chapter.

as the ministers of God] There is an ambiguity in the A. V. here. The Apostle means 'we, as ministers of God, recommend ourselves to those to whom we minister' in the way afterwards mentioned, not that the Apostles prove themselves *to be* ministers of God by their conduct. Tyndale renders *let us behave ourselves as the ministers of God*.

in much patience] Dean Stanley divides the means by which the

sities, in distresses, in stripes, in imprisonments, in tumults, 5
in labours, in watchings, in fastings; by pureness, by know- 6
ledge, by longsuffering, by kindness, by the Holy Ghost, by

Apostle commended himself into four classes: (1) from patience (or rather **endurance**) to 'fastings,' referring to the bodily sufferings of the Apostle; (2) from 'pureness' to 'love unfeigned,' referring to the virtues, that is, the manifestations of the Divine presence in St Paul; (3) from 'by the word of truth' to 'by evil report and good report,' referring to the means whereby he was enabled to prove himself to be a true minister of God; and (4) the remainder, relating to the acceptation in which the Apostles were held, and its contrast with the reality. Bengel also would subdivide the first class into three triplets of sufferings. But this is perhaps somewhat fanciful.

in afflictions] The word thus rendered is translated indifferently by *tribulations* (Wiclif so renders it here) and *afflictions* in the A. V. See note on ch. iv. 8.

in distresses] See note on ch. iv. 8.

5. *in stripes*] Cf. ch. xi. 23, 24; Acts xvi. 23.

in imprisonments] Cf. ch. xi. 23. The Acts of the Apostles, up to this date, records only one such, namely that at Philippi, Acts xvi. 23—40. But the Acts is far from recording all the events of St Paul's life. See notes on ch. xi. and on ch. i. 8.

in tumults] The word in the original signifies primarily *unsettlement*. Cf. margin of A. V., *tossings to and fro*. St Chrysostom would interpret it of the uncertain dwelling-place of the Apostle. But the word came to mean disorder or tumult. See Luke xxi. 9; 1 Cor. xiv. 33; James iii. 16, as well as ch. xii. 20, where the word occurs. In these passages moral disorder, not local unsettlement, is clearly implied. For the tumults which the Apostle went through see Acts xiii. 50, xiv. 5, 19, xvi. 22, xvii. 5, xviii. 12, xix. 23—41.

in labours] i.e. (1) the toils by which he supported himself (cf. Acts xviii. 3, xx. 34; 1 Thess. ii. 9; 2 Thess. iii. 8); and (2) his labours for the cause of Christ (cf. Rom. xvi. 12; 1 Tim. iv. 10).

in watchings] Literally, **sleeplessnesses**, caused by "manual labour, teaching, travelling, meditating, praying, cares and the like." Meyer.

in fastings] Since St Paul himself distinguished these fastings from ordinary hunger and thirst (ch. xi. 27) we must do so also. "Not fasting from want, but a voluntary exercise of abstinence." Calvin. Fasting, we know, was practised under the new Covenant as well as the old. See Acts xiii. 2, 3, xiv. 23.

6. *by pureness*] The preposition in the Greek is not changed here, though the Apostle turns from outward to inward signs of his sincerity, a change marked in our version by the use of 'by' for 'in.' Wiclif and the Rhemish, following the Vulgate, give the more restricted sense *chastity* here. But see 1 Tim. v. 22; 1 Pet. i. 22; 1 John iii. 3.

by the Holy Ghost] i.e. by Whom we are inspired in our whole mind and conduct. Cf. Rom. viii. 4, 5; Gal. v. 16, 25.

7 love unfeigned, by the word of truth, by the power of God, by the armour of righteousness on the right hand and on 8 the left, by honour and dishonour, by evil report and good 9 report: as deceivers, and *yet* true; as unknown, and *yet* well known; as dying, and behold, we live; as chastened, 10 and not killed; as sorrowful, yet alway rejoicing; as poor,

unfeigned] Love might easily enough be feigned for selfish purposes. St Paul could appeal to his own career to shew that his love was as real as its expression was ardent. Cf. *v.* 11 and note. Also Rom. xii. 9, where the Greek is the same as here.

7. *by the word of truth*] i.e. the Gospel of reconciliation, with which he was entrusted. Cf. Gal. ii. 5; Eph. i. 13, iv. 21; Col. i. 5; 2 Tim. ii. 15; James i. 18.

by the power of God] This is an expression very common in the N.T.; and, as Acts viii. 10 shews, was not confined to the Christian Church. See Matt. xxii. 29; Luke ix. 43; Rom. i. 16; 1 Cor. i. 18, 24, &c. Also 1 Cor. iv. 19, 20, v. 4, and ch. xiii. 10.

by the armour of righteousness] Rather **weapons** (*arma*, Vulgate). The translation in the text—which we owe to Tyndale—is possibly suggested by passages such as Eph. vi. 11, 13; 1 Thess. v. 8. Cf. ch. x. 4.

on the right hand and on the left] i.e. offensive and defensive, shield as well as spear.

8. *by honour and dishonour*] The preposition is here changed in the original, and *not* in our version. It means either *by means of*, or *by endurance of*, both of which senses are given by our English *through*. The sense is that not only did he persevere through evil report and good report, but that both were overruled to the furtherance of the Gospel.

as deceivers, and yet true] The Apostle now reaches the last division of the modes in which he sets forth the genuineness of his mission. This consists in the contrast between the *ideas* of his person and work formed by the world without, and the *fact* of which he was conscious within. The world (Matt. xxvii. 63) held Jesus Christ to be a deceiver, and 'the disciple is not above his master.'

9. *as unknown, and yet well known*] The passage would be better without the 'yet' interpolated by our translators (following Tyndale). St Paul was 'unknown' to some, and 'well known' to others. Cf. ch. iii. 1, 2, iv. 2, v. 11.

as dying, and behold, we live] See ch. iv. 10, 11. Also Rom. viii. 36, 37; 1 Cor. iv. 9, xv. 31; Eph. ii. 6; Col. ii. 13, iii. 1—4.

as chastened, and not killed] Cf. Ps. cxviii. 18, which was no doubt in the Apostle's mind. Also ch. vii. 4.

10. *as sorrowful, yet alway rejoicing*] Or *afflicted*, see ch. ii. 2. What the afflictions of the Apostle were, is obvious enough. His fount of joy was independent of things external. See Rom. v. 3, 11; Phil. ii. 16, 17, iv. 4; 1 Thess. v. 16, and ch. xii. 10.

yet making many rich; as having nothing, and *yet* possessing all *things*.

11—VII. 1. *Such a Ministry demands a suitable response on the part of those on whose behalf it is exercised.*

O *ye* Corinthians, our mouth is open unto you, our heart 11 is enlarged. Ye are not straitened in us, but ye are strait- 12

making many rich] With the riches of the Gospel. See Eph. i. 7, 18, ii. 7, iii. 8, 16, &c.
possessing all things] The whole passage bears a close similarity to 1 Cor. vii. 29—31, where, however, the turn given to the thought assumes a converse form. It was in Christ that His ministers could be said to possess all things. Cf. Rom. viii. 32; 1 Cor. iii. 22, 23. Also Phil. iv. 13.

11—VII. 1. SUCH A MINISTRY DEMANDS A SUITABLE RESPONSE ON THE PART OF THOSE ON WHOSE BEHALF IT IS EXERCISED.

11. *our mouth is open unto you*] i.e. we have spoken with perfect frankness on all points, keeping nothing back, because we love you. Chrysostom. Cf. ch. iii. 12.
our heart is enlarged] Rather, **hath been** enlarged, i.e. in what has been said. Chrysostom quotes Rom. i. 11, 13; Gal. iv. 19; Eph. iii. 14; Phil. i. 7, iv. 1; Col. ii. 1, 2; 1 Thess. ii. 7, 8, 19 as instances of St Paul's love of the faithful. Cf. also Rom. xv. 32; 2 John 4; 3 John 3, 4. The expression refers to the expansive effect of love and sympathy in the affections, just as we speak of a man of wide sympathies as 'large-hearted.' The passages cited from the O.T. by Dean Stanley (1 Kings iv. 29; Ps. cxix. 32; Isai. lx. 5) seem to have a somewhat different signification, that of the enlargement and exaltation consequent on the possession of intellectual, spiritual, or, in the last passage, it may be even *material* advantages. Robertson observes here, "Now what makes this remark wonderful in the Apostle's mouth is that St Paul had received a multitude of provocations from the Corinthians. They had denied the truthfulness of his ministry, charged him with interested motives, sneered at his manner, and held up to scorn the meanness of his appearance. In the face of this his heart expands!"
12. *Ye are not straitened in us, but ye are straitened in your own bowels*] i.e. "our heart is large enough to receive you and give you full possession of our affections, but yours is too narrow to receive any one but yourselves;" for such would seem to be the meaning hinted at, though not fully expressed, by the Apostle. The word *bowels* is a Hebraism for loving-kindness. As instances of its use in the O.T., take Cant. v. 4; Isai. xvi. 11; and in the New, Phil. ii. 1. For *straitened* (*angwischid*, Wiclif) see note on ch. iv. 8. The original meaning of the word is to *coop up in a narrow space*. The word *strait* in the sense of *narrow* (Latin, *strictus*) was a common phrase when the A.V. was made.

13 ened in your own bowels. Now for a recompence in the same, (I speak as unto *my* children,) be ye also enlarged. 14 Be ye not unequally yoked together with unbelievers: for what fellowship hath righteousness with unrighteousness? 15 and what communion hath light with darkness? and what concord hath Christ with Belial? or what part hath he that

e.g. Matt. vii. 13. It survives in modern English in such words as *straits, strait-waistcoat*.

13. *Now for a recompence in the same*] "St Paul details the circumstances of his ministry, and he asks in return, not the affection of the Corinthians, nor their admiration, but this: that they 'receive not the grace of God in vain,' and again 'be ye also enlarged.'" Robertson. Tyndale, whom Cranmer follows, has a curious mistranslation here, *I promyse you lyke rewarde with me as to my children*.

be ye also enlarged] i.e. return my affection by shewing a similar sympathy with mine for all who are Christ's.

14. *Be ye not unequally yoked together with unbelievers*] Dean Stanley observes on the "remarkable dislocation of the argument here." But the connection of thought is not difficult to trace. The only reward (see last verse) St Paul sought from the Corinthians was conduct in accordance with the Gospel of Christ. This was the best form their sympathy with him could take. Therefore he touches on some of the points on which they were in the habit of doing most violence to their Christian profession. They did not keep sufficiently aloof from unbelievers, but even went so far as to 'sit at meat' with them 'in the idol-temple' (see 1 Cor. viii., x., and notes) and thus become partakers with them in their idolatry, whereby they were the cause of infinite mischief to the souls of their brethren. The reference in the words 'unequally yoked together' is to the precept in Deut. xxii. 10, a precept, like many similar ones in the same chapter (*vv*. 9, 11, 12) and elsewhere in the Mosaic laws, manifestly figurative in its character. The Apostle's words must not be confined to intermarriages with the heathen, though of course it includes them in the prohibition. It refers to all kinds of close and intimate relations. "They are yoked together with unbelievers, who enter into close companionship with them." Estius.

what fellowship] The word thus rendered here is not the same as that rendered *communion* below, a word which (see notes on 1 Cor. i. 9, x. 16) is itself rendered indifferently by *communion* and *fellowship* in the N.T., but is derived from the word signifying to partake (*partynge*, Wiclif), e.g. in 1 Cor. x. 17. See Eph. v. 7; also 1 Maccabees i. 13—15 and 2 John 11.

unrighteousness] Literally, **lawlessness**, the normal condition of the heathen man, Rom. vi. 19, while the Christian is endowed with 'God's righteousness,' ch. v. 21.

light with darkness] Cf. John i. 5, iii. 19, the one signifying the condition of man in Christ, the other his condition without Christ. See also Eph. v. 8; 1 Thess. v. 5; and ch. iv. 4.

15. *Belial*] This word, derived from two Hebrew ones signifying 'of

believeth with an infidel? and what agreement hath the 16
temple of God with idols? for ye are the temple of the
living God; as God hath said, I will dwell in them,
and walk in *them;* and I will be their God, and
they shall be my people. Wherefore come out from 17
among them, and be ye separate, saith the Lord, and

no profit,' was used in the O.T. (e.g. Deut. xiii. 13; 1 Sam. ii. 12) in
the phrase 'child,' 'son' or 'daughter of Belial,' to signify a worthless
person, and generally (as in Deut. xv. 9, in the Hebrew) as a substantive
signifying worthlessness. It seems to have been personified among the
later Jews (some such personification seems clearly indicated by the
language of the Apostle), and to have become a synonym for Satan.
Similarly we find the idea of Belial presented in Judges xix. 22 personified by Milton in *Paradise Lost*, Book I. 490. But we must guard
against importing the imaginations of the poet into the interpretation of
the Scriptures.

16. *what agreement hath the temple of God with idols?*] Cf. 1 Cor.
iii. 16, 17, vi. 19, 20, viii. 10, x. 14—21. St Paul does not lay stress on
the abuse of liberty to which he devotes so large a portion of the first
Epistle (see note on *v.* 14), but we may gather from this hint that there
was still some need of improvement in this particular as well as in the
general relations of Christians with heathens.

for ye are the temple of the living God] Cf. 1 Cor. iii. 16; Eph.
ii. 21, 22; 1 Tim. iii. 15; Heb. iii. 6; 1 Pet. ii. 5.

as God hath said] The Apostle here combines, as was customary
among Jewish teachers, Lev. xxvi. 11, 12 with Ezek. xxxvii. 26, 27,
xliii. 7 (cf. also Zech. ii. 10, 11). The citation is in many respects
verbally accurate, but it is a citation, no doubt, from memory. The
Apostle has, however, given a Christian turn to his translation. The
Hebrew cannot be shewn to mean more than 'I will dwell *among* them.'
The LXX., in the remarkable word ἐμπεριπατήσω, seems to have anticipated the Christian idea of the indwelling of God in His people. But the
Apostle was evidently also thinking of some words of Christ, known to
him by tradition, and afterwards recorded by the Evangelist St John in
such passages as John vi. 56, xvii. 21, 23.

and I will be their God, and they shall be my people] St Paul here
boldly transfers the prophecies that relate to the earthly Israel to the
spiritual Israel, the Christian Church. Cf. Rom. ix. 25, 26; 1 Cor.
x. 1—11; Gal. iv. 26; Heb. xii. 22; 1 Pet. ii. 9, 10; Rev. iii. 12,
xxi. 2, 10.

17. *Wherefore come out from among them*] A combination of Isai.
lii. 11 with Ezek. xx. 34. This passage must be read in conjunction
with 1 Cor. v. 10, and must be understood not of absolute separation,
but of abstinence from any kind of *intimacy.* "Wherever union in the
highest cannot be, wherever *idem velle atque idem nolle* is impossible,
there friendship and intimate partnership must not be tried." Robertson.

touch not the unclean *thing;* and I will receive you,
18 and will be a Father unto you, and ye shall be my sons and
7 daughters, saith the Lord Almighty. Having therefore
these promises, dearly beloved, let us cleanse ourselves
from all filthiness of the flesh and spirit, perfecting holiness
in the fear of God.

2—16. *Exhortation to set aside all suspicion and to confide in
the Apostle's love and zeal for their spiritual well-being.*

2   Receive us; we have wronged no *man,* we have cor-

and touch not the unclean thing] The passage (see Isai. lii. 11) refers
to the priests and Levites, and relates to the ceremonial defilement
caused by contact with whatever was unclean. See for instance Lev.
xi. 8, 24, 31—40; also Rev. xviii. 4.
18. *saith the Lord Almighty*] Another combination of various
passages. See 2 Sam. vii. 14; Isai. xliii. 6; Ezek. xi. 20, xiv. 11,
xxxvii. 27.
CH. VII. 1. *Having therefore these promises*] Literally, **promises
such as these** (*soche promeses,* Tyndale and Cranmer), i. e. those that
have just been mentioned.
let us cleanse ourselves from all filthiness] Rather, **defilement** (see last
note but two), sin taking the place of 'the unclean thing' under the law.
For what is meant by defilement in the case of a Christian, see Matt.
xv. 18—20; Mark vii. 20—23, where, however, the word translated
'defile' means to *make common,* i.e. to reduce to the same condition as
the rest of mankind. Here it is the *stain* of sin which is the predominant idea.
of the flesh and spirit] i.e. inward as well as outward. See 1 Sam.
xvi. 7; Matt. xii. 34, 35. The outward defilement is caused by sins of
the *flesh,* or bodily part of man, the inward by those of the spirit, such
as pride, unbelief, and the like.
perfecting holiness in the fear of God] Perfection, and nothing less, is
to be the aim of the Christian. Cf. Matt. v. 48; Rom. xii. 2; Col. i. 22,
28, iv. 12. With this view he is to cleanse himself daily by sincere repentance from every defilement of sin, and to watch that he offend not
in like kind again. Cf. also 1 Thess. iv. 3; 1 Pet. iii. 15. The fear of
offending God (cf. ch. v. 11) is a very necessary element in the process
of sanctification. "We cannot do without awe: there is no depth of
character without it. Tender motives are not enough to restrain from
sin." Robertson.

2—16.   EXHORTATION TO SET ASIDE ALL SUSPICION AND TO
  CONFIDE IN THE APOSTLE'S LOVE AND ZEAL FOR THEIR
  SPIRITUAL WELL-BEING.

2. *Receive us*] Literally, **Make room for us** ('capaces estote nostri,'
Erasmus and Calvin. Tyndale and Cranmer, incorrectly, *understonde*

rupted no *man*, we have defrauded no *man*. I speak not 3
this to condemn *you*: for I have said before, that you are
in our hearts to die and live with *you*. Great *is* my bold- 4

us). The word here used is to be found in the sense of *having room for*
in Mark ii. 2; John ii. 6, xxi. 25. These words have reference to ch. vi.
12, 14, where see notes. The connection of what follows with what
has just preceded is to be found in the thought which underlies the
whole, that St Paul's only desire is the spiritual advancement of his
flock.

*we have wronged no man, we have corrupted no man, we have defrauded
no man*] Perhaps these words should be rendered 'we wronged,
corrupted, defrauded no man,' i e. during the course of our ministry at
Corinth. St Paul here refers to the charges brought against him. He
had been accused of *wronging* the Corinthians by claiming an authority
to which he had no right, and which he turned to his own account (see
1 Cor. ix. 1—6; 2 Cor. i. 12—17, v. 12, vi. 3, 4, 12, x. 7—11, xi. 7,
xii. 14); of *corrupting* them by preaching false doctrine, ii. 17, iv. 2 (unless, with Thomas Aquinas, we interpret it of *bad example*); of *defraud-
ing* them, xii. 17, 18, where the word here used is translated 'make a
gain of.' To this he replies by challenging them to prove their asser-
tions, to name a single instance in which he had done either. Dr
Plumptre regards the words 'corrupted' and 'defrauded' as referring to
sensual sin, and illustrates by the revolting charges of immorality
brought against the Christians by those who misinterpreted their
brotherly and sisterly affection. It is true that the word here translated
'defrauded' seems to have a reference to something more than mere greed
of gain. See note on 1 Cor. v. 10, 11. Still, the word translated 'corrupted' and its derivatives do not appear to have had any such restricted
sense in St Paul. See, for instance, 1 Cor. iii. 17, ch. xi. 3 of this
Epistle; and, in a less degree, Eph. iv. 22. And, however common
such charges were in the days of Minucius Felix and Tertullian, they
are not hinted at elsewhere in Scripture, but rather the contrary. See
1 Pet. iv. 4; 2 Pet. ii. 2.

3. *I speak not this to condemn you*] "It might seem as if this were
spoken *at* them with indirect reproach. Therefore he adds, 'I am not
reproaching you for past injustice: I only say these things to assure you
of my undiminished love.'" Robertson.

for I have said before] See ch. i. 6, iv. 10—12, 15, v. 11, 13—15.

you are in our hearts to die and live with you] "There is one thing in
the character of St Paul which often escapes observation. Carlyle calls
him an 'unkempt Apostle Paul,' and some say of him, 'he was a man rude,
brave, true, unpolished.' We all know his integrity, his truth, his
daring, his incorruptible honesty. But besides these, there was a refined
and delicate courtesy, which was for ever taking off the edge of his
sharpest rebukes, and sensitively anticipating every pain his words might
give." Robertson. He refers to Philemon 8, 12, 14, 17—20; Acts
xxvi. 29; and Phil. iii. 18. See also 1 Cor. iv. 14; 2 Cor. vi. 11—13,
ix. 4, and the whole of the present chapter. Robertson's whole com-

ness of speech toward you, great *is* my glorying of you : I am filled with comfort, I am exceeding joyful in all our ⁵ tribulation. For, when we were come into Macedonia, our flesh had no rest, but *we were* troubled on every *side;* with-⁶ out *were* fightings, within *were* fears. Nevertheless God, that comforteth *those that are* cast down, comforted us by

mentary on this chapter is invaluable to any one who desires to grasp the full meaning of the Apostle. For the expression 'in our hearts,' see Phil. i. 7. The commentators have pointed out a similar expression to that in the text in Horace, *Odes,* III. 9. 24, " Tecum vivere amem, tecum obeam libens." Wordsworth refers to the Theban sacred band, and to a similar passage in Athenaeus. But a deeper meaning is suggested by a comparison of ch. iv. 10, 11, 12 and notes. Also cf. ch. iii. 2.

4. *Great is my boldness of speech toward you*] Cf. note on ch. iii. 12.

great is my glorying of you] See notes on ch. i. 14 and ch. v. 12. The word here signifies not the *ground* of rejoicing or boasting, but, as A. V., the act itself. St Paul explains his boldness of speech by the confidence he has that it will not be misplaced. This is another instance of the delicate tact of the Apostle referred to above.

comfort] For this word and *tribulation,* see notes on ch. i. 3, 4. So also below in *vv.* 6, 7.

I am exceeding joyful] Literally, **I abound overmuch with joy.** The English word *exceedingly* has lost much of its original force.

5. *For, when we were come into Macedonia*] See Acts xx. 1, and ch. ii. 13.

our flesh had no rest] The word translated *rest* means rather *ease, remission of care.* The phrase is precisely the same as in ch. ii. 13, with the substitution of 'flesh' for 'spirit.' The change of expression is noticeable, and must imply that St Paul's inward anguish, like that of other men, seriously affected his bodily health. See Robertson's note. There is a peculiar vividness in the Greek and in ch. ii. 13 here, which can hardly be reproduced in a translation.

without were fightings, within were fears] Literally and more emphatically, **fightings without, fears within** (*without forth figtyngis and dredis withynne,* Wiclif). The first were probably controversies with gainsayers such as always attended St Paul's fervent preaching of the Gospel. A 'door,' we read, had been opened to him at Troas (see note on ch. ii. 12). What results were likely to follow from this we learn from Acts xiii. 45, xiv. 4, 5, 19, xvi. 19, xvii. 5—8, 13, &c. What the fears were scarcely needs explanation. They related to the mission of Titus and its reception by the Corinthians.

6. *those that are cast down*] The word ταπεινός, says Dean Stanley, never (except in metaphors in the N.T.) has the meaning of 'humble,' but only acquired such a meaning in later times to express the Christian grace of humility. It occurs in Matt. xi. 29; Luke i. 52; James iv. 6; 1 Pet. v. 5. In Rom. xii. 16 and in James i. 9 it is translated *men of low degree,* or *estate.* See also note on ch. x. 1. The *substantive* formed

the coming of Titus; and not by his coming only, but by 7 the consolation wherewith he was comforted in you, when he told us your earnest desire, your mourning, your fervent mind toward me; so that I rejoiced the more. For though 8 I made you sorry with a letter, I do not repent, though I did repent: for I perceive that the same epistle hath made you sorry, though *it were* but for a season. Now I rejoice, 9

from it is translated *humility* and *humbleness of mind*, save in Phil. ii. 3, where we have *lowliness* of mind; while the *verb* is used in Luke iii. 5 of the hills being made low, and in Phil. ii. 8 of what is called the 'humiliation' of Christ.

by the coming of Titus] "'By the *coming and presence* of Titus,' as in the frequent use of the word to describe the Advent of Christ." Stanley. See Matt. xxiv. 3; 1 Cor. xv. 23; 1 Thess. ii. 19, iii. 13, iv. 15; 2 Thess. ii. 1, &c.

7. *and not by his coming only, but by the consolation*] See ch. ii. 14, which is explained by this passage. It was not the mere *presence* of Titus, but the tidings he brought, which so rejoiced the Apostle.

fervent mind] Literally, **zeal** (*loue*, Wiclif). Our translation is due to Tyndale, who seems to have borne in mind the derivation of the word from a verb signifying *to boil up*. Meyer translates it 'your warm interest in me,' and explains by 'to appease me, to obey me and the like.' The word has also an evil sense in Scripture—*jealousy*, as in 1 Cor. iii. 3; Gal. v. 20; and ch. xii. 20. There is an instance of an intermediate sense in ch. xi. 2. It seems to signify any warm or strong feeling with regard to a person, whether for good or for evil.

8. *with a letter*] Rather, **by the letter**, i. e. the First Epistle.

though I did repent] "There was a moment in the Apostle's life when he half regretted what he had done. To some persons this would be perplexing. They cannot understand how an inspired Apostle could regret what he had done: if it were done by inspiration, what room could there be for misgivings? And if he regretted an act done under God's guidance, just as any common man might regret a foolish act, how could the Apostle be inspired? But this, which might perplex some, exhibits the very beauty and naturalness of the whole narrative. God's inspiration does not take a man and make a passive machine of him. When God inspires, His spirit mixes with the spirit of man in the form of thought, not without struggles and misgivings of the human element. Otherwise it would not be inspiration *of* the man, but simply a Divine echo *through* the man." Robertson. Similar conflicts of the human with the Divine in the inspired writers may be seen in Exod. iv. 10—14, vi. 12; Jer. i. 6—9, xiv. 13, xx. 7—9, 14—18, and in the whole book of Jonah.

for I perceive that the same epistle hath made you sorry] There are a good many various readings here, and the editors have adopted various punctuations, possibly from the difficulty mentioned in the last note. But in truth there need be no such difficulty. The right course was

not that ye were made sorry, but that ye sorrowed to repentance: for ye were made sorry after a godly manner, that ye might receive damage by us in nothing. For godly sorrow worketh repentance to salvation not to be repented of: but

that taken in the First Epistle, under the inspiration of the Holy Spirit. But after the Epistle was sent, the tender human heart of St Paul doubted whether he had done right, whether he had not given unnecessary pain, and the like, and his mind was not fully set at rest on the point until the arrival of Titus shewed him clearly the hand of God in the matter. Such self-questionings are constantly going on in the mind of every conscientious man, even when he has been acting most thoroughly under the guidance of God's Spirit. The word here translated *made sorry*, which is owing to Wiclif, is the same word which in ch. ii. is rendered 'caused grief' and 'grieved.'

9. *Now I rejoice, not that ye were made sorry*] Another instance of the tender consideration of St Paul (see note on *v.* 3). He will not run the risk of being supposed, even for a moment, to have taken pleasure in others' pain.

repentance] It cannot be too strongly insisted upon that the Greek word translated repentance (*penaunce*, Wiclif and the Rhemish Version) contains neither the idea of sorrow nor of penitential discipline. The word means *change of mind* or *purpose*. Sorrow may or may not accompany it. In most cases, as in this, it will do so. But the essence of Gospel repentance is not the sorrow it produces, but the change it works. The word translated *repent* in *v.* 8 is a different word, and has precisely the meaning usually in our days attached to the word *repentance*. It, or its cognate verb, only occurs here and in Matt. xxi. 29, 32, xxvii. 3, and Heb. vii. 21. It is a misfortune that the A. V. has employed the same word to express two very different ideas.

after a godly manner] The original is stronger, *according to God*, i.e. in such a manner as He had commanded or would approve. Cf. Rom. viii. 27.

receive damage] The word signifies to suffer injury or loss. See Matt. xvi. 26, where it is translated *lose;* Luke ix. 25, where it is translated *cast away*. See also 1 Cor. iii. 15. Wiclif renders here *suffer pairement;* Tyndale, *ye were hurte;* the Rhemish, well, *suffer detriment*.

10. *For godly sorrow worketh repentance*] Rather, **For the sorrow** which is **according to God** (*that is aftir God*, Wiclif) **worketh change of mind**. The difference between the true repentance and the false remorse may be illustrated by the cases of David and Saul, St Peter and Judas.

to salvation not to be repented of] Or *not to be regretted*, the word here used involving the idea of sorrow or anxiety. It is by most commentators connected with salvation, as though that were the result not to be regretted. But it may as naturally be referred to the change of mind. "The beautiful law is," says Robertson, "that in proportion as the repentance increases, the grief diminishes. 'I rejoice,' says St Paul,

the sorrow of the world worketh death. For behold this 11 selfsame *thing*, that ye sorrowed after a godly sort, what carefulness it wrought in you, yea, *what* clearing of yourselves, yea, *what* indignation, yea, *what* fear, yea, *what* vehement desire, yea, *what* zeal, yea, *what* revenge! In all *things* ye have approved yourselves to be clear in *this* matter. Wherefore, though I wrote unto you, *I did it* not 12 for his cause that had done the wrong, nor for his cause

'that I made you sorry, though it were *but for a time.*' Grief for a time, but repentance for ever."

but the sorrow of the world] i.e. of the world untouched and unregenerated by the Spirit of God—the sorrow of the natural man, "the opposite of the sorrow according to God." Stanley. See 1 Cor. ii. 14.

worketh death] Death of the *body*, sometimes, as when despair tempts to suicide, or brings on deadly sickness. Death of the *soul*, when sorrow fails to melt the heart, but leads it to that state of rebellious stubbornness, of entire alienation from God, which is expressed in the words "hardness of heart and contempt of His word and commandment." Cf. Prov. xvii. 22.

11. *after a godly sort*] See note on last verse. Also *v.* 9.

what carefulness] Literally, **diligence** (so Tyndale and Cranmer; *bisynes*, Wiclif; *moral earnestness*, Robertson). See Mark vi. 25; Luke i. 39, where it is translated *haste*.

what clearing of yourselves] Literally, **defence** or **excuse**, but a better translation than that in the text is impossible.

indignation] or *vexation*, a sort of feeling between indignation and disgust at themselves for having been 'puffed up,' and not having 'rather mourned that he that had done this deed had not been taken away from among them.' 1 Cor. v. 2.

fear] *Ne cum virga venirem*. Bengel. See 1 Cor. iv. 21, and *v.* 15. Or, perhaps, fear of God's wrath. See *v.* 1. But cf. note below.

vehement desire] Rather, **longing**, i.e. for St Paul's presence (see Phil. i. 8, ii. 26; 1 Thess. iii. 6; also ch. v. 2, ix. 14). The same word in *v.* 7 is translated *earnest desire*. Theophylact detects here another instance of the anxiety of the Apostle not to lay too much stress on his authority. To the idea of fear he immediately subjoins that of affection.

zeal] (*a fervent mynde*, Tyndale). See note on *v.* 7.

revenge] *punysshment*, Tyndale. The word is used of punishment inflicted by judicial process. See Luke xviii. 3. Also ch. x. 6. Such a process had taken place in this case. Cf. 1 Cor. v. 4, 5, with 2 Cor. ii. 6. Bengel remarks that the six results mentioned by the Apostle fall into six pairs. The first two relate to their feelings towards themselves, the next to their feelings towards the Apostle, the last to their feelings towards the offender and his offence.

12. *for his cause that had done the wrong*] See 1 Cor. v. 1.

that suffered wrong, but that our care for you in the sight of
13 God might appear unto you. Therefore we were comforted
in your comfort: *yea*, and exceedingly the more joyed we
for the joy of Titus, because his spirit was refreshed by you
14 all. For if I have boasted any *thing* to him of you, I am
not ashamed; but as we spake all *things* to you in truth,
even so our boasting, which *I made* before Titus, is found a
15 truth. And his inward affection is more abundant toward
you, whilst he remembereth the obedience of you all, how
16 with fear and trembling you received him. I rejoice therefore that I have confidence in you in all *things*.

nor for his cause that suffered wrong] From this it has been inferred that the father of the offender was *still alive*.
but that our care for you in the sight of God might appear unto you] Many MSS., versions, and editors read *that your care for us might appear to you*. Whichever be the true reading, the alteration has either sprung from a desire to alter the passage into conformity with the supposed meaning of the Apostle, or from similarity of sound, in the case of a copyist writing from oral dictation. Either reading would make good sense, but that in the text is more probable for two reasons: (1) the Apostle has been all along insisting on the purity of his motives and on his unfeigned affection for his Corinthian converts (ch. ii. 17, iv. 2); and (2) it seems rather unlikely that he should have wished the Corinthians to manifest their earnestness in his behalf *unto themselves*. See, however, on the other hand, ch. ii. 9, and cf. Calvin, who says "St Paul congratulates the Corinthians on having learned at length by this test, how they were disposed towards him." The word here translated *care* is the same as that rendered *carefulness* in the last verse.
13. *Therefore we were comforted in your comfort*] Most modern editors punctuate as follows: 'Therefore we were comforted. And in addition to (or in consequence of) our comfort we rejoiced a very great deal more at the joy of Titus,' 'our' being read for the 'your' of the A. V.
exceedingly the more] See note on *v*. 4.
14. *I am not ashamed*] Rather, 'I **was** not ashamed,' i.e. at his return.
but as we spake] i.e. when we were with you.
15. *his inward affection*] Bowels, margin. See note on ch. vi. 12. The translation here is Tyndale's.
more abundant] Literally, **more exceeding**. See note on *v*. 4.
the obedience of you all] Cf. ch. ii. 9, and x. 6.
16. *I rejoice therefore*] Our translation follows the Geneva version here. There is no 'therefore' in the best MSS. and versions. It is found neither in Wiclif, Tyndale, nor Cranmer. And the somewhat abrupt conclusion is in harmony with St Paul's style. Cf. 1 Cor. v. 13, where a similar attempt has been made by some copyist to soften down the abruptness.

CH. VIII., IX. *The Collection for the poor Saints at Jerusalem.*

Moreover, brethren, we do you to wit of the grace of God 8
bestowed on the churches of Macedonia; how that in a 2
great trial of affliction the abundance of their joy and their

that I have confidence in you] Tyndale and Cranmer translate *that I may be bolde over you.* Our version here again follows the Geneva Bible. Wiclif renders *trist.* But the word is not that usually rendered 'have confidence' in the N. T. The Apostle's meaning is rather, *that in every thing I am of good courage in consequence of your conduct.* From this chapter, says Robertson, we learn "the value of explanations. Had St Paul left the matter unsettled, or only half settled, there never could have been a hearty understanding between him and the Corinthians. Whenever there is a misunderstanding between man and man, the true remedy is a direct and open request for explanation." Cf. Matt. xviii. 15—17.

CH. VIII., IX. THE COLLECTION FOR THE POOR SAINTS AT JERUSALEM.

The somewhat abrupt commencement of this chapter is explained by a reference to 1 Cor. xvi. See notes there (and also Acts xxiv. 17; Rom. xv. 25—27). The plain directions there given by the Apostle render it unnecessary for him to enter into any explanation of his meaning here. Therefore the Corinthians are simply stirred up by the example of other Churches, and by considerations drawn from the nature of the Christian religion, to be forward in that good work.

1. *we do you to wit*] The translation is Tyndale's. Wiclif translates literally, **we make known to you.** Cranmer, *I certifye you* (cf. Calvin, *certiores vos facio*). The word *wit* is derived from the Anglo-Saxon *witan,* the German *wissen,* Shakespeare's *wis,* to know, and *do* is here used in the sense of *make.* Cf. 1 Cor. xii. 3, xv. 1, and Gal. i. 11, where the same Greek word is used.

the grace of God] i.e. the favour He had shewed them in thus making them partakers of His Spirit.

bestowed on] Rather, **in.** (*Given in,* Tyndale. So Wyclif and the Rhemish Version.) St Paul would imply that though given by God, it is manifested in their conduct.

the churches of Macedonia] The Thessalonians and the Philippians, and probably the Beroeans. It is observable that a holy emulation is a spirit quite consistent with the principles of the Gospel. Though we are not to seek the praise of men, we may not despise their example. "I wish you to know, how much good God has wrought in them." Estius.

2. *trial*] The Greek word is always used of that which has been tried and has stood the test. See notes on 1 Cor. xi. 19 and James i. 12 in this series. The meaning here is that tribulation has brought out the

deep poverty abounded unto the riches of their liberality.
3 For to *their* power, I bear record, *yea*, and beyond *their*
4 power *they were* willing of themselves; praying us with
much intreaty that we would receive the gift, and *take upon*
5 *us* the fellowship of the ministering to the saints. And *this*

genuine Christian qualities of the Macedonian Churches. For this tribulation see 1 Thess. i. 6, ii. 14; Acts xvii. 5.

affliction] Translated more usually **tribulation.** See note on ch. i. 4. The Apostle refers to the persecutions which they shared with him, which, if not endured in the proper spirit, would have shut them up in the contemplation of their own sorrows, instead of making them anxious to relieve those of others.

the abundance of their joy and their deep poverty] Cf. 1 Cor. i. 26. "In spite of their troubled condition they had displayed great joyfulness, and in spite of their poverty they had displayed great liberality." De Wette. The Geneva Version instead of 'deep poverty' has *the poverty which had consumed them even to the very bottom*. The literal rendering of *deep* is **down to the depth,** or **according to depth.** "Munificence," says Chrysostom, "is determined not by the measure of what is given, but by the mind of those who bestow it." Cf. Luke xxi. 3. "The condition of Greece in the time of Augustus was one of great desolation and distress... It had suffered severely by being the seat of the successive civil wars between Caesar and Pompey, between the triumvirs and Brutus and Cassius, and lastly, between Augustus and Antonius... The provinces of Macedonia and Achaia petitioned in the reign of Tiberius for a diminution of their burdens, and were considered deserving of compassion." Arnold's *Roman Commonwealth*. Corinth (see Introduction to First Epistle), from its position, would no doubt recover more speedily from such a condition of depression.

the riches of their liberality] (*singleness*, Tyndale and Cranmer, *simplicity*, Rhemish, after Vulgate). It is worth remarking that nowhere, save in 1 Tim. vi. 17, does St Paul use the word *riches* of material, but, with that one exception, solely of moral or spiritual wealth. Dean Stanley remarks on the fact that both the Greek word translated *liberality*, and its English equivalent, have a double meaning, the original meaning of the Greek word being *singleness of heart*, absence of all selfish motives (see ch. i. 12), and that of the English word the habit of mind engendered by a state of freedom.

3. *willing of themselves*] *Willynge of their owne accorde*, Tyndale. Literally, **of their own choice,** not excluding, however, as Meyer well remarks, Divine, but only human, influence in the matter. Cf. *v*. 17.

4. *intreaty*] *Monestynge*, Wiclif; *instaunce*, Tyndale. *Exhortation*, Rhemish. See note on ch. i. 3.

that we would receive the gift, and take upon us the fellowship] A more literal rendering would be, **praying of us the gift and fellowship** (perhaps we may take this as a Hebraism, meaning 'the favour of the fellowship'), i.e. that the Apostle would allow them to take part in the good work. The word here translated *gift* is the same which is usu-

they did, not as we hoped, but first gave their own selves to the Lord, and unto us by the will of God. Insomuch that 6 we desired Titus, that as he had begun, so he would also finish in you the same grace also. Therefore, as ye 7 abound in every *thing*, *in* faith, and utterance, and knowledge, and *in* all diligence, and *in* your love to us, *see* that ye abound in this grace also. I speak not by com- 8

ally translated *grace* in the N.T. See note on ch. i. 12. And the words 'that we would receive' are not in the best MSS. and versions.

5. *And this they did*] The words *this they did* are not in the original. They were added by Tyndale in order to explain the meaning of the passage. The construction of the Greek is not clear, but the general sense is that by the readiness of their offers of service and by their devotion to God, the Macedonians had surpassed St Paul's expectations.

first gave their own selves] *First* here may be a reference to the order of time, but it is better, with most commentators, to understand it of the order of importance; 'above all.' Alford. For a similar expression see the Greek of John i. 27, 30.

and unto us] The sense requires 'and *then* unto us,' i.e. as God's ministers and representatives. Cf. Acts xv. 28.

by the will of God] See note on *v.* 3. It was God's Will that they should have the power to act thus, if they were willing to carry out His Will. Cf. 1 Thess. iv. 3, v. 18; 1 Tim. ii. 4.

6. *Insomuch that we desired Titus*] Titus, it seems clear by the words 'as he had begun,' went a *second* time to Corinth before the Apostle arrived there (see, however, note on *v.* 18). His first visit began, his second completed the collection for the saints. For *desired* see ch. i. 3, the word receiving a great variety of translations in the N.T. Perhaps **incited** (or *urged*) would be the best translation here.

finish] Literally, **complete**.

in you] Literally, **unto you.** "Erga vos." Estius.

the same grace also] See note on *v.* 4. The Greek word is the same in both instances. The grace or favour is either (1) (see last note) the work of love which St Paul had accomplished in Macedonia, that of stirring up their zeal in giving; or (2) it may refer to the good work which God performed in their souls by means of His ministers, in drawing out all the best qualities of their renewed humanity.

7. *as ye abound*] Cf. 1 Cor. i. 5.

in all diligence] See note on ch. vii. 11.

your love to us] Some copies read *our love to you*.

this grace also] The word here, as in the last verse, seems to bear more the signification known to us in the phrase 'Christian graces' than in most places in which it occurs. The passage should perhaps run **see that ye also abound** (literally **exceed**, see note on ch. vii. 4) **in this grace**, i.e. act of favour or kindness (see last verse). We

mandment, but by occasion of the forwardness of others, ⁹ and to prove the sincerity of your love. For ye know the grace of our Lord Jesus Christ, that, though he was rich, yet for your sakes he became poor, that ye through his ¹⁰ poverty might be rich. And herein I give *my* advice: for this is expedient for you, who have begun before, not only

may observe that faith and utterance and the like were of little avail without love. See 1 Cor. viii. 1, xiii.; 2 Pet. i. 5—7.
   8. *I speak not by commandment*] The Apostles "never spoke as dictators." Robertson. See ch. i. 24, and *v.* 10, as well as 1 Cor. vii. 6, 25; Philemon 8, 9, 13, 14, and 1 Pet. v. 3.
   by occasion of the forwardness of others] Because other are so fervent. Tyndale.
   sincerity] Literally, **genuineness**. Cf. Phil. iv. 3; 1 Tim. i. 2; Tit. i. 4. The original meaning is *of legitimate* as opposed to illegitimate birth.
   9. *For ye know the grace of our Lord Jesus Christ*] In St Paul's eyes "Christ is the reference for everything. To Christ's life and Christ's Spirit St Paul refers all questions, both practical and speculative, for solution." Robertson. For *grace* see above, *vv.* 4, 6. Tyndale and some of the other versions render it here by *liberality*, and Estius interprets by *beneficentia*.
   though he was rich, yet for your sakes he became poor] Rather, **being** rich (cf. St John iii. 13 in the Greek and ch. xi. 31). There is no *was* in the original. Jesus Christ did not cease to be rich when He made Himself poor. He did not cease to be God when He became Man. For *became poor* we should perhaps translate, **made Himself a beggar**. The aorist refers to the moment when He became Man; and the word translated *poor* seems rather to require a stronger word. ("Apostolus non dixit pauper sed egenus. Plus est egenum esse quam pauperem." Estius.) The word (which seems "to have almost superseded the common word for poverty in the N.T." Stanley) is connected with the root *to fly, to fall*, and yet more closely with the idea of *cowering*, and seems to indicate a more abject condition than mere poverty. For the word, see Matt. v. 3, also ch. vi. 10, and *v.* 2 of this chapter. For the idea cf. Matt. viii. 20; Phil. ii. 6—8.
   that ye through his poverty might be rich] We could only attain to God by His bringing Himself down to our level. See John i. 9—14, 18, xii. 45, xiv. 9; Col. i. 15; Heb. i. 3. And by thus putting Himself on an equality with us He enriched us with all the treasures that dwell in Him. Cf. Eph. i. 7, 8, ii. 5—7, iii. 16—19; Col. ii. 2, 3, &c., as well as Phil. ii. 6—8 just cited.
   10. *And herein I give my advice*] See *v.* 8.
   for this] Either (1) 'that I advise and not command,' or (2) 'this proof of your love.'
   expedient] Rather, **profitable**. The word *expedient* in the A.V. is never, as in modern English, opposed to *right*. See note on 1 Cor.

to do, but also to be forward a year ago. Now therefore 11
perform the doing *of it;* that as *there was* a readiness to
will, so *there may be* a performance also out of that which
you have. For if there be first a willing mind, *it is* accepted 12
according to that a man hath, *and* not according to that
he hath not. For *I mean* not that other *men* be eased, and 13
you burdened: but by an equality, *that* now at *this* time 14

vi. 12. Wiclif and the Rhemish Version render here by *profitable.*
See Luke xvi. 9 and 1 Tim. vi. 18, 19.
begun before] i.e. before the Macedonian Churches. See ch. ix. 2.
but also to be forward] Literally, **to will** (margin, *be willing*). There
is much difference of opinion among the commentators concerning the
apparent inversion of the natural order in this sentence. But it would
seem that the Apostle, as we might expect from such passages as ch. iii.
3, 6, Rom. vii. 6, &c., attaches more importance to the *motive* than to
the action. They not only had begun to do the work, but they had
resolved to do so upon a full persuasion that it was the right thing to
do. Their conduct was due to no mere transitory impulse, but was the
deliberate conviction of the heart. To this "readiness to will" (see
next two verses) the Apostle appeals, and invites them to further
action on the ground that the principle on which they acted was just
as true now as it had been in the previous year. See note on ch.
ix. 7.
a year ago] Better, perhaps, **last year** (*the former yeere.* Wiclif;
ab anno priore. Vulgate). St Paul probably speaks as a Jew. But it
is uncertain whether he refers to the Jewish civil or ecclesiastical year,
the former of which began with the month Tisri, answering to part of
our September and October, the latter with the month Abib or Nisan.
The former is more probable, for the Apostle must have been writing
too near the commencement of the latter to give any force to his
remark. See 1 Cor. xvi. 5, 8, and ch. ii. 12, 13.
11. *Now therefore perform the doing of it*] The words *perform,
performance,* in this verse should rather be rendered **complete, completion.** See ch. vii. 1, where the participle of the same verb is rendered
perfecting, also *v.* 6 of this chapter. The sense is, 'you made a resolution last year to do a certain work. Carry out that resolution now,
and let the completion of the task bear witness, as far as your ability
goes, to the genuineness of the resolution you then made.'
out of that which you have] i.e. according to your means. See note
on *v.* 2.
12. *For if there be first a willing mind*] Literally, **For if willingness** (or *readiness*) **is present.** See Heb. vi. 18. The word translated
willing mind here is rendered *readiness* in *v.* 11 and *ready mind* in
v. 19.
13. *that other men be eased, and you burdened*] This translation is
partly due to the Geneva Version and partly to Tyndale. Literally it
runs, **that other men should have relief** (see note on ch. vii. 5) **and**

your abundance *may be a supply* for their want, that their abundance also may be *a supply* for your want: that there
15 may be equality: as it is written, He that *had gathered* much had nothing over; and he that *had gathered* little had no lack.
16 But thanks *be* to God, which put the same earnest care

ye tribulation. (*That it be remissioun to other men and to you tribulation.* Wiclif. Similarly the Rhemish Version.) "Again, in St Paul's spirit of entreaty we remark the spirit of reciprocity. It might have been supposed that because St Paul was a Jew he was therefore anxious for his Jewish brethren; and that in urging the Corinthians to give liberally, even out of their poverty, he forgot the unfairness of the request, and was satisfied so long as only the Jews were relieved—it mattered not at whose expense." Robertson.

14. *but by an equality*] Cf. 1 Cor. xii. and Acts ii. 41—47, iv. 32—37. Dean Stanley remarks on the similarity between this passage and several in the 5th book of Aristotle's *Ethics*, and no doubt St Paul here uses the word in Aristotle's sense of *fairness, reciprocal advantage*. Many of the English translators connect these words with those that succeed, *but by an equality at the present time.*

your abundance] i.e. as we should now say, *super*abundance. See note on ch. vii. 4, where the word in the Greek is derived from the same root. The English word *abundance* is derived from the Latin *unda*, a wave, and signifies originally an *overflowing quantity*.

that their abundance also may be a supply for your want] Literally, **might be.** There are two interpretations of this passage. The first, which is supported by the ancient interpreters, refers it to the spiritual return made by the Jews in the fact that it was men of their nation who preached the Gospel to the heathen. Cf. ch. ix. 14. The second, which has found favour with the moderns, is that the allusion is to earthly gifts. The chief difficulty which besets the latter interpretation is the impossibility of conceiving of what those earthly gifts could consist, unless, with De Wette, we regard it as referring to a communication of earthly goods "at another time, and under other possible circumstances." But Estius refers to Luke xiv. 12—14, as decisive against any reference to temporal recompense.

15. *as it is written*] In Exod. xvi. 18. "In this miracle St Paul perceives a great universal principle of human life. God has given to every man a certain capacity and a certain power of enjoyment. Beyond that he cannot find delight. Whatever he heaps or hoards beyond that, is not enjoyment but disquiet." Robertson.

16. *But thanks be to God*] The word translated *thanks* here is that translated *grace, gift,* in other places of this Epistle. We learn from *vv.* 6, 17, that Titus, moved by the strong interest in the Corinthians which his first mission had excited, and being requested by the Apostle to undertake the work of stimulating their energy in the charitable work they had undertaken (*v.* 10), determined of his own accord to

into the heart of Titus for you. For indeed he accepted the 17 exhortation; but being more forward, of his own accord he went unto you. And we have sent with him the brother, 18 whose praise *is* in the gospel throughout all the churches;

visit Corinth, instead of writing (this seems the only way in which we can reconcile *v.* 6 with *v.* 17), and thus to stir up the Corinthians by his personal presence to a holy emulation of the good deeds of the Churches of Macedonia. Titus can hardly, as some have thought, have been entrusted with this Epistle on the occasion of which the Apostle speaks, for St Paul speaks in the past tense of this mission. See notes on *v.* 18 and ch. xii. 18.

which put] "Opera bona Dei dona." Estius. The received Greek text here has 'putteth,' but a large number of MSS. read as in the text.

the same earnest care] i.e. the same as I have myself. For *earnest care* (*bisynesse*, Wiclif, *good mynde*, Tyndale and Cranmer) see notes on ch. vii. 11, 12, viii. 7, where the same Greek word is used.

17. *For indeed he accepted the exhortation*] The Greek implies that Titus did indeed receive an exhortation from St Paul, but that he did more than he had been asked to do. For *exhortation* compare *entreaty*, *v.* 4, and see note on ch. i. 3.

but being more forward] Literally, 'more **diligent**,' i.e. than I had desired him to be. See note on *earnest care* above.

18. *And we have sent with him*] Literally, **we sent with him**, unless the tense be what is known as the epistolary aorist (see above, ch. ii. 9), in which case these messengers were also the bearers of this Epistle.

the brother, whose praise is in the gospel] Innumerable guesses have been made as to who this was. We can but briefly glance at them. First of all it is clear that it was no obscure member of any of the various communities who is here mentioned. He was thoroughly well known to the Churches. Secondly, we may remark that it was not *Barnabas*, as many of the early Fathers have supposed, since we never hear of Paul and Barnabas as travelling together after their misunderstanding in Acts xv., nor *Silas*, for he does not appear to have been with the Apostle after his departure from Corinth for Jerusalem related in Acts xviii. 18. We learn from the next verse that the 'brother' here referred to was a delegate of the Churches, and deputed to accompany St Paul on his journey to Jerusalem with the proceeds of the collection. He must either have been a delegate of the Ephesian or the Macedonian Christians. If the latter, it must have been (1) St Luke, for he *did* travel with St Paul on this occasion, as we learn from Acts xx. 5. And though he did not join the Apostle till he reached Philippi from Corinth, and did not accompany him on his visit to Corinth (Acts xx. 1—5), this is no reason against his having accompanied Titus on his visit to Corinth. See note on *v.* 16. And St Luke answers in many ways better than any one else to this description. But ch. ix. 4 seems to imply that the brother was not of Macedonia (though Meyer thinks

19 and not *that* only, but who was also chosen of the churches to travel with us with this grace, which is administered by us to the glory of the same Lord, and *declaration of* your 20 ready mind: avoiding this, that no *man* should blame us in

that the whole context shews him to have been a Macedonian). Nor can the words 'whose praise is in the Gospel' be pressed (so St Chrysostom and the Collect for St Luke's Day) as signifying the Gospel of St Luke. For the word gospel is never used in the Scripture of any of the biographies of Christ, but solely of the good tidings proclaimed by His ministers. The earliest phrase by which the Gospels are designated is 'memoirs.' (See Justin Martyr's *First Apology*, ch. 67.) If the brother were an Ephesian delegate, he must have been either (2) Trophimus or (3) Tychicus. *Both* these left Greece with St Paul. The former was 'an Ephesian' and accompanied him to Jerusalem. (Acts xxi. 29.) The latter was '*of Asia*' (Acts xx. 4), and probably of Ephesus, for he was *twice* sent thither by St Paul (Eph. vi. 21; 2 Tim. iv. 12). And he evidently stood high in the estimation of the Apostle (Eph. vi. 21, 22; Col. iv. 7, 8) for his qualities as a minister of Christ. *Both* these, however, if the deputies were Ephesians, would most likely have been the messengers. See note on *v.* 22.

19. *and not that only*] i.e. not only is he praised throughout all the Churches.

but who was also chosen of the churches] i.e. chosen by the Churches. See note on 1 Cor. xiv. 24, ch. i. 16, ii. 6, 12 of this Epistle, and Heb. xii. 5, &c. The word here used signifies *chosen by show of hands*. So also in Acts xiv. 23. Voting by show of hands was the custom among the Greeks as among ourselves. See Xenophon, *Anabasis*, Book III. ii. 33. For the choosing by the Churches see 1 Cor. xvi. 3, 4 and note.

to the glory of the same Lord] The word 'same' is omitted by many MSS. and editors.

and declaration of your ready mind] Nearly all the MSS. and versions read 'our.' (*To the glorie of the Lord and to our ordeyned wil.* Wiclif.) The words 'and declaration of' are not in the Greek.

20. *avoiding this*] The word is used in Greek of furling the sails of a vessel to avoid a disaster. It occurs again in the N.T. in 2 Thess. iii. 6. But it may perhaps be translated **making this arrangement**.

that no man should blame us] Chrysostom and Calvin remark on the care taken by the Apostle to avoid giving the slightest cause for suspicion. He did not, says the former, send Titus alone. "He was not," says the latter, "so satisfied with himself as to think it unworthy of his dignity to avoid calumny." And he adds, "certainly nothing exposes a man to unpleasant insinuations more than the management of public money." "In this is to be observed St Paul's wisdom, not only as a man of the world, but as a man of God. He knew that he lived in a censorious age, that he was as a city set on a hill, that the world would scan his every act and his every word, and attribute all conceivable and even inconceivable evil to what he did in all honour. It was just be-

this abundance which is administered by us: providing *for* 21 honest *things*, not only in the sight of the Lord, but also in the sight of men. And we have sent with them our bro- 22 ther, whom we have oftentimes proved diligent in many *things*, but now much more diligent, upon the great confidence which *I have* in you. Whether *any do inquire* of 23 Titus, *he is* my partner and fellow-helper concerning you: or our brethren *be inquired of, they are* the messengers of the churches, *and* the glory of Christ. Wherefore shew ye to 24

cause of St Paul's honour and innocence that he was likely to have omitted this prudence." Robertson.

abundance] The Greek word occurs only here in the N.T. It comes from a root meaning *firm, solid, compact*, or perhaps with some lexicographers, *large*, and hence *extensive, abundant*.

21. *providing*] Most MSS. and editors here read **for** *we provide*, or rather, **take care beforehand to do**, i.e. it is our custom to give no occasion for suspicion. See Rom. xii. 17, where the same words occur. They are, as Dr Plumptre has reminded us, a quotation of Prov. iii. 4. Cf. also Rom. xiv. 6; 1 Tim. v. 14, vi. 1; Tit. ii. 8. Also ch. vi. 3.

honest things] Rather, **what is honourable**. The word implies what is of good repute among mankind, and hence what is honourable and noble in itself. See note on ch. iv. 2.

also in the sight of men] It is not enough for the Christian to have a clear conscience. He must give no man an opportunity of insinuating that his conscience is *not* clear. See Matt. v. 14—16.

22. *And we have sent with them*] Literally, as before, *v.* 18, **we sent** with them, i.e. with the other two.

our brother, whom we have oftentimes proved diligent] See for this *third* brother, the note on *v.* 18. Dr Plumptre suggests Clement, as one dear to St Paul and known to the Philippians (Phil. iv. 3).

upon the great confidence which I have in you] The margin, '*he* hath,' is to be preferred. This brother had no doubt been at Corinth, and was quite certain that the Corinthians, in spite of all shortcomings, would in the end come up to St Paul's highest anticipations.

23. *he is my partner*] Literally, **sharer**. See notes on the words *communion* and *fellowship* in the first Epistle. 'The sharer of my labours and cares.'

and fellow-helper concerning you] Better, **and as regards you, my fellow-worker**.

the messengers of the churches, and the glory of Christ] The word '*and*' is not in the original, and detracts from the force of the sentence. The word here translated 'messengers' is *Apostles* in the original. But here, as in Phil. ii. 25, it does not signify the official rank in the Church of the persons referred to, but simply the fact that they were sent. For 'the glory of Christ' see *v.* 19 and 1 Cor. xi. 7. A man is the glory of Christ when he manifests Christ's glory, which is done

them, and before the churches, the proof of your love, and of our boasting on your behalf.

9 For as touching the ministering to the saints, it is super-
2 fluous for me to write to you: for I know the forwardness of your mind, for which I boast of you to them of Macedonia, that Achaia was ready a year ago; and your zeal
3 hath provoked very many. Yet have I sent the brethren,

either by displaying His power, or the holiness which comes from Him. Cf. John i. 14, ii. 11, xi. 40; Gal. i. 24, and Acts xxi. 19, 20; also ch. iii. 18. *Both* the brethren would seem from this passage to have been 'chosen of the Churches.'

24. *before the churches*] To which they belong, and of which they are the representatives, *vv.* 19, 23. The spirit shewn by the Corinthians would of necessity be reported by these delegates to the Churches which had commissioned them. For the expression, literally **in the face of,** cf. ch. ii. 10, iv. 6, v. 12 and notes.

our boasting on your behalf] See ch. ix. 2.

CH. IX. **1.** *For*] i.e. I am not writing to you about the ministry to the saints, for that is unnecessary. I am writing about your reception of the brethren, and your being ready when they come. See *v.* 3.

the ministering] Literally, **the ministry.** See note on ch. iii. 3. *Anything* which conveyed God's good gifts from one member of the Church to another, was in the Apostle's eyes a *ministry*, a *diaconate*, for the words rendered *minister, ministry*, are in Greek διάκονος, διακονία. See also note on *v.* 12 and on ch. viii. 4.

it is superfluous for me to write to you] "Observe the tender wisdom of this proceeding. The charity which finds us unprepared is a call as hateful as that of any creditor whom it is hard to pay. St Paul knew this well; therefore he gave timely notice." Robertson. It was unnecessary to write to them about the collection itself. It was not unnecessary to remind them as a matter of Christian prudence that they must not allow themselves to be taken unawares, lest the amount of their bounty should hardly correspond to what men had a reason to expect. Cf. 1 Cor. xvi. 2. Calvin, however, thinks that the Apostle wavered between confidence and anxiety. He knew their readiness, but he feared the instability of human nature.

2. *for I know the forwardness of your mind*] Rather, **readiness** (*your redynesse of minde*. Tyndale). See note on ch. viii. 12. And therefore I need not write about the collection.

I boast] The Apostle, then, says Bengel, was already in Macedonia. *Achaia*] See note on ch. i. 1.

a year ago] Rather, **last year.** See ch. viii. 10. The Vulgate renders here by *ab anno praeterito.*

and your zeal hath provoked very many] "We did not advise, we did not exhort; we only praised you, we only boasted of you; and this was enough for exhortation of them." Chrysostom. For *zeal*, see notes on ch. vii. 7, 11. Perhaps the Apostle means to say here the

vv. 4, 5.] II. CORINTHIANS, IX. 97

lest our boasting of you should be in vain in this behalf; that, as I said, ye may be ready: lest haply if they of Mace- 4 donia come with me, and find you unprepared, we (that we say not, you) should be ashamed in this *same* confident boasting. Therefore I thought it necessary to exhort the 5

emulation arising from your conduct, since the word rendered 'your' is literally, **arising from you**. The word here translated 'provoke' is used in a bad sense in Col. iii. 21. The English word *provoke*, from the Latin *provoco, to call forth*, is usually in these days used in a bad sense. But it was not so at the time when the A. V. was made. Cf. Heb. x. 24. The meaning here is *stirred up*. For *very many*, the original has *the majority*.

3. *Yet have I sent*] Although instructions to make the collection were needless, it was not needless for me to send the brethren. See note on *v.* 1. For *I have sent*, the Greek has *I sent*. But see notes on ch. viii. 18, 22, and Introduction.

our boasting] Literally, 'our **ground of** boasting,' but see ch. v. 12. It was not that St Paul expected no result from the collection, but feared that it might be one out of all proportion to what his expressions of confidence in the Corinthian Church would have led other Churches to expect.

in this behalf] Rather, **in this respect**, i.e. in regard to the matter of the collection. He had not hesitated to speak of their other good qualities. See 1 Cor. i. 4—8; and for the expression see ch. iii. 10.

4. *lest haply*] The earlier editions have *happily* (*paraventure*, Tyndale), with the same meaning as in the text.

they of Macedonia] We should rather say in English **any Macedonians**. From this it has been inferred that the brethren sent previously were not Macedonians. See ch. viii. 17—24.

we (*that we say not, you*)] The 'we' is emphatic. We have another instance here of what we might call the gentlemanly instinct of the Apostle. See note on ch. vii. 3. 'I should be ashamed of my confidence, and, might I not add, you also would be ashamed that I should have expressed it.'

confident boasting] The word '*boasting*' is omitted by most recent editors. It is absent from the best MSS. and versions, and has probably been introduced from ch. xi. 17. The rendering in this case must be '*in this confidence*,' i.e. which I have had in you. Some would render by 'foundation' or 'substance' (*in hac substantia*, Vulg.), the latter being the literal rendering of the word (see Heb. xi. 1, also i. 3 where it is translated *person*); but in Heb. iii. 14, as in Classical Greek and in the LXX., it means and is rendered *confidence*. It means originally (1) that on which one takes one's stand; or (2) that which stands beneath us. Hence in later Greek theology it came to mean *person*, as the underlying entity at the root of all apparent being. Compare our English words *understand, understanding*, which however, like the Latin *substantia*, have had a different history, and have arrived at a different signification.

brethren, that they would go before unto you, and make up beforehand your bounty, whereof *ye* had notice before, that the same might be ready, as *a matter of* bounty, and not as 6 *of* covetousness. But this *I say*, He which soweth sparingly shall reap also sparingly; and he which soweth boun- 7 tifully shall reap also bountifully. Every man according as he purposeth in *his* heart, *so let him give;* not grudgingly, or 8 of necessity: for God loveth a cheerful giver. And God *is* able to make all grace abound towards you; that ye, always

5. *the brethren*] i.e. those mentioned in the last chapter.
go before] i.e. before the Apostle.
your bounty, whereof ye had notice before] Rather, according to the best MSS., 'your **previously announced** bounty,' i.e. either (1) announced by me to the Macedonian Churches; or (2) generally, promised beforehand. The word translated *bounty* is more usually translated *blessing* (Vulg. *benedictio*). See 1 Cor. x. 16; also Gen. xxxiii. 11; 1 Sam. xxx. 26 in the LXX. The gifts of the Corinthians are called a *blessing*, because they are so to others, and because they call down a blessing on those who impart them. See Dean Stanley's note, who quotes the well-known passage from the *Merchant of Venice*, where Portia says that mercy is "twice blessed; it blesseth him that gives and him that takes."
as a matter of bounty] Rather, **so as to be a blessing**.
and not as of covetousness] Rather, perhaps, **greed**; i.e. to be given in a generous and not in a grudging spirit. But Dr Plumptre regards it as possibly referring to St Paul, 'as a work of *your* bounty, not of *my* claims upon your purses.' Ch. vii. 2, xii. 17, 18, which he cites, are decidedly in favour of this interpretation. For *covetous, covetousness*, see 1 Cor. v. 10 (note).

6. *He which soweth sparingly*] "He calls it sowing," says Chrysostom, "in order that we may learn by the figure of the harvest that in giving we receive more than we give." Cf. Gal. vi. 7—9; also Prov. xi. 18.
bountifully] Literally, **with blessings** (*in benedictionibus*, Vulg.). In both cases the Greek word is the same.

7. *purposeth*] The word, as used in Aristotle, denotes *deliberate choice*, without any constraint of any kind, as well as free from the impulse of the passions.
grudgingly] Literally, **from sorrow**, i.e. out of a sorrowful or unwilling heart. Cf. Exod. xxv. 2; Deut. xv. 10.
cheerful giver] Cf. Rom. xii. 8; Tobit iv. 7; Ecclus. xxxv. 9; and the LXX. of Prov. xxii. 8.

8. *all grace*] See notes on *grace* elsewhere, esp. ch. viii. 6 and v. 15 of this chapter; also cf. 1 Cor. xvi. 3. The meaning here is 'God is able to make every gift of His loving-kindness to abound to you, that you, being thus enriched, may impart of His bounty to others.'

having all sufficiency in all *things*, may abound to every good work: (as it is written, **He hath dispersed abroad;** 9 **he hath given to the poor: his righteousness remaineth for ever.** Now he that ministereth seed to the 10 sower both minister bread for *your* food, and multiply your seed sown, and increase the fruits of your righteousness;)

sufficiency] This is translated *contentment* in 1 Tim. vi. 6, while the corresponding adjective is rendered *content* in Phil. iv. 11. But 1 Tim. vi. 8 explains the meaning of the word. It is the state of mind which, needing nothing but the barest necessaries, regards all other things as superfluities, to be parted with whenever the needs of others require them. This is the force of the words 'all' twice repeated, and 'always.' At all times, save when he is actually deprived of food and raiment, the Christian ought to regard himself as having enough. It is worthy of remark that this *self-sufficingness* was a favourite virtue with heathen philosophers, though destitute, in the case of the Stoics, of all the gentler and more attractive aspects in which it has been wont to present itself among Christians. The use of this word, as of the word noticed in *v.* 7, seems to shew that St Paul was well acquainted with the philosophy of Aristotle. See also note on ch. viii. 14.

9. *as it is written*] In Ps. cxii. 9.

the poor] The word here is the usual one in Classical Greek. See notes on ch. viii. 9.

his righteousness remaineth for ever] As this passage is simply quoted from the O. T., it seems unfair to build any theological argument upon it, especially as on points like these the Hebrew language has by no means the precision of the Greek. It probably means no more than this; that a good and charitable deed remains such for evermore. The parenthesis, which in the A. V. includes *v.* 10, ought to include this verse only.

10. *Now he that ministereth*] The word used twice in this verse has the original signification of *leading a chorus.* Hence it came to mean to *defray the expenses* of a chorus, since when a wealthy man was appointed to any office of importance in his city, it was usual for him to provide festal displays for the citizens. Hence it came to have the general meaning of *furnish, provide,* as here.

both minister] In the best MSS. these verbs are in the future indicative, i.e. *will* minister; *will* multiply; *will* increase (so Wiclif and Tyndale); not, as the received Greek text, in the optative.

bread for your food] In the Greek these words seem to belong to the former verb, 'Now he that supplieth seed to the sower and bread for food will supply and multiply,' &c. The words here are a quotation from the LXX. version of Isai. lv. 10.

increase the fruits of your righteousness] Cf. 1 Cor. i. 30, iii. 6. The words are taken from the LXX. version of Hos. x. 12. The metaphor is taken from the natural processes of growth just referred to.

11 being enriched in every *thing* to all bountifulness, which 12 causeth through us thanksgiving to God. For the administration of this service not only supplieth the want of the saints, but is abundant also by many thanksgivings unto 13 God; whiles by the experiment of this ministration they glorify God for your professed subjection unto the gospel

God supplies the seed of works of mercy; He multiplies it, and good works in plenty are the crop.

11. *bountifulness*] (*symplenesse*, Wiclif; *syngleness*, Tyndale). The Greek word here is the same as in ch. i. 12, viii. 2, where see notes. The word 'bountifulness' was first introduced by our translators, who however have *liberality* in the margin.

which] i.e. the 'bountifulness' or 'singlemindness' just spoken of.

causeth through us thanksgiving] i.e. your singleness of heart, your absence of all secondary and selfish motives, provides us with the means of alleviating the distresses of others, and thus elicits from them thanks to God out of the fulness of a grateful heart.

12. *For the administration of this service*] Literally, **For the ministry** (see note on *v.* 1) **of this public service** (*the mynysterie of this public office*, Wiclif; *the office of this ministracion*, Tyndale). The word translated *service* means any public work. "The λειτουργοί," says Potter in his *Grecian Antiquities*, "were persons of considerable estates, who were ordered to perform some public duty or to supply the commonwealth with necessaries at their own expenses." See also Smith's *Dictionary of Antiquities*, Art. Liturgia. Hence comes our word Liturgy, which originally signified any public function, but afterwards became restrained to the Holy Communion only. See, for the word, Luke i. 23; Phil. ii. 17, 30; Heb. viii. 6, ix. 21. The verb derived from the same source is used of the public services of the Church in Acts xiii. 2; Heb. x. 11. In Rom. xv. 27 it is used in the same sense as here.

is abundant] Rather, **exceedeth**, or **aboundeth**. See note on 'exceeding joyful,' ch. vii. 4; also ch. i. 11, iv. 15.

by many thanksgivings] Cf. ch. i. 11, iv. 15.

13. *experiment*] Rather, **proof** (*probatio*, Vulg.), i.e. the proof afforded by the conduct of the Corinthians that they were Christians, not in name only, but in deed. See ch. ii. 9, viii. 2, 8.

glorify] Cf. Matt. v. 16; John xv. 8; 1 Pet. ii. 12.

your professed subjection] The translators of the A.V. have regarded this sentence as a Hebraism. Literally, it is **the subjection of your confession**, or **profession**, i.e. of Christianity. See 1 Tim. vi. 12, 13 (margin); Heb. iii. 1, iv. 14, x. 23. The brethren at Jerusalem glorified God for the fact that the profession of Christianity made by the Corinthians was in strict accordance with the precepts of the Gospel. It is obvious that this cannot be predicated of every individual, or even of every Church, and cannot therefore be assumed as a matter of course. It is, however, to be observed (see Meyer's note) that 'to the Gospel'

of Christ, and *for your* liberal distribution unto them, and unto all *men;* and by their prayer for you, which long after you for the exceeding grace of God in you. Thanks *be* unto God for his unspeakable gift. 14 15

1—6 *St Paul's intention of overcoming all opposition to the Gospel.*

Now I Paul myself beseech you by the meekness and 10

should perhaps be translated 'towards the Gospel,' i.e. towards the work of furthering it.

and for your liberal distribution] Literally, **and for the liberality of your contribution.** The word here rendered *distribution* in the A.V. is that usually rendered by *communion*, or *fellowship*. Here it clearly has the active sense of *communication*. The Vulgate renders *simplicitate communicationis*. See notes on 1 Cor. i. 9, x. 20. For *liberality* see *v.* 11.

and unto all men] Because the principle thus admitted by the Corinthians was equally applicable to all.

14. *and by their prayer for you, which long after you*] The construction in the Greek is somewhat obscure. Some would render (1) as A.V., and regard this verse also as depending upon the word *glorify*. Others suppose (2) that St Paul has abruptly changed the construction, and would render *they themselves, with prayer, earnestly longing to see you*. If we accept (1), which also involves a change in the construction of the sentence, the sense is that the prayer of the Jewish Christians and their affection for the Corinthians redounded to the glory of God. If (2), it simply means that the result of the Corinthian bounty would be to draw out a corresponding fervency of affection on the part of the Church at Jerusalem. It is worthy of remark that the Apostle, in his vivid anticipation of the future, regards it as already present.

15. *Thanks*] The word is the same which is elsewhere translated *grace*.

for his unspeakable gift] This, as Dean Alford suggests (after Chrysostom), can be none other than Jesus Christ Himself. No other gift could correspond to the word 'unspeakable,' which suggests (like Rom. xi. 33; Eph. iii. 18, 19) the idea of God. And in Jesus Christ 'dwelleth all the fulness of the Godhead bodily' (Col. ii. 9). From Him all gifts of nature or grace proceed. And what the gift is which is above all others, we learn from such passages as Rom. v. 15, vi. 23; Heb. vi. 4. So Bengel. "Deus nobis dedit abundantiam bonorum internorum et externorum, quae et ipsa est inenarrabilis, et fructus habet consimiles." See also Rom. viii. 32.

CH. X. 1—6. ST PAUL'S INTENTION OF OVERCOMING ALL OPPOSITION TO THE GOSPEL.

1. *Now I Paul myself*] "Until now, Paul has addressed himself preeminently to the better intentioned in the Christian Church, but

gentleness of Christ, who in presence *am* base among you,
2 but being absent am bold toward you: but I beseech *you*,
that I may not be bold when I am present with *that* confidence, wherewith I think to be bold against some, which

henceforth he addresses himself to those who had sought to lower his dignity and weaken his authority by representing him as weak in personal influence," as well as in bodily strength and consistency of purpose, "although courageous and full of self-commendation in his letters." Olshausen. The word 'myself' is difficult to explain. Deans Stanley and Alford explain it (1) of St Paul's intention to enter upon personal matters. St Chrysostom seems to imply (2) that it refers to the emphasis with which he speaks, and he cites Gal. v. 2, Philem. 19. But (3) it seems more probable that it means 'I, the very man who in absence am said to be bold, shew my consistency by preferring meekness even in my letters. I am meek, not because I am afraid, but because I ought to be meek. But if meekness fails, then I must be severe.' Cf. *vv*. 2, 9, 10; also 1 Cor. iv. 21. It must be remembered that one main purpose of this Epistle is to vindicate the consistency of the Apostle. See ch. i. 17—19.

beseech] Rather, **exhort**. See note on ch. i. 3.

meekness and gentleness] *Myldnesse and softnesse*, Wiclif. Tyndale introduced the translation *meekness*. The word *gentleness* is due to our translators. But it is not the exact equivalent of the original. Derived from a word signifying *like the truth*, and therefore *fair, equitable*, it came to be the equivalent (see Aristotle, *Ethics* V. 10, and VI. 11) for the habit of mind engendered by the practice of regarding the rights of other people as well as our own. Aristotle describes it as the principle which underlies justice and tempers it, and as resulting in sympathy. Its nearest equivalents in English are *fairness, considerateness, reasonableness*. It and the cognate word occur in the N.T. only in Acts xxiv. 4; Phil. iv. 5; 1 Tim. iii. 3; Tit. iii. 2; James iii. 17; 1 Pet. ii. 18. For *meekness* cf. Matt. xi. 29, 30; Isai. xlii. 2, 3, liii. 7.

in presence] Some translate by *in personal appearance*. See *v.* 7, and margin here. But the word seems in this verse to be opposed to *absence*. See *v.* 11. Also the Greek of Acts iii. 13, xxv. 16.

base] See note on ch. vii. 6, where the word in the Greek is the same as here. The word *base* signifies originally *low in position*. Cf. the word *basement* and the French *bas*. See also Acts xvii. 5. So Spenser, in his *View of the State of Ireland*, distinguishes between the "lords and chief men," and the "peasants and *baser people*."

2. *I beseech you, that I may not be bold*] Literally, **I entreat the not being bold**. Compliance or non-compliance with this request rested entirely with the Corinthians. The word here translated *beseech* is not the same as the one used in the last verse.

with that confidence, wherewith I think to be bold] It does not clearly appear from this passage what St Paul meant to do when he arrived at Corinth. He speaks of 'pulling down of strongholds,' of 'casting down whatever exalteth itself' against Christ. But he never says what he in-

think of us as if we walked according to the flesh. For 3 though we walk in the flesh, we do not war after the flesh: (for the weapons of our warfare *are* not carnal, but mighty 4 through God to the pulling down of strong holds;) casting 5 down imaginations, and every high thing that exalteth itself

tends to do. Calvin (1) interprets the passage of excommunication. Others (2) of bodily punishments, such as those inflicted on Elymas (Acts xiii. 6—11), or on Ananias and Sapphira (Acts v. 1—10). Or (3) we may regard it as referring to the authoritative proclamation of the Gospel by one fully inspired, which must of necessity bring about in the end the disappearance of error. This is thought to be implied by *v.* 11, which implies the immediate exercise when present, of the same power which when absent is exercised by letter. But a comparison of *v.* 11 with 1 Cor. iv. 21, v. 1—5 would lead to the idea of a formal delivery over to Satan of those who wilfully corrupted the doctrine of Christ, and gainsaid the authority of His Apostle. See note on 1 Cor. v. 5. The word rendered 'bold' here is not the same as that in the former part of the verse. It implies (1) to dare, (2) to bear oneself boldly, i.e. to *others,* while the former word seems to imply confidence in *oneself.*

against some] i.e. the false teachers.

according to the flesh] See ch. v. 16; Rom. viii. 1.

3. *in the flesh*] To walk *in* the flesh is to possess the fleshly nature with its many infirmities (see Rom. vii.). To walk *after* the flesh is to neglect the dictates of the higher spiritual nature, and to live as though the desires of the body were the only ones that needed satisfying.

war after the flesh] The metaphor of a warfare, as applied to the Christian life, is a common one with St Paul, though it is more usually used of the internal conflict of the Christian soul than of the external warfare waged against the evil around. See 1 Cor. ix. 26; Eph. vi. 10—17; 1 Thess. v. 8; 1 Tim. i. 18, vi. 12; 2 Tim. ii. 3, 4, iv. 7. Bp Wordsworth remarks on the fact that "the armies of Imperial Rome, her camps and her campaigns," and the rest, were "objects that presented themselves to St Paul in his travels, and were very familiar to his readers." Cf. ch. ii. 14—16.

4. *carnal*] See note on *v.* 2. Also on 1 Cor. iii. 1.

mighty through God] Either (1) as in the text, or (2) mighty *to* God, i.e. in His sight, or (3) mighty *for* God, i.e. on behalf of Him, or perhaps (4) an Hebraistic construction, like the one in Acts vii. 20, where it is equal to *exceeding,* just as Nineveh is called 'a great city of God' (Jonah iii. 3 and notes).

strong holds] or *fortifications,* from a Greek word signifying *to fortify.*

5. *casting down*] This is not spoken of the *weapons,* but of the *Apostles.*

imaginations] Rather, as margin, **reasonings** (*consilia,* Vulgate, *counceilis,* Wiclif). The rendering 'imaginations' comes from Tyndale. St Paul refers to the efforts of human reason to deal with things beyond it, the best corrective of which is and always will be the simple proclamation of God's message to man.

against the knowledge of God, and bringing into captivity
6 every thought to the obedience of Christ; and having in a
readiness to revenge all disobedience, when your obedience
is fulfilled.

7—18. *Caution to those who judge by outward appearance.*

7 Do ye look on *things* after the outward appearance? If
any *man* trust to himself that *he* is Christ's, let him of him-

exalteth itself] Or, is *exalted*.
against the knowledge of God] For this phrase see Prov. ii. 5; Hos.
vi. 6; 1 Cor. xv. 34; Col. i. 10, and the kindred phrase in Isai. xi. 9;
2 Pet. ii. 20. Here it signifies that by which we know God, i. e. the
Gospel. See 1 Cor. ii. 16, xiii. 12; Gal. iv. 9.
bringing into captivity] Another military metaphor. See note on
v. 3.
every thought] The word is the same as in ch. ii. 11, iii. 14, iv. 4.
It occurs only in Phil. iv. 7 and in this Epistle.
6. *and having in a readiness*] The expression is equivalent to our
holding ourselves in readiness.
to revenge] Better, **to avenge**. Literally, **to do justice, execute
sentence** upon.
when your obedience is fulfilled] St Paul was ready to wait until his
exhortations and rebukes had had time to work. He would not 'come
to them in heaviness' (ch. ii. 1). He called 'God to witness that if he
did delay to come to Corinth it was to spare them' (ch. i. 23). He
wrote while absent that he might not have to use sharpness when
present (ch. xiii. 10). But when all had been done that could be done,
it was his intention to come and 'not spare' those who refused to listen
to his voice (ch. xiii. 2).

7—18. CAUTION TO THOSE WHO JUDGE BY OUTWARD
APPEARANCE.

7. *Do ye look on things after the outward appearance?*] The words
here translated *outward appearance* are translated *when I am present* in
v. 2. They may be rendered in three ways, (1) as in the text, (2) *ye
look on things after the outward appearance*, or (3) as some interpreters
prefer to render, *look at what lies plainly before your eyes*, i.e. the
genuineness of St Paul's Apostolic mission. The Vulgate and Rhemish
versions render thus. So also Wiclif, *See ye the thingis that ben aftir
the face*. Either (1) or (2) is preferable to (3), which not only does not
suit the context (cf. also 1 Cor. ii. 5, iii. 21, and St John vii. 24,
where however the Greek is not the same as here, and viii. 15), but is
contrary to the spirit of St Paul's writings, which invariably glorify what
does *not* lie on the surface, at the expense of what *does* so. The meaning of the last of the three renderings is that if the Corinthians regard
their teachers from an exclusively fleshly point of view, St Paul has no
need to shrink from the comparison. Cf. ch. xi. 18—33.

self think this again, that, as he *is* Christ's, even so *are* we Christ's. For though I should boast somewhat more of our 8 authority, which the Lord hath given us for edification, and not for your destruction, I should not be ashamed: that 9 I may not seem as if *I* would terrify you by letters. For 10 *his* letters, say they, *are* weighty and powerful; but *his* bodily presence *is* weak, and *his* speech contemptible. Let 11

as he is Christ's, even so are we Christ's] St Paul proceeds to give four proofs of this. He shews (1) that he was unquestionably the founder of the Corinthian Church (*v.* 13—18, cf. 1 Cor. iv. 15, ix. 2, and ch. iii. 2, 3); (2) that if he refused to be maintained by them, it was for no other reason than his desire for their benefit (ch. xi. 1—15, cf. 1 Cor. ix. 12, 15, 18); (3) that his life was a sufficient proof of his sincerity (ch. xi. 21—33); and (4) that the supernatural revelations vouchsafed to him were vouchers for his inspiration (ch. xii. 1—6).

8. *boast*] The word is translated 'glory,' 'rejoice,' elsewhere. See note on ch. i. 12.

somewhat more] Literally, **somewhat in excess.**

edification] Literally, **building up.** The English word comes from two Latin words signifying to *build a house*. See note on 1 Cor. viii. 1, and cf. 1 Cor. vi. 12, x. 23, 33, xiv. 5, 6, 12.

and not for your destruction] The word is translated *pulling down* in *v.* 4, and the verb from which it is derived *casting down* in *v.* 5. Cf. ch. ii. 2, vii. 8—11.

I should not be ashamed] Literally, **I shall not be ashamed,** or perhaps **shamed,** i.e. brought to shame. "Shall not be pointed out as a liar or a vain boaster." Chrysostom. See note on last verse.

9. *that I may not seem as if I would terrify you by letters*] Literally, by means of **the** letters, i.e. this and the two former. See note on 1 Cor. v. 9. The connection of thought is not clear at first sight, but a little consideration will serve to bring it out. St Paul is about to boast of his authority. This boast is no *brutum fulmen*. He means to act upon it in all seriousness when he comes to Corinth. He wishes them to understand that it will not be confined to words, but will be shewn in deeds when he arrives. See note on *v.* 6.

10. *his bodily presence is weak*] The bodily weakness of the Apostle seems clearly indicated by many passages in Scripture. We may perhaps gather from Acts xiv. 12 (though this is doubtful) that he was of less dignified presence than St Barnabas. He refers to his infirmity in 1 Cor. ii. 3. It was probably the thorn in the flesh of which he speaks in ch. xii. 7 (see Introduction), and the 'temptation' which was 'in his flesh' in Gal. iv. 13, 14. There is an admirable note on St Paul's personal appearance at the end of Dr Plumptre's Commentary on the Acts of the Apostles in the Bishop of Gloucester's *New Testament for English Readers*.

and his speech contemptible] Literally, **despised.** *Rude*, Tyndale.

such a one think this, that, such as we are in word by letters when we are absent, such *will we be* also in deed when we are present.

12 For we dare not make *ourselves* of the number, or compare ourselves with some that commend themselves: but they measuring themselves by themselves, and comparing

Wiclif, *worthi to be dispisid*. This is the proper meaning of the word *contemptible*. Whatever St Paul's fervour and mental and spiritual power may have been, it is evident that he lacked the conventional gifts of the orator, the powerful voice, the fluent and facile delivery, the arts whereby to enchain attention. It was not the manner of his speech, but its matter, which attracted his hearers to him.

11. *such a one*] i.e. the man who speaks in this way. See note on ch. ii. 7.

that, such as we are in word by letters] It is evident that St Paul's opponents were not very measured in their opposition to him. Not only did they deny his Apostolic authority (1 Cor. ix. 1, 6), not only did they ridicule his appearance, but they even charged him with the grossest cowardice. For nothing is more contemptible than to utter loud threats when at a distance, and to subside into silence and meekness when confronted with an adversary. See note on *v.* 1.

12. *For we dare not make ourselves of the number, or compare ourselves*] i.e. ironically, *we dare not venture to number or compare ourselves* with certain persons who have of late been claiming great authority among you. After St Paul's manner (see ch. i. 13, iii. 2) there is a play upon words here, which is difficult to translate.

commend themselves] As has been said, the Greek word here used has in the N. T. the sense of *praise;* but probably here the leading idea as in ch. iii. 1 is of *recommending* themselves, by such means as are indicated in chapters i.—iii. of the first Epistle, and of having their own selfish objects in view in so doing.

but they measuring themselves] The idea suggested by the A.V. is of men whose motives are centred in self. They judge themselves by their own standard, they take advantage of other men's labours, they even, St Paul seems to hint (v. 16), boast of other men's labours, they give other men no credit for what they have done. And all this, like the Galatian teachers (Gal. iv. 17), that they may occupy the principal place in the Corinthian Church. There is another reading here, however, which is accepted by many editors and preferred by Dean Stanley, which gives an entirely different turn to the sentence. Omitting the words '*are not wise, but we*' the passage runs, '*but measuring ourselves by ourselves, and comparing ourselves with ourselves, we do not boast beyond measure.*' This reading may have been caused by the transcriber's eye passing from ΟΤΣ to ΟΥΚ in the Greek, and omitting the intervening words, while it is difficult to see how St Paul can describe himself as avoiding the danger of boasting beyond measure by the very process which experience shews to be the commonest mode of causing such boasting, namely by taking oneself as the sole standard of com-

vv. 13, 14.] II. CORINTHIANS, X. 107

themselves amongst themselves, are not wise. But we will 13
not boast of *things* without *our* measure, but according to
the measure of the rule which God hath distributed to us, a
measure to reach even unto you. For we stretch not our- 14
parison. And the testimony of MSS. and versions is much in favour of
the received text. See however next note but two.

by themselves] Literally, **in** themselves, i.e. if we accept the A.V.,
having their thoughts perpetually turned inwards in complacent self-
contemplation. Meyer quotes the expression *Metiri suo modulo* from
Horace *Ep.* I. 7. 98.

amongst themselves] Rather, **with** themselves.

are not wise] These words are omitted by the Vulgate and Wiclif.
It must be confessed that they are not in the Apostle's manner, and
that they have a suspicious appearance of having been inserted to fill up
some supposed deficiency in the sense. But see last note but two. If
we omit them, together with the words 'But we' in the next verse,
the Apostle's meaning will be, 'We do not compare ourselves with
some who have lately appeared among you. We keep within the
bounds of our own labours, of the work that God has marked out for
us. We do not 'build on another man's foundation' (Rom. xv. 20)
or challenge comparison by intruding into another man's sphere of
work.' See also *vv.* 15, 16. The balance of probability, in spite of the
difficulties enumerated above, is in favour of this reading. St Paul seems
to imply that he avoids *all* comparison by keeping within his own
bounds. See Analysis, Introduction, ch. II.

13. *of things without our measure*] Literally, **unto the measureless
things**, i.e. 'beyond the measure which God has meted out to us,'
'beyond the region of our own work, which was ever, save in the case
of Rome, among Churches which we ourselves have founded.' Nor
was Rome really an exception. For the Church there seemed not to
have been formally founded by any one, but to have grown up of itself
through the gravitation of persons from all parts to the great metropolis.
This is why St Paul, on his way into Spain, desires to 'impart some
spiritual gift' to a Church which had not had the privilege of the personal superintendence of an Apostle. See Rom. i. 11, xv. 23, 24.

rule] This word is translated *line* in *v.* 16. It means (1) a measuring
rod and then (2) the line marked out by such means. It has become an
English word familiar to our ears (3) as a rule or precept of Ecclesiastical
Law, known as a *Canon*. A cognate word in English is *cane*.

which God hath distributed to us, a measure] Better, **a measure
which God apportioned**, i.e. which is *His* work, not man's.

to reach even unto you] That God had done this was very evident.
The Corinthians owed their existence as a Church to St Paul. See
ch. iii. 2, 3; 1 Cor. iii. 6, 10, ix. 2. The metaphor, says Estius, is
derived from handicraftsmen, who have a rule prescribed to them by
the master, which they are not permitted to go beyond.

14. *For we stretch not*] The meaning is, For we are not straining
ourselves beyond our due limits in claiming you as our charge, for it is
an undeniable fact that we came (the tense is the simple past in the

selves beyond *our measure*, as though we reached not unto you: for we are come as far as to you also in *preaching* the
15 gospel of Christ: not boasting of *things* without *our* measure, *that is*, of other *men's* labours; but having hope, when your faith is increased, that *we* shall be enlarged by you
16 according to our rule abundantly, to preach the gospel in the *regions* beyond you, *and* not to boast in another *man's*
17 line of *things* made ready to our hand. But he that glo-

original and the word has the sense of *anticipating others* in coming) as far as you in our work of preaching the Gospel. Corinth was the farthest point the Apostle had yet reached.

15. *not boasting of things without our measure*] The Apostle now repeats what he has before said in *v.* 13, but directs his remarks more pointedly against the false teachers by adding '*in other men's labours.*' For they, as Meyer remarks, were adorning themselves with strange feathers as they intruded themselves into other men's spheres of work. See also for St Paul's line of conduct Gal. ii. 9.

when your faith is increased] Two reasons may be assigned for this reservation; (1) that as we have seen (ch. ii. 12, 13), St Paul could not settle himself to any other work while the Corinthian Church was in such an unsatisfactory condition, and (2) that the consistent conduct of one Christian community was an immense help to the first missionaries of the Gospel in founding another. See Tit. ii. 8; 1 Pet. ii. 12.

enlarged] The Apostle seems to identify himself with his work as he has before identified himself with the Corinthian Church. See ch. iii. 2, vii. 3. He is enlarged when the Church is enlarged by his means.

by you] Literally, **in** or **among** you. Some connect these words with 'when your faith is increased,' i.e. among yourselves.

abundantly] Literally, **unto superabundance.**

16. *to preach the gospel in the regions beyond you*] i.e. the rest of Greece, Italy and Spain. Cf. Rom. xv. 19, 24, 28. St Paul here attributes his further progress in the Gospel not to his own energy, but to their faith, another instance of his identification of himself with those in whom the same life dwelt. Cf. ch. i. 11.

and not to boast in another man's line] Literally, and not **to have** boasted. Both this word and the words translated *enlarged* and *preach the gospel* are in the past tense. St Paul here again reflects indirectly, but most severely upon his opponents. *Our* hope is first that your faith may increase, and then that we may congratulate ourselves on having carried the good tidings of the Gospel to those who as yet have not heard them, not, as others do, on the successes which by intruding into another man's work, we have found ready made for us.

17. *But he that glorieth*] See note on *v.* 8. This passage occurs in 1 Cor. i. 31, where it is prefaced by the words 'it is written.' It is in fact a paraphrase of Jer. ix. 24. Meyer remarks that a noble example of this kind of glorying is given by St Paul himself in 1 Cor. xv. 10. Cf. also ch. xii. 10.

rieth, let him glory in the Lord. For not he that 18 commendeth himself is approved, but whom the Lord commendeth.

1—17. *St Paul's Defence of himself against his accusers.*

Would *to God* you could bear with me a little in *my* 11 folly: and indeed bear with me. For I am jealous over 2 you with godly jealousy: for I have espoused you to one husband, that *I* may present *you as* a chaste virgin to

18. *For not he that commendeth himself is approved*] St Paul's self-commendation is only wrung from him by circumstances. The Corinthians will not judge of things except 'after the appearance' (*v.* 7). St Paul, bearing in mind the wise man's advice to 'answer a fool according to his folly' (Prov. xxvi. 5), shews that even from that point of view the new teachers could not arrogate to themselves any superiority over him. But he takes care to remark that the only true ground of approval is to do the work of God.

CH. XI. 1—17. ST PAUL'S DEFENCE OF HIMSELF AGAINST HIS ACCUSERS.

1. *Would to God*] The words 'to God' are not in the original.
bear with me a little in my folly] i.e. the folly of boasting, which (ch. x. 8, xi. 16—18, xii. 11) the Apostle regards as a necessity laid upon him by the present condition of the Corinthian Church. Cf. also 1 Cor. iii. 1.
and indeed bear with me] Most recent editors translate as Chrysostom, *but you really do bear with me. Ye* (i.e. *yea*), *ye do also forbeare me*, Cranmer. The imperative rendering, however, harmonizes best with what follows, 'Nay, indeed I beseech you to bear with me, for I am zealous,' &c.
2. *with godly jealousy*] Literally, **with a jealousy of God**, i.e. either (1) which comes from Him, or (2) which is pleasing in His sight, or (3) as Chrysostom, with the jealousy with which God is jealous, or (4) with a jealousy for God "like that of the paranymph," Estius (see next note). The literal rendering in this verse is *zealous, zeal.* See notes on ch. vii. 7, 11, ix. 2.
for I have espoused you] Rather, **I espoused you,** i.e. at your conversion, it being the *act*, rather than its completion, to which St Paul asks attention. Cf. Matt. xxii. 2; John iii. 29; Eph. v. 25, 27; Rev. xxi. 2, 9, xxii. 17. Also Isai. liv. 5; Jer. iii. 14; Ezek. xvi. 8; Hos. ii. 19, 20. St Paul, like St John the Baptist, here represents himself as the friend of the bridegroom, who often (see Art. Marriage in the *Dictionary of the Bible*) took a prominent part in the negotiation of the marriage.
to one husband] The reference is to such passages as Jer. iii. 1; Ezek. xvi. 15. St Paul betrothed them to Christ, but they gave heed to 'divers and strange doctrines,' Heb. xiii. 8, 9.

3 **Christ.** But I fear, lest by any means, as the serpent beguiled Eve through his subtilty, so your minds should be
4 corrupted from the simplicity that is in Christ. For if he that cometh preacheth another Jesus, whom we have not preached, or *if* ye receive another spirit, which ye have not

present you as a chaste virgin to Christ] i.e. at His coming. Cf. Eph. v. 27, where Christ is said *Himself* to present the Church to Himself. The betrothal, in St Paul's day, as in some Christian countries at the present time, preceded the marriage sometimes by a considerable interval. There is a reference here also to the passages from the O.T. cited above, and to Ezek. xxiii. &c.

3. *as the serpent beguiled Eve*] The Church, as a second Eve, is espoused to Christ, the new Adam (1 Cor. xv. 45). She must beware lest, like Eve, she listen to the voice of the same tempter, who ever lieth in wait to deceive, and so lose the privileges she was destined to enjoy. See ch. ii. 11.

through his subtilty] See ch. iv. 2, and note. A similar sentiment will be found in Col. ii. 4—8. For the serpent, see Gen. iii. 1; and cf. Wisd. ii. 23, 24; Rev. xii. 9, 14, 15.

your minds] See note on ch. ii. 11, where the same word is used as here.

from the simplicity] Rather, **singlemindness.** See ch. i. 12, viii. 2, ix. 11, 13. Most editors here add *and the chastity*. No doubt the words *and the chastity* have been left out from the close similarity of the two Greek words in this passage. A word only differing in the Greek from this by one letter has been substituted for the word *simplicity* by many editors in ch. i. 12.

that is in Christ] Literally, 'that is **unto** Christ' (*that ye had toward Christ*, Cranmer). "This is an expression commonly mistaken. People suppose simplicity means what a child or ploughman can understand. Now if this be simplicity, the simplicity of the Gospel was corrupted by St Paul himself. 'Simple,' according to St Paul, means unmixed or unadulterated." Robertson. See notes on passages cited in last note. The meaning therefore is 'your single-minded devotion to Christ.'

4. *he that cometh*] This shews that the false teachers came from elsewhere, whence they brought their corruptions. Chrysostom. Cf. Acts xv. 1, 24; Gal. ii. 4, 12. Otherwise, says Olshausen, they would have been excommunicated.

another Jesus] The word is not the same as that translated *another* below. In this case it means the *same* Jesus ("the historical Jesus," Stanley), but preached in such a way as to produce a different impression. Cf. the Greek in Gal. i. 6, 7.

or if ye receive another spirit, which ye have not received] Literally, **whom (or which) ye did not receive.** The preaching of Jesus after quite another fashion, that of bondage to law (Acts xv. 1; Gal. iv. 21), would involve the communication of a *different* spirit (see last note) to

received, or another gospel, which ye have not accepted, ye might well bear with *him*. For I suppose *I* was not a whit behind the very chiefest apostles. But though *I be* rude in

the spirit of liberty made known by St Paul (Rom. viii. 2, 15). For the nature of the false teaching at Corinth, see Introduction to the First Epistle, p. 11, and *v.* 22.

another gospel] i.e. a *different* Gospel. See last note.

ye might well bear with him (or *it*)] These words have generally been regarded as ironical, *nobly would ye bear with him* (Alford, Plumptre), and explained of the ready reception which the false teachers had met with. But a comparison with Gal. i. 7, difficult as that passage is, makes it probable that no irony whatever is intended. "Had they preached another Gospel altogether, there would have been some reason in listening to them." But they do *not* do this. They profess to preach the *same* Lord and the *same* Gospel, only they depreciate the authority of him from whom you first received it. Such men have no *raison d'être*, no standing-ground among you. They have none in my position in the Church, for it is equal to that of any of the Apostles (*v.* 5). They have none in my disregard of the technical rules of oratory, for I am not lacking in knowledge. They have none, in fact, in any way, for I challenge the closest investigation into my conduct (*v.* 6). In one point, I admit (*v.* 7), they have an apparent advantage. But even that vanishes on investigation. See notes below.

5. *For I suppose*] The connection of thought seems to be as above. If they had been preaching another Gospel, you might have borne with them, but when preaching the same Gospel they can arrogate no superiority over me, for I am on an equality with the very highest.

I was not a whit behind] Rather, **I have not fallen short in any way**, i.e. I neither have been, nor am now, in the least inferior.

the very chiefest apostles] Cf. ch. xii. 11. Most modern editors render by "these surpassers of the Apostles" (Alford), "those Apostles extraordinary" (Plumptre) (literally, **the overmuch Apostles**), regarding the Greek as ironical and interpreting the passage as referring to the false teachers. Chrysostom and the ancient interpreters refer it to St Peter and the rest of the twelve. But possibly there is no personal reference at all. St Paul may mean that no Apostles existed anywhere, however great they might be, who could claim superiority over him. Cf. Gal. ii. 6, 9. Robertson has some interesting remarks on the common interpretation: "Some cannot understand the feeling which prompts an expression like this. Shallow men would call it egotism, vanity, folly, as if egotism consisted only in speaking of oneself. True Christian modesty is not the being ignorant of what we are, neither does it consist in affecting ignorance. It consists in this—in having a high and sublime standard set before us, so that we feel how far we are from attaining to *that*."

6. *But though I be rude in speech*] The word (see note on 1 Cor. xiv. 16, and cf. Acts iv. 13; 1 Cor. i. 17, ii. 1, 4, 13, and ch. x. 10) signifies one not specially instructed in an art. "It does not mean one who is not

speech, yet not in knowledge; but we *have been* throughly
7 made manifest among you in all *things*. Have I committed
an offence in abasing myself that you might be exalted, be-
8 cause I have preached to you the gospel of God freely? I
robbed other churches, taking wages *of them*, to do you ser-

eloquent, but one who has not learned eloquence by the rules of rhetorical schools." Bp Wordsworth. See ch. x. 10. Some have regarded it as meaning 'untrained in Rabbinical learning.' But this could hardly be said of the pupil of Gamaliel (Acts xxii. 3). St Paul seems here to be combating *all* his antagonists, whether of Jewish or Gentile tendencies.

yet not in knowledge] Cf. 1 Cor. ii. 6 and note. Also Eph. iii. 4.

made manifest] See notes on ch. i. 12—14, ii. 17, iv. 2, v. 11, vii. 12, and on v. 4. St Paul continually appeals to his conduct as the best witness of the genuineness of his mission. Most modern editors read the active instead of the passive participle here. We must then translate *made things manifest.*

7. *Have I committed an offence*] Literally, **committed sin** (*don sinne*, Wiclif. *Did I therein synne?* Tyndale, Cranmer and the Geneva version). This passage is ironical. The Corinthians had allowed St Paul's anxious desire not to be burdensome to them to be used against him (see 1 Cor. ix. 1—14). He asks if such an anxiety for their welfare was to be imputed to him as a sin. Cf. the very similar passage in ch. xii. 13.

abasing myself] i.e. by working for his living, when he might have enjoyed what men are apt to regard as a dignified ease at their expense. For the word see note on ch. x. 1.

that you might be exalted] He speaks, not of temporal exaltation, for his coming made no difference, unless perhaps for the worse, in their temporal condition, but of the "height of Christian salvation" (Meyer) to which they had been lifted.

freely] Cf. 1 Cor. ix. 12—18; 1 Thess. ii. 9; Matt. x. 8. There is a contrast intended between the greatness of the gift, the Gospel of God, and the cost for which it was imparted, *for nothing* (literally, **as a gift**). Cf. Isaiah lv. 1.

8. *I robbed other churches*] "An hyperbolical expression" (Meyer). And yet in one sense it was true, for the Corinthians were just as much bound to support the Apostle when at Corinth as any other Churches were when the Apostle was with them. And, therefore, if when at Corinth he availed himself of assistance from those other Churches, he was taking from them what they ought not to have been called upon to supply. *Why* he did so we are told in v. 12.

taking wages of them] The Philippian Church, we learn from Phil. iv. 15, 16 (cf. next verse), is the Church referred to. Their liberality, St Paul felt, was not likely to be cast in his teeth, therefore he readily accepted it. In later days he again received their bounty with a willingness which would not, he knew, be misconstrued. This is an instance of that minute but undesigned agreement in points of detail which consti-

vice. And when I was present with you, and wanted, I was 9 chargeable to no *man*: for that which was lacking to me the brethren which came from Macedonia supplied: and in all *things* I have kept myself from being burdensome to you, and *so* will I keep *myself*. *As* the truth of Christ is in 10 me, no *man* shall stop me of this boasting in the regions of Achaia. Wherefore? because I love you not? God know- 11

tutes so strong an argument for the genuineness of most of the Scriptures of the N.T. For the word translated *wages* see St Luke iii. 14; Rom. vi. 23; 1 Cor. ix. 7. It was most commonly used of a soldier's pay, when given *in kind*.

to do you service] Rather, **towards my support in my ministry to you.**

9. *and wanted*] Rather, **was in want.** The same word is used in *v*. 5. See note on 1 Cor. i. 6.

I was chargeable to no man] Greuous, Tyndale. Our translation is Cranmer's (though Wiclif's is almost identical, '*chargeous*'). The Geneva version is nearer to the original, *I was not slothful to the hinderance of any man*. The original word is remarkable. It signifies originally to *benumb thoroughly*, and our word *narcotic* comes from this root, as also *narcissus* from the narcotic qualities of the plant. The torpedo, from its benumbing properties, had in Greek the name of νάρκη, from whence some have translated it, 'I attached myself to no man like the torpedo attaches itself.' But as it is doubtful whether the fish gave the name to the sensation or the sensation to the fish, it will be sufficient to render by I *disabled*, or *paralysed*, no man, by throwing my maintenance on him.

from Macedonia] See note on last verse. "The principal fact set forth in this passage, the arrival at Corinth of brethren from Macedonia during St Paul's residence in that city, is explicitly recorded, Acts xviii. 1, 5." Paley.

and so will I keep myself] Cf. 1 Cor. ix. 18.

10. *As the truth of Christ is in me*] Rather, **the truthe of Crist is in me** (Wiclif, whom the Geneva and Rheims versions follow here) or *if the truth* (Tyndale and Cranmer). "There is no oath" (Dean Alford, who refers to Rom. ix. 1). "The mind of Christ is in him (1 Cor. ii. 16), the heart of Christ beats in him (Phil. i. 8), Christ speaks in him (ch. xiii. 3), and all this through the Spirit of Christ which dwells in him." Meyer.

stop me] *This boasting shall not be stopped in me*, margin. The Greek word signifies to *wall* or *fence* round. Bp Wordsworth thinks that an allusion is here made to the Isthmian Wall, and refers to several passages in ancient history which speak of the value of such a fortification in the defence of the Peloponnesus. But it is possible that no such allusion was intended. The word is used in the N.T. (as in Rom. iii. 19; Heb. xi. 33) of *stopping the mouth*.

11. *Wherefore? because I love you not?*] See *v*. 7 and note. The

12 eth. But what I do, that I will do, that I may cut off occasion from them which desire occasion; that wherein
13 they glory, they may be found even as we. For such *are* false apostles, deceitful workers, transforming themselves
14 into the apostles of Christ. And no marvel; for Satan him-
15 self is transformed into an angel of light. Therefore *it is* no great *thing* if his ministers also be transformed as the minis-

same ironical tone is adopted. 'Can you suppose that *this* is a proof of my indifference towards you?' And then the Apostle suddenly becomes serious, and appeals to God who knows the heart.

12. *occasion*] See ch. v. 12.

that wherein they glory, they may be found even as we] These words seem to imply that the Corinthian false teachers did *not* accept money or maintenance for their services. But then it is difficult to see how they could have made that very practice an argument against St Paul. It is, therefore, better to suppose, that they boasted of their disinterestedness, in spite of their willingness to enrich themselves at the Corinthians' expense (see next verse), and that St Paul was determined that they should have no solid ground for insinuations of this kind against him (though such were made nevertheless, ch. xii. 16, 17, by those who judged of the Apostle by themselves). So he steadfastly refused to take a farthing of money from the Corinthians, preferring to undergo privations (*v.* 9) rather than give an opportunity to his opponents to assert of him, what was true of themselves, that his professed disinterestedness was only a pretence. There are a number of interpretations of this passage, for which the student may consult the commentaries of Deans Stanley and Alford.

13. *For such*] The link of connection is as follows. You cannot believe them in their boasting. They are false and deceitful in all their doings. They have not *your* interest at heart, but their own. Cf. ch. ii. 17.

false apostles] See Rev. ii. 2; also note on *v.* 26.

deceitful workers] St Paul is indirectly aiming at such persons in ch. iv. 2, as well as more directly in ch. ii. 17. Cf. Rom. xvi. 17, 18; Phil. iii. 2. The word *workers* is in the original equivalent to our word *workmen* or *artisans*. The reference is to workmen who shirk, or as it is called 'scamp' their work, instead of dealing fairly by their employer.

14. *And no marvel*] *No wondre*, Wiclif, where we may remark that the older English expression has held its ground against the French equivalent.

Satan himself is transformed] Cf. ch. ii. 11. Not that he is *really* so transformed, but that he appears to be so, to those who judge 'according to the appearance,' ch. x. 7; Gal. vi. 12; Phil. i. 15, iii. 18; Tit. i. 10, 11. "*Transformed* into, not *becoming*." Chrysostom. He reads '*if* Satan himself.'

15. *whose end shall be according to their works*] Cf. Prov. xxiv. 12;

ters of righteousness; whose end shall be according to their works.

I say again, Let no *man* think me a fool; if other 16 wise, yet as a fool receive me, that I may boast myself a little. *That* which I speak, I speak *it* not after the Lord, 17 but as *it were* foolishly, in this confidence of boasting.

Matt. xvi. 27; Rom. ii. 6—11; 1 Cor. iii. 8; Phil. iii. 19; 2 Tim. iv. 14; Rev. xx. 12, &c.

16. *I say again*] Cf. ch. x. 8, xi. 1, 6. "Three times he has attempted to begin his boast. First he is interrupted by the recollection of the hollowness of the boast of his opponents: again, he is checked by the difficulty of pressing it on men so perverted by the influence of their false teachers; and again, when he is led aside to answer the charge arising from his refusal of support. Now once more he returns to the point, and now for the first time carries it through." Stanley.

Let no man think me a fool] This reiterated appeal to the Corinthians is due to the fact that St Paul keenly feels the unsuitableness of such boasting to the Christian character. See ch. xii. 6, and notes on ch. x. 8, xi. 1. "Observe how, when about to enter upon his own praises, he checks himself." Chrysostom.

if otherwise] *Or else* (Tyndale, Cranmer, Geneva), i.e. but even if you do regard me as a fool.

yet as a fool receive me] i.e. 'Receive me, even though you must receive me as a fool.'

that I may boast myself] Rather (with Vulgate, Cranmer, Geneva, Rhemish) that **I also**, i.e. as the false teachers have done (see the first four chapters of the first Epistle). Our version copies Tyndale here.

a little] The original is stronger; 'a little bit,' as we say.

17. *not after the Lord*] i.e.(1) according to the example of the Lord; see for similar forms of expression 1 Cor. iii. 3, xv. 32; 2 Cor. i. 17, x. 3 (in the Greek); or (2) not *inspired by the Lord* (cf. 1 Cor. vii. 12, 25, 40). "There are many things"—he mentions war, self-defence, generous resentment—"which are not exactly *after* Christ, and yet are not contrary to the Spirit of Christ." Robertson. "By itself it is not after the Lord, but it becomes so by the intention." Chrysostom. "Like an oath, self-praise may under certain circumstances become necessary, especially for those who, like St Paul, have the public duties of a sacred ministry to discharge." Wordsworth. St Paul was resolved 'by all means to save some' (1 Cor. ix. 22). If there were those at Corinth who raised objections to his ministrations, he took them on their own ground, and shewed that, low and unworthy as that ground was, even there they had no sufficient justification for their conduct. It is often necessary to adopt such a course, on the principle laid down by our Lord in Matt. vii. 6. Appeals to the higher spiritual instincts of men who have never cultivated those instincts are useless. We must deal with mankind as they are, and hope thus to lead them to become what at present they are not. And if it be asked how we are to know when to walk 'after the

18—33. *St Paul permits himself to enumerate his labours for the Gospel's sake.*

18 Seeing that many glory after the flesh, I will glory also. 19 For ye suffer fools gladly, seeing ye *yourselves* are wise. For 20 ye suffer, if a man bring you into bondage, if a man devour

Lord,' and when to condescend to the folly of mankind, the answer is, whenever we conscientiously believe it to be for their benefit.
in this confidence of boasting] i.e. on which I am now about to enter. Cranmer translates *in this matter of boasting* (*substantia*, Vulgate; *substaunce*, Wiclif and the Rhemish). So Chrysostom. But it seems better to translate as the A.V. St Paul regards what he is about to say as an outburst of foolish self-confidence, ridiculous in itself, but rendered necessary by the thoroughly low and carnal ideas of many of his Corinthian converts. Foolish as they are, he hopes to redeem them from their folly by shewing that he possesses even the qualifications on which they set so exaggerated a value, in greater measure than those for whom they had deserted him.

18—33. ST PAUL PERMITS HIMSELF TO ENUMERATE HIS LABOURS FOR THE GOSPEL'S SAKE.

18. *after the flesh*] See note on *after the Lord*, and Phil. iii. 4. Also note on ch. x. 3. St Paul means after the manner of those who judge only by what is outward and visible, or perhaps he may mean boasting of things, such as "high birth, wealth, wisdom, of being circumcised, of Hebrew ancestry, of popular renown" (Chrysostom), on which fleshly men set high value.
I will glory also] "It is remarkable that St Paul does not glory in what he has *done*, but what he has *borne*." Robertson.
19. *For ye suffer fools gladly, seeing ye yourselves are wise*] Literally, **For gladly do ye tolerate men without understanding, being prudent** (or perhaps better **sensible men**). The word here translated *suffer* is translated *bear with* in v. 4. The translation here is Wiclif's. It is a question (see next note) whether *either* of the two members of this sentence is to be taken literally. But that its general purpose is ironical there can be no doubt. Cf. 1 Cor. iv. 10.
20. *For ye suffer*] (*susteynen*, Wiclif). "This may be understood in three ways. (1) He may be understood as reproving the Corinthians ironically, because of their inability to bear with anything, or (2) as charging them with sluggishness of spirit, because they had shamefully enslaved themselves to the false Apostles, or (3) he repeats in the person of another what was maliciously affirmed regarding himself, namely, that he claimed a tyrannical authority over them." Calvin. If, with him and many ancient commentators, we adopt (2), the sense is, as Calvin goes on to say, 'You bear with all kinds of indignities from others, why not with far less from me, who am in every respect their equal, if not their superior, in the very qualifications by which you set so much store?' This interpretation agrees best with the context (see

you, if a man take *of you*, if a man exalt himself, if a man smite you on the face. I speak as concerning reproach, as though we had been weak. Howbeit whereinsoever any is bold, (I

next verse). The connection of this verse with the former will then be as follows: 'You pride yourselves on being sensible people, and certainly you have immense toleration for folly. You even endure the foolish—or worse than foolish—insults of men who have no claim whatever to lord it over you. Why then not bear with me, when I condescend for a moment to the level of their folly? You will crouch to worthless pretenders, why resist the voice of real authority?'

if a man bring you into bondage] Literally, **enslave you**. Our translation is Tyndale's. Cf. Gal. ii. 4, iv. 9, v. 1.

devour you] Cf. Matt. xxiii. 14; and the LXX. of Isai. ix. 12. These false teachers were animated by none of St Paul's delicacy as regards money matters. It could not be said of *them* that they were no Apostles, because they had no claim to be maintained by the Churches.

take of you] Rather, **seize** you, i. e. as a hunter his victim, or a man his property (cf. ch. xii. 16). The earlier versions rendered simply by *take*, as though doubtful of the meaning. It was the Geneva that first added 'your goods.'

smite you on the face] An utterly extraordinary and inconceivable piece of presumption, according to our modern notions. But we do not habitually realize the immense extent to which Christianity has leavened our habits. Dean Stanley refers us to 1 Kings xxii. 24; Matt. v. 39; Luke xxii. 64; Acts xxiii. 2; 1 Tim. iii. 3; Tit. i. 7; and to the canon of the Council of Braga (A.D. 675), which orders that no bishop at his will and pleasure shall strike (the original, however, seems to imply *scourging*) his clergy, lest he lose the respect which they owe him. He might have referred also to the famous Latrocinium, or Robber-Synod of Ephesus, in which one patriarch of the Church and his adherents literally stamped another to death, and even to a period so late as the Council of Trent, in which it is admitted, even by the Jesuit historian Pallavicino, that scenes of personal violence occurred among those who were or should have been teachers of religion. See his History of the Council of Trent, Book VIII. ch. 6.

21. *I speak as concerning reproach, as though we had been weak*] Literally, **after** reproach (or dishonour, see ch. vi. 8, and see note on *v*. 17), "to my reproach" (Stanley), or perhaps 'about the dishonour that has been cast upon me,' that *I* ventured to do none of these things, because I dared not. The 'we' is emphatic. *We*, the true ministers of Christ, incurred the reproach of weakness while among you (see ch. x. 10, and 1 Cor. iv. 10), for *we* ventured upon no such evidences of our power. And this 'weakness' has been alleged against us as proof positive that we are no true Apostles of Christ. 'As though' implies that St Paul does not admit the justice of the accusation. But he passes it by, and proceeds to shew that he, too, can shew boldness upon occasion.

whereinsoever any is bold] There is no ground upon which the 'false Apostles' have based their authority which St Paul could not also ad-

22 speak foolishly,) I am bold also. Are they Hebrews? so *am*
I. Are they Israelites? so *am* I. Are they the seed of
23 Abraham? so *am* I. Are they ministers of Christ? (I speak
as a fool) I *am* more; in labours more abundant, in stripes

vance: there are few on which his title to the respect of his flock is not greater than theirs.

I am bold also] St Paul is not here so much thinking of his boldness in asserting his Apostolic authority (ch. x. 2, 11) as of his boldness in asserting his personal claims on the allegiance of the Corinthian Christians; for now, though not 'after the Lord,' but 'after the flesh,' he commences that eloquent and impassioned description of his ministerial labours and experiences, which has done more than any other passage in Scripture to bring the person of the great Apostle before us, and to endear him to the Christian conscience.

22. *Are they Hebrews?*] We may take the words Hebrew, Israelite, seed of Abraham, as referring (1) respectively to the *nationality, theocratic condition*, and *Messianic rights* of the Jewish people. Thus the *Hebrew* would not only be one who was of pure descent, but whose attachment to Jewish nationality caused him to cling to the Jewish language (see Acts vi. 1, xxi. 40, xxii. 2; and Phil. iii. 5). The *Israelite* would be a man attached to the covenant privileges of his nation (cf. St John i. 47; Acts ii. 22, iii. 12, v. 35, xiii. 16, xxi. 28; and especially Rom. ix. 4). *Seed of Abraham* must refer to the pure Abrahamic descent of St Paul, and his consequent title to all the promises made to Abraham. See Rom. ix. 7, xi. 1.

23. *Are they ministers of Christ?*] St Paul here cannot be content with the simple 'so am I.' These men (see ch. x. 7; 1 Cor. i. 10) claimed to be in some special sense Christ's ministers. But when the Apostle thinks of the singleness of his devotion to Christ's cause, of which he had so frequently boasted (ch. ii. 17, iv. 5, vi. 4—10, vii. 2, &c.), and of the nature of his services as compared with theirs, his spirit rises within him. 'I may speak like a madman,' he cries (see next note), 'but I cannot contain myself at such a charge. What have *they* done for the cause of Him whose name they falsely arrogate to themselves, compared to the services I have rendered? I use no mere words of vaunting, but appeal to the devotion of a life to His Gospel.'

I speak as a fool] Rather as a *madman* (*scarse wise*, Rhemish. Our translation is Tyndale's). The word in the original is stronger than that in *vv.* 16, 19. St Paul is not thinking here so much of the impression his words may produce on the Corinthians, as of the fact that all 'boasting' in God's sight is 'excluded' by the 'law of faith' (Rom. iii. 27; cf. Luke xvii. 10). Mad indeed is it to boast of anything as constituting a claim on God for reward. But facts are facts, and they may be appealed to, not for self-glorification, but (ch. xii. 11) to confute pretensions which ought never to have been advanced.

in labours more abundant] Cf. 1 Cor. xv. 10. He now commences the proof of this assertion, and it consists not in words but in deeds. He appeals to "a life hitherto without precedent in the history of the world.

above measure, in prisons more frequent, in deaths oft. Of 24 the Jews five times received I forty *stripes* save one. Thrice 25 was I beaten with rods, once was I stoned, thrice I suffered

Self-devotion at particular moments, or for some special national cause, had been often seen before; but a self-devotion involving sacrifices like those here described, extending through a period of at least fourteen years, and in behalf of no local or family interest, but for the interest of mankind at large, was up to this time a thing unknown." Stanley. De Wette would translate *more abundantly* (the word is an adverb in the original) and connect it with what has gone before, 'in labours I am more abundantly a minister of Christ than they.'

in prisons more frequent] "What is left out is more than is enumerated." Chrysostom. There is but *one* imprisonment mentioned up to this time in the Acts (ch. xvi. 23). So there is but *one* beating with rods (see below). The Acts of the Apostles, being written with a special purpose (see note on ch. i. 8, vi. 5), does not attempt to give a *full* account of St Paul's labours and sufferings. See Stanley's note on *v.* 21 and Paley, *Horae Paulinae, Ep. to Corinth.* 9. Estius accounts it a proof of St Paul's modesty that he had never mentioned these things even to a friend so intimate as St Luke.

in deaths oft] Cf. ch. i. 9, 10, iv. 11; 1 Cor. xv. 31. "Perils *containing* death," i.e. as a possible event. Chrysostom.

24. *Of the Jews*] Literally, **Under Jews**, as though it were a disgrace to them to have treated one of their brethren thus. Cf. St Matt. x. 17.

forty stripes save one] Cf. Deut. xxv. 3. The Mishna (*Makkoth,* III. 10 [9]) prescribes that one below the number there mentioned were to be given, clearly, as Maimonides (Commentary *in loco* and *Mishneh Torah, Hilckhoth Synhed·in,* XVII. 1) explains, lest by a mistake the prescribed number should be exceeded. Others refer it to the *three cords* of the scourges, which could only inflict stripes to the extent of some multiple of three. Josephus, *Antiq.* IV. 8. 21, mentions the custom.

25. *Thrice was I beaten with rods*] See Acts xvi. 22, 23, and note on *v.* 23. *This* punishment is also said frequently to have caused the death of the victim. It was inflicted by the Romans on those who did not possess the privilege of Roman citizenship, Acts xxii. 25. A precisely similar scene to that in the Acts is recorded in Cicero *in Verrem* V. 62, where the victim is said to have uttered the well-known words, *Civis Romanus sum.* Cicero here invokes the 'lex Porcia,' by which the beating a Roman citizen with rods, which had been formerly lawful, was forbidden. See Livy, X. 9, "gravi poena si quis verberasset necasseteve civem Romanum," and cf. Sallust, *Catilina,* c. 51.

once was I stoned] See Acts xiv. 19. Clement of Rome, St Paul's companion and friend (Phil. iv. 3), says in a somewhat obscure passage (*Ep.* 1. 5) that St Paul was "*seven* times imprisoned, put to flight and stoned."

26 shipwrack, a night and a day I have been in the deep; *in* journeyings often, *in* perils of waters, *in* perils of robbers, *in* perils by *my own* countrymen, *in* perils by the heathen, *in*

thrice I suffered shipwrack] The shipwreck related in Acts xxvii. is not one of these, but occurred some time afterwards. We have no other account of those referred to here.
 a night and a day] The Apostle here speaks of some terrible peril, compared to which even the shipwreck related in Acts xxvii. was a trifling one. Probably for twenty-four hours he was exposed to the dangers of the ocean, with but a plank between him and death. The Acts of the Apostles, we are once more constrained to remark, gives us but a scanty account of the labours and perils undergone by this undaunted soul. The word translated 'a night and a day' is but a single word in the original, and signifies a period of twenty-four hours, commencing with sunset. Some have thought that the expression here, 'in the deep,' is the same as the LXX. of Exod. xv. 5, and that St Paul *went down* with the ship, and was delivered by a Divine interposition. So Wiclif, Tyndale and the Geneva and Rheims versions, following the Vulgate, seem to have interpreted this passage (*in the depnesse of the see*, Wiclif; *in the depe of the see*, Tyndale). But the expressions here and in Exod. xv. 5 (LXX.) are *not* identical. Cranmer renders, *in the deepe see*. So Chrysostom, who explains it, '*swimming on the sea*,' and the Syriac version, which translates, 'without a ship in the sea.'
 26. *in perils of waters*] Literally, **rivers** (*flodis*, Wiclif). Cf. 1 Cor. xv. 30. When bridges were rare, such perils were frequent. What they are, even now, in less civilized regions, the recent loss sustained by our troops in Afghanistan (in April, 1879) by a sudden *spate*, after several regiments had crossed the same river in perfect safety, may serve to shew us. Stanley refers also to the fate of Frederick Barbarossa at a place not far from Tarsus. See also Conybeare and Howson's *St Paul*, I. 457.
 in perils of robbers] What these were in Judaea in those times we may learn from the well-known parable recorded in St Luke x. The danger to the traveller in Palestine and the neighbourhood from bands of wandering Bedouins is still almost as great if the traveller in those parts ventures about without the protection afforded by a caravan. Mr Cyril Graham and other recent travellers have recorded their detention by the Arabs until rescued or ransomed.
 in perils by my own countrymen] (*of kyn.* So Wiclif, literally. Cf. Acts vii. 19; Gal. i. 14, in the Greek). These were not the least among the dangers St Paul had to encounter, as Acts ix. 23, 29, xiii. 50, xiv. 5, 19, xvii. 5, 13, xviii. 12 testify. And doubtless there are many such dangers which have been allowed to remain entirely unrecorded, but which may be imagined from what we read, and above all from the yet more serious dangers which befel the Apostle in consequence of his visit to Jerusalem, recorded in Acts xxi., the record of

perils in the city, *in* perils in the wilderness, *in* perils in the
sea, *in* perils among false brethren; in weariness and pain- 27
fulness, in watchings often, in hunger and thirst, in fastings
often, in cold and nakedness. Besides those *things* that are 28

which takes up the remainder of the book. Cf. 1 Thess. ii. 15, 16, St
Paul's first extant Epistle, written, be it remembered, from Corinth.

by the heathen] See Acts xvi. 19—39, xix. 23—34.

in the city] See last note, and Acts ix. 23, 29, as well as *v.* 32 of
this chapter.

in the wilderness] Translated *desert* in Acts viii. 26. Cf. St Matt.
xiv. 13, 15. It means any place void of inhabitants. Hunger and
thirst, as well as robbers, were among the perils thus to be endured. If
any one should object that the Apostle thus repeats himself, it may be
observed that the expressions here used are arranged in pairs, and are
intended to shew that wherever he was, and whatever he did, the
Apostle was in danger.

in the sea] Not a mere repetition. "There are many perils in the
sea,"—pirates, for instance, especially in days long past—"short of
shipwreck." Alford.

among false brethren] Cf. Gal. ii. 4 and *v.* 13 of this chapter. It
refers, no doubt, chiefly to the Judaizing teachers (see *v.* 22), but need
not be confined to them. Any one who falsely pretends to be a disciple
of Christ may be thus described. Cf. Acts xx. 29; 2 Peter ii. (throughout);
1 John ii. 18, 19, 22, iv. 3; 2 John 7, 9; 3 John 9; Jude 4, 7—16; Rev.
ii. 2, 15, 20.

27. *in weariness and painfulness*] *In laboure and travayle* (Tyndale),
more literally. So Cranmer also. Our translators followed the Geneva
version. Cf. 2 Thess. iii. 8, where the words in the Greek are the same
as here.

in watchings] Literally, **in sleeplessnesses**, i.e. in repeated nights
of sleeplessness, whether from anxiety or other causes.

in hunger and thirst] Cf. 1 Cor. iv. 11; Phil. iv. 12.

in fastings often] "Voluntary ones, as he has before spoken of hunger
and want." Calvin. Cf. ch. vi. 5.

in cold and nakedness] Dr Plumptre reminds us of the sharp contrast
between this view of the greatness of a teacher and that current among
the Jews, who had a proverb that "a goodly house, a fair wife, and a
soft couch" were the prerogatives of the "disciples of the wise." He
refers to Matt. xxiii. 6. See also Matt. viii. 20.

28. *Besides those things that are without*] The six principal English versions interpret this expression (1) of *external* trials, of which the Apostle
has hitherto been speaking—"the thynges which outwardly happen unto
me" (Tyndale). As the Apostle now begins to speak of *inward* troubles
this rendering would seem quite natural. But Chrysostom (2) interprets it
of *things left out of the enumeration*. And this interpretation is supported
by the only two other passages in which the word occurs in the N. T.,
namely, Matt. v. 32; Acts xxvi. 29. Cf. Heb. xi. 32. If this interpretation be followed, we must connect the words, not only with what

without, that which cometh upon me daily, the care of all
29 the churches. Who is weak, and I am not weak? who is
30 offended, and I burn not? If I must needs glory, I will
31 glory of the *things* which concern mine infirmities. The God
and Father of our Lord Jesus Christ, which is blessed for

follows, but with what precedes. 'And besides a host of other things, which I cannot now mention, there is the daily pressure of anxiety arising from the Churches under my care.'

that which cometh upon me daily] There is a various reading here. If we follow the received text, which is that of the Peshito Syriac in the second century and is followed by Chrysostom, we must understand it of the daily *concourse* of troubles arising from this source. If we follow that which is proposed to be substituted for it, which is that of the Vulgate and of the most ancient MSS. (though it may not improbably have arisen from the copyist's eye having passed from ΣΤ to ΣΤ), it must be rendered "that which *presseth* on me" (*instantia*, Vulgate; *my daily instance*, Rhemish). Tyndale, Cranmer and the Geneva render, *I am combred dayly*.

the care] Rather perhaps, **the anxiety**, as we speak of *care* in the abstract, the Greek word being derived from a verb signifying *to part asunder*, and implying that the mind is *torn asunder* as it were by conflicting emotions.

of all the churches] This must not perhaps be pressed (as Döllinger in his *Last Age of the Church*) so far as to assert that each Apostle considered himself individually responsible for the care of the whole Church of Christ. That there was some division of responsibility appears from Gal. ii. 7. St Paul probably means the care of *all the Churches which he had planted*, surely no inconsiderable burden.

29. *Who is weak, and I am not weak?*] St Paul goes on to explain in what that care consisted. It consisted in taking upon himself the anxieties of every individual member of the flock. We may see how true his words are by a reference to Rom. xiv. 1—xv. 7; 1 Cor. i. 11, v. 1—5, vi. 1, vii. 1, viii. 1—13, ix. 22, x. 25—33; the whole Epistle to the Galatians; Phil. iv. 2, 3, as well as ch. ii. 5—11, vii. 12 of this Epistle.

30. *If I must needs glory*] See note on ch. i. 14, v. 12.

I will glory of the things which concern mine infirmities] Cf. ch. xii. 5, 9, xiii. 9. If St Paul turns aside for a few moments to boast 'according to the flesh,' his thoughts soon flow back into a channel more customary to one who has been 'created anew' in Christ. He is obliged to boast somewhat. But it has become more natural to him to boast of those things which to the natural man (see v. 21) are weakness.

31. *The God and Father of our Lord Jesus Christ*] St Paul is now about to give a remarkable proof of the truth of what he has just said, and one which he confirms by a solemn asseveration (cf. ch. i. 18, 23). That these words belong to what follows, and not to what precedes, is

evermore, knoweth that I lie not. In Damascus the go- 32
vernor under Aretas the king kept the city of the Damascenes *with a garrison*, desirous to apprehend me: and 33
through a window in a basket was I let down by the wall,
and escaped his hands.

the opinion of commentators so widely differing as Chrysostom, Calvin, Meyer, Bp Wordsworth, Deans Stanley and Alford. A strong argument appears to be brought against this view by the fact that the incident related does not warrant so strong an affirmation. But as Meyer reminds us, the visions and revelations related in ch. xii. 1—4 are an *interruption* of his enumeration of his infirmities, which he resumes in ch. xii. 5. And perhaps eighteen centuries of Christianity have somewhat dimmed our perception of the immense difference between this vaunt, and those customary among the inflated teachers of St Paul's day. *They* enlarged upon their triumphs, their influence with the rich and great, the success of their oratory, the number of their disciples, and this with an arrogance which in our days would be justly contemptible. St Paul, while he shews his sincerity by the fact that his life was exposed to danger, narrates nothing but his escape, a circumstance not likely in itself to raise his reputation among men who judged according to outward appearance (we may compare the reproaches cast upon Cyprian for a similar flight), and not rendered more dignified by the manner in which it was accomplished. See Dean Alford's note.

which is blessed for evermore] Literally, **existing, blessed unto the ages.**

32. *In Damascus*] Cf. Acts ix. 23—25.

the governor] Literally, the **Ethnarch** (ruler of the nation—the title of an Oriental provincial governor. See 1 Macc. xiv. 47, xv. 1, &c.).

under Aretas the king] Aretas (see Josephus' *Antiquities*, XVIII.) was the king of Arabia Petraea. His daughter had been divorced by Herod Antipas in order that he might marry Herodias, 'his brother Philip's wife' (see Matt. xiv. 3—5). This and some disputes about the frontier led to war being proclaimed, and a battle was fought (A. D. 36) in which Herod's army was entirely destroyed. It is thought by some that Aretas profited by this circumstance to seize on Damascus, and that it was just at this juncture (A. D. 37) that St Paul returned to Damascus from his stay in Arabia. Others, however, place this event about the year 39, after Herod Antipas had been banished to Gaul, and think that Aretas, taken into favour by Caligula, had obtained Damascus, among the various changes which the new Emperor made in the arrangements of his eastern provinces. Aretas seems to have been a common name among the Arabs, like Ptolemy in Egypt, or Seleucus and Antiochus in Syria. Josephus mentions more than one. Cf. also 2 Macc. v. 8.

kept the city of the Damascenes with a garrison] Literally, **was guarding** the city of the Damascenes.

33. *in a basket*] The word literally means a **plaited cord.** Hence a basket made of cords. The word in Acts ix. 25 is not the same.

1—6. *The Visions and Revelations vouchsafed to St Paul.*

12 It is not expedient for me doubtless to glory. I will
₂ come to visions and revelations of the Lord. I knew a

was I let down by the wall] Theodoret well remarks, "He shews the greatness of the danger by the mode of his flight." The peroration of Chrysostom's homily here is an eloquent picture of the magnanimity of the great Apostle.

CH. XII. 1—6. THE VISIONS AND REVELATIONS VOUCHSAFED TO ST PAUL.

1. *It is not expedient for me doubtless to glory. I will come*] The Greek text here is in the most utter confusion. Out of the seven Greek words which commence this chapter, the genuineness of only three is guaranteed by the agreement of the MSS. and versions. Some MSS. read, instead of as the A. V., *I must glory, it is not expedient for me, for—* (or *yet*). Others again, *I must glory, it is not, I grant, expedient, yet—*. The Vulgate begins with *if* (*if it bihoveth to have glorie, it spedith not, but I schal come,* Wiclif), no doubt from ch. xi. 30. The A. V. avoids the difficulty of choosing between *for* and *but* before *I will come* by leaving out both. The usual rule in the case of a doubtful reading is to prefer the more difficult one, on the ground that a transcriber was more likely to evade what seemed to him to be a difficulty by the substitution of an easier word, than of his own accord to add to the difficulty of the passage. This rule is inapplicable here, where the alterations have clearly proceeded from an inability to comprehend the passage as it stood. The reading is therefore to be preferred which falls in best with the general scope of St Paul's argument. As regards the first portion of the sentence it makes very little difference to the sense whether we follow the A. V. and render *I am quite aware* (δή) *that it is not well for me to boast*, or with other authorities, *I must boast, I know it is not good for me.* With regard to *for* or *but*, the latter seems to fall in best with the context. If we read *for*, we must regard St Paul as intending to give an additional proof of the undesirableness of boasting, as shewn by the fact that (*v.* 7) even when there be anything to boast of, it is invariably in the end a source of weakness. If we read *but*, we must suppose St Paul to feel himself compelled to boast, lest the incident to which he has just referred (ch. xi. 31—33) should be turned into an accusation of cowardice. Therefore in spite of himself he gives a proof which few would venture to challenge, that he has a right to speak in the name of God, in order that his confessions of weakness might not be used against him. For *expedient* and *glory* see ch. viii. 10 and v. 12.

visions and revelations of the Lord] *Visions* are the sight of things ordinarily beyond our mortal ken, whether waking or in dreams. *Revelations* (see 1 Cor. i. 7 in the Greek, and Gal. i. 12, 16, ii. 2) are here the mental and spiritual discoveries resulting from such visions.

2. *I knew a man*] That this is the Apostle is proved by *v.* 7. The word *knew* should, both here and in *v.* 3, be rendered **know**.

man in Christ above fourteen years ago, (whether in the body, I cannot tell; or whether out of the body, I cannot tell: God knoweth;) such a one caught up to the third heaven. And I knew such a man, (whether in the body, 3 or out of the body, I cannot tell: God knoweth;) how that 4 he was caught up into paradise, and heard unspeakable

in Christ] i.e. after his conversion, when he had become united to Christ.

above fourteen years ago] And yet, as Chrysostom and Calvin remark, he had kept silence about it all this time. The secret raptures of the soul should be matters between it and God, not subjects of boasting save where necessity compels it. After all the main point (*v.* 6) is what a man *is*, not what he has seen, even of things beyond the sphere of sense. Whether this were the 'revelation' spoken of in Gal. i. 12, ii. 2, we cannot tell. St Paul had many such revelations (see note on 1 Cor. ix. 1), and he gives here no distinct intimation of the time at which the vision occurred.

whether out of the body] "The Apostle here by implication acknowledges the possibility of consciousness and receptivity in a disembodied state." Alford.

I cannot tell] The *fact* of the vision was certain enough. He saw clearly what God gave him permission to see, but whether the soul was rapt from his body left without life, or whether body and soul were caught up together to the third heaven and to Paradise, was known only to God.

the third heaven] Some commentators have explained this passage by the Jewish tradition (see Dean Stanley *in loc.*) of *seven* heavens. But if St Paul had this in his mind, he here meant the *clouds*, a notion combated by Irenaeus, who (see next note) had unusually good opportunities of knowing the Apostle's meaning. He says distinctly (*Adv. Haer.* II. 30) that the third heaven is regarded by St Paul as a place preeminently exalted, and he rejects the idea of the seven heavens as taught by the Valentinian heretics, regarding it as absurd to suppose that four heavens remained as yet unexplored by St Paul. Some of the Jewish teachers held that there were *two*, others that there were *seven* heavens. So in *Chagigah* f. 12 b, "R. Jehuda said there are two heavens, as it is said in Deut. x. 14, 'the heavens and the heaven of heavens.' Rish Lakish said there were seven, &c." See also *Debarim Rabba*, § 2, fol. 253. 1. Rashi on Isai. xliv. 8 says, "ye are my witnesses because I have opened to you the seven heavens (firmaments)," i.e. I have disclosed to you all that pertains to the knowledge of God.

4. *how that he was caught up into paradise*] Was this a second vision, or only an extension of the first? St Paul's language makes the latter more probable. Early tradition is not very clear upon the subject, but the general opinion seems to have been that St Paul was not only caught up to the highest heaven, and there saw visions of God like those of Isaiah and St John, but that he was transported among the saints departed to that particular region of heaven called Paradise, and was permitted to hear the words there uttered. The word Para-

⁵ words, which *it is* not lawful for a man to utter. Of such a one will I glory: yet of myself I will not glory, but in mine ⁶ infirmities. For though I would desire to glory, I shall not

dise is probably an Aryan word, and is found in Sanscrit and Persian as well as in Greek. But it is also found in Hebrew, Arabic and Syriac. It signifies originally a park or pleasure-ground. It is used apparently in this sense in Rev. ii. 7. But in St Luke xxiii. 43 it clearly means the place (or rather *state*, since it is difficult to predicate *place* of a disembodied spirit) of rest and refreshment to which the Lord conducted the soul of the penitent thief as well as (1 Pet. iii. 19, iv. 6, cf. Iren. *Adv. Haer.* IV. 27) the souls of those who were waiting in the unseen world for the revelation of Him. So says Irenaeus (*Adv. Haer.* V. 5), who, quoting as he often does the words of the Elders who had seen the Apostles, with whom he had often conversed, describes Paradise as a state of things "prepared for righteous men and men led by the Spirit, who remain there until the consummation, as a preparation for immortality." Some have thought that Paradise is a yet more exalted place than the third heaven. But if we are right in regarding the third as the highest heaven, it is scarcely possible to see in Paradise something higher still. For visions of this kind cf. Isai. vi. 1; Ezek. iii. 14, 22, 24, viii. 1, xi. 1, 24, xxxvii. 1, xl. 1—3, xliii. 5; Rev. i. 10, and in a lesser degree Acts viii. 39.

unspeakable words] Literally, **unspoken** words, which may in this case have been the fact, since if St Paul were out of the body, as he himself tells us he may have been, the words could not have been *spoken* in our sense of the word. But the epithet usually has the sense which the context attaches to it here, *words not to be uttered*. Calvin asks to what purpose then were they uttered to St Paul, and replies that he needed such spiritual consolation to sustain him in the heavy load of afflictions and cares which was laid upon him. We may also hence learn, he continues, that there are depths in the counsels of God which we must not hope or even wish to penetrate while here on earth. Dean Stanley contrasts the reticence of St Paul with the full details of his supposed visions given by Mahomet, and he might have added many others who have given detailed accounts of things seen in their ecstasies.

5. *Of such a one will I glory: yet of myself I will not glory*] St Paul desires to put the fact in the background that it is of himself he is speaking (see next verse). He has been compelled by the folly and perversity of certain among the Corinthians to touch on these proofs of Divine favour, but he just glances at the topic and passes it by; nay, he even seems to make a distinction between himself as he is and the man once so highly glorified by God, and returns to a kind of boasting more in accordance with his own sense of propriety. So he expatiates on the thorn in the flesh as an instance of how human weakness does but serve to manifest the power of God.

6. *For though I would desire to glory*] St Paul here identifies himself with the man who saw the visions. 'I shall not be foolish, even if I do boast, for I shall only be speaking the truth. But I refrain.'

be a fool; for I will say the truth: but *now* I forbear, lest any *man* should think of me above *that* which he seeth me *to be*, or that he heareth of me.

7—10. *The Thorn in the Flesh.*

And lest I should be exalted above measure through the 7 abundance of the revelations, there was given to me a thorn in the flesh, the messenger of Satan to buffet me, lest I should be exalted above measure. For this *thing* I besought 8 the Lord thrice, that it might depart from me. And he 9 said unto me, My grace is sufficient for thee: for my

forbear] See ch. i. 23, ix. 6, xiii. 2, where the word is the same in the Greek. Also 1 Cor. vii. 28, and Rom. viii. 32, xi. 21.

lest any man should think] It is not visions or revelations, however exalted, for which a man ought to be esteemed, but his conduct and the message with which he is entrusted.

7—10. THE THORN IN THE FLESH.

7. *And lest I should be exalted above measure*] Rather, 'lest I should be **too much** exalted.'

a thorn in the flesh] See Introduction.

the messenger of Satan] Or, **an angel** of Satan. Cf. St Matt. xii. 45, xxv. 41; Rev. xii. 7, 9.

8. *For this thing I besought the Lord thrice*] Literally, **Concerning** this. For the word translated *besought* see ch. i. 3, viii. 6, and v. 18 of this chapter. With St Paul's prayer here compare St Matt. xxvi. 39—44 and the parallel passages in the other Gospels. It is not wrong to offer such petitions, or our Lord would not have done so. But humanity in its weakness often shrinks from trials which God in His wisdom knows to be best for it. The only requisite for such prayers is that they shall be offered in a spirit of submission to a Higher Will. Dean Stanley remarks on St Paul's vivid sense of a Personal Lord, to Whom all difficulties may be taken, and Who never fails to answer such appeals.

the Lord] Jesus Christ. We may compare St Paul's imitation of his Master with that of St Stephen. See Acts vii. 59, and cf. St Luke xxiii. 46.

that it might depart] Or *he* might depart. See above.

9. *And he said unto me*] Jesus Christ said it, "but *how* the answer from Christ was received, whether through an inner voice or by means of a vision, is entirely unknown to us." Meyer.

My grace is sufficient for thee] "Gratia mea, id est, favor ac benevolentia mea qua tibi volo benefacere," Estius, which is the case with every one who is in covenant with Christ. The meaning is 'Trust all to me. I will never fail thee nor forsake thee. Even that which thou feelest to be a hindrance will be overruled into a source of strength.' *This* was the answer; the thorn was not taken away, but strength was given to bear it.

strength is made perfect in weakness. Most gladly therefore will I rather glory in my infirmities, that the power of 10 Christ may rest upon me. Therefore I take pleasure in infirmities, in reproaches, in necessities, in persecutions, in distresses for Christ's sake: for when I am weak, then am I strong.

11—18. *Continuation of the Defence.*

11 I am become a fool in glorying; ye have compelled me:

my strength is made perfect in weakness] Rather, **power**. The word is the same as that rendered *power* below. This is a paradox very common with St Paul. See ch. iv. 7, 10, xiii. 4. Also 1 Cor. i. 21—30, ii. 1—4; Heb. ii. 10. The extraordinary results which God has worked in all ages through means apparently most insufficient are the best commentary on these words, and the best answer to despondent thoughts, when men are weighed down with the sense of their own insufficiency. Many MSS. and editors follow the Vulgate here, omitting the word *my*, and render *for strength is perfected in weakness.* So Wiclif, *for vertu is perfigtly made in infirmity.* "We learn to regard the Apostle not as sustained by a naturally indomitable strength of mind and body, but as doing what he did by an habitual struggle against his constitutional weakness." Stanley.

Most gladly therefore will I rather glory] Better, **boast**. This intimation from our Lord gives St Paul an additional reason why he should boast in his infirmities. When compared with the results of his labours they furnish the most decisive proof (cf. ch. iv. 7, and 1 Cor. ii. 5) that the work he has been doing is of God.

that the power of Christ may rest upon me] Rather, **tabernacle upon me**. Cf. St John i. 14. The five other versions render *dwell in me.* The true meaning combines the two translations, 'come down upon, and dwell in me.' St Paul would have us understand that if he boasted of his own powers, he could not expect to be endowed with power from on high, but that if he gave God all the glory by laying stress on his infirmities, he might hope that Christ would dwell and work in him.

10. *in reproaches*] Rather, perhaps, **insults**.

in distresses] See note on ch. vi. 4.

for Christ's sake] This refers to *all* the preceding list of things endured.

strong] Perhaps better, **powerful** (*migty*, Wiclif), as the word is cognate with *power* above. The word *strong* is scarcely adequate.

11—18. CONTINUATION OF THE DEFENCE.

11. *I am become a fool in glorying*] Or perhaps, with some, *Have* I become a fool? The words *in glorying* are not in the best MSS. and versions. Thus Wiclif, following the Vulgate, translates, *I am made unwitti, ye constreineden me.*

ye have compelled me] Literally, **ye compelled me**, as Wiclif above.

for I ought to have been commended of you: for *in* nothing am I behind the very chiefest apostles, though I be nothing. Truly the signs of an apostle were wrought among you in all patience, in signs, and wonders, and mighty deeds. For what is it wherein ye were inferior to other churches, except *it be* that I myself was not burdensome to you? forgive me this wrong.

Behold, the third *time* I am ready to come to you; and

The word *ye* is emphatic. It was not *my* desire, but *your* conduct that led me to boast. See notes on ch. xi.

for I ought to have been commended of you] See ch. iii. 1, v. 12, x. 12, 18. The word *I* is emphatic. The reason is given in the next verse. They had had abundant evidences of his true Apostleship, and yet they needed that he should himself recal them to their minds.

the very chiefest apostles] See note on ch. xi. 5.

though I be nothing] Cf. 1 Cor. xv. 8—10. Chrysostom connects these words with what follows, and the meaning certainly then comes nearer to the passage just cited from the First Epistle. The Apostle arrogates no greatness to himself, but nevertheless that mighty deeds had been wrought by his means was undeniable.

12. *Truly the signs of an apostle*] Rather, of the Apostle, i.e. of him who is an Apostle. These are of two kinds, (1) inward, consisting in endurance for the Gospel's sake, and (2) outward, in credentials of his mission given from on high.

signs, and wonders] These words are continually conjoined in Scripture not only by St Paul and St Luke, but by the other three Evangelists. The first refers to miraculous works, considered as signs of a Divine power dwelling in the worker; the second is perhaps equivalent to our word *portents*.

and mighty deeds] Literally, **powers**, referring to the inner power which worked them. Dean Stanley remarks on the claim to miraculous powers here made by St Paul. Cf. Acts xiii. 11, xiv. 10, xvi. 18, xix. 11, 12.

13. *For what is it wherein ye were inferior to other churches*] (*hadden lesse than*, Wiclif). There is no need to regard this, with some commentators, as "bitter irony." There is nothing bitter about it. Ironical indeed it is, but it is irony of the very gentlest kind. 'Everything that an Apostle can do has been done amongst you, except the throwing himself upon you for his maintenance' (which had been made by the Apostle's opponents one of the 'signs of an Apostle;' see 1 Cor. ix. 5, 6). 'Surely this is an offence which you might very readily forgive.'

I myself] St Paul's resolution to decline maintenance at the hands of the Corinthians seems to have concerned himself alone, and not to have extended to his companions.

burdensome] See ch. xi. 9.

14. *Behold, the third time*] We can either interpret this (1) with most commentators, of some unrecorded visit to Corinth, or (2) with

I will not be burdensome to you: for I seek not yours, but you: for the children ought not to lay up for the parents, 15 but the parents for the children. And I will very gladly spend and be spent for you; though the more abundantly 16 I love you, the less I be loved. But be it so, I did not burden you: nevertheless, being crafty, I caught you with

Paley, that St Paul is speaking here and in ch. xiii. 1 of the *intention* merely of visiting Corinth, such as we know (ch. i. 15—17) was frustrated once, and probably more than once. (1) is rendered improbable by the fact that St Paul had carefully avoided visiting Corinth for some time. The whole tenor of the Epistles, moreover, implies that he had not been to Corinth since his long stay there, since it would have been hardly possible, had such a visit been paid, that some more distinct notice of it should not appear in letters so overflowing with personal details as these. On the other hand, it must be admitted that our information (see notes on ch. xi.) of St Paul's movements is extremely incomplete.

I am ready] The phrase is almost the same as in ch. x. 6. St Paul does not say here that he has been to Corinth twice before, but simply that this is the third time in which he is holding himself in readiness to come. Whether he comes or not will depend upon their conduct. See ch. xiii. 10. Also ch. xiii. 1.

not yours, but you] Not their money, nor their praise, nor even their affections (see next verse), but simply to induce them to give themselves to Christ.

but the parents for the children] Cf. 1 Cor. iv. 15. The treasures which were laid up by St Paul for his converts were the inexhaustible stores of Divine love and mercy given us in Jesus Christ. See Rom. ix. 23; Eph. i. 7, 18, ii. 7, iii. 8; Col. ii. 9, &c.

15. *very gladly*] Or *most* gladly.

spend and be spent] St Paul regards himself but as a gift of Christ's love, in that he has been made a channel of His grace. Simply as such, as a means whereby Christ is enriching them with Himself, he will not only spend himself, but be spent by others, just as money is, which is worthless in itself, and is only valuable for what it enables us to obtain.

though the more abundantly I love you] This passage shews us how the *man* valued and yearned for affection, even while the *Apostle* knew it to be right to do his duty, without expecting the least return of any kind.

16. *But be it so*] St Paul returns to the charge in *v.* 13. He supposes his antagonists to admit that, as far as he himself is concerned, he has given it a satisfactory answer. But he is prepared for any amount of unjust insinuations. He expects (see note on *v.* 13, on the words 'I myself') that they will attempt to charge him with making use of others to do what he boasted of not doing himself.

nevertheless, being crafty, I caught you with guile] These words are frequently quoted as though the practice here referred to were a defen-

guile. Did I make a gain of you by any of them whom I 17
sent unto you? I desired Titus, and with *him* I sent a bro- 18
ther. Did Titus make a gain of you? walked we not in the
same spirit? *walked we* not in the same steps?

XII. 19—XIII. 10. *The Apostle's intentions on his arrival.*

Again, think you that we excuse ourselves unto you? we 19

sible one. The next verse shews that St Paul repudiates such an impu-
tation with the utmost distinctness. For *crafty* see ch. iv. 2, xi. 3.

17. *make a gain of you*] See ch. ii. 11.

by any of them whom I sent unto you] They may have been maintained at the expense of the Churches, but they certainly made no
attempt to enrich St Paul by their mission. In their disinterested labours
they followed implicitly the example of the great Apostle. Some have
thought that there is a reference here to the collection for the poor
Christians at Jerusalem, but this can hardly be, for the mission of Titus
was simply for the purpose of urging the Corinthians to complete their
preparations. St Paul had anticipated all objections as to his making
use of that money for his own purposes by arranging (see 1 Cor. xvi. 3)
that it should be sent in the charge of brethren selected by the Corinthian
Church itself. See also ch. viii. 19, 21. We must therefore understand
the words as an appeal to the conduct of Titus and his companions
while at Corinth, and as a refutation of a charge which St Paul thought
might possibly be brought, that he had endeavoured in an underhand
manner to obtain money from Corinth through them.

18. *I desired Titus*] See ch. viii. 6. This has also been thought to
be the Epistolary aorist, and to have a present signification, as though the
present letter had been sent by Titus, but the rest of the verse seems
to point to some *past* occasion. See also ch. xiii. 2, 10, in the Greek.

a brother] Literally, **the** brother. See ch. viii. 18, 22.

in the same spirit] i.e. the Holy Spirit. Cf. Gal. v. 16.

in the same steps] Perhaps those of Christ. See 1 Pet. ii. 21. At
least the expression marks the precise accordance between the conduct
of the Apostle and his messengers.

XII. 19—XIII. 10. THE APOSTLE'S INTENTIONS ON HIS
ARRIVAL.

19. *Again, think you that we excuse ourselves*] Rather, **Do
ye think that we are defending ourselves again?** Many MSS. and
versions read, *Do you think* (or *You think*) *that we have been defending
ourselves to you this long time?* The word *excuse* gives a false impression,
as though the Apostle were exculpating himself from blame rather than
meeting accusations by sufficient answers. If we take the first reading
the reference will be to the former Epistle or the commencement of this
one. Cf. ch. iii. 1. If the second, the meaning will be 'you think that
I have been making a long and perhaps tedious defence of myself, yet
I can assure you that I shall not stand upon my defence when I come.

speak before God in Christ: but *we do* all *things*, dearly
20 beloved, for your edifying. For I fear, lest, when I come, I
shall not find you such as I would, and *that* I shall be found
unto you such as ye would not: lest *there be* debates, envyings, wraths, strifes, backbitings, whisperings, swellings, tu-
21 mults: *and* lest, when I come again, my God will humble

I only desire your improvement. But if words will not suffice, I shall have, when I come, to proceed to deeds.'
we speak before God in Christ] This sense of saying and doing everything in the sight of God and Christ, Who will avenge all deceit by unmasking the deceiver, is a characteristic of St Paul's whole nature, but is never more clearly displayed than in this Epistle. See ch. i. 18, 23, ii. 17, iii. 4, iv. 2, 6, v. 11, vii. 12, viii. 21, xi. 10, 11, 31.
edifying] See 1 Cor. viii. 1, and ch. v. 1, x. 8.
20. *For*] The connection of thought is, 'I do this for your edification, of which there is much need, for there are many disorders among you.'
such as ye would not] "He here completely and finally throws off the apologist and puts on the Apostle." Alford. He will rule by love rather than by fear, if possible. But if it be *not* possible, in the last resource he must use his Apostolic power. See notes on ch. x. 8, 11.
debates] Rather, **strifes**. The word *debate*, however, derived from the French *débattre*, had, like the French *débat*, a stronger meaning than it has now. So Shakespeare, *K. Hen. IV.* Pt. II. Act IV. Scene iv.:

"Now, lords, if Heaven doth give successful end
To this *debate* that bleedeth at our doors."

envyings] See note on ch. vii. 7.
strifes] Our translators have been misled by an apparent similarity between this word and that rendered *debates* above. It is derived from a word signifying a hired labourer, and may either mean (1) *party spirit*, (2) *personal aims* in public life, in which sense Aristotle seems to have used the word in his *Politics*, and hence (3) *self-seeking* in general, and (4) faction. The word occurs in Rom. ii. 8; Gal. v. 20; Phil. i. 16, ii. 3; James iii. 14, 16.
backbitings, whisperings] "Open slanders, secret revilings." Alford. Wiclif renders *detracciouns, privie spechis of discord*. He is followed by the Rhemish in the rendering *detractions*. Tyndale, Cranmer and the Geneva render as A. V. See 1 Pet. ii. 1 for the first word, which is there rendered *evil speakings*. Its literal meaning is *speakings against*, but no idea of secrecy is implied, as in our version, but rather the contrary. *Whisperings*, on the other hand, imply secrecy as a matter of course.
swellings] Rather, **puffings up** (Wiclif, well, *bolnyngis in pride*). See 1 Cor. iv. 6, 18, 19. The word and its cognates occur only in these two Epistles and in Col. ii. 18.
tumults] See ch. vi. 5.

me among you, and *that* I shall bewail many which have sinned already, and have not repented of the uncleanness and fornication and lasciviousness which they have committed.

This *is* the third *time* I am coming to you. In the mouth of two or three witnesses shall every word be established. I told *you* before, and foretell *you*, as if I were present the second *time;* and being absent now

13

2

21. *among you*] Or, with some interpreters, *in reference to* you. The literal translation is to you.

which have sinned already] Literally, those who have sinned before, i. e. either (1) before their conversion and who did not cast off their evil habits when they became Christians, or (2) those who sinned before the Apostle's letter came, and who did not pay any attention to his rebukes. The latter seems to fall in best with the tenor of the first Epistle and with ch. ii., vii., and x. 1—6.

and have not repented] This makes it clear that, as 1 Cor. vi. 12—20 would imply, there were other offenders in the particular sin here mentioned beside the incestuous person. It also appears that the Apostle was willing to forgive such offenders as soon as they had abandoned their sin. For *repentance* see ch. vii. 9. The literal rendering of this sentence is many of those who have sinned and did not repent. Many commentators have asked, Why *many* and not *all?* But they have overlooked the difference of tense in the original. There were many who had sinned, and who, up to the arrival of the second Epistle, had not repented. But it is quite clear that St Paul hoped that his second Epistle would have much influence upon those whom his first Epistle and the visit of Titus had failed to move.

lasciviousness] The term in the original has reference to the unnatural condition of restless excitement which licentious habits produce in their victim.

CH. XIII. 1. *This is the third time I am coming to you*] See note on ch. xii. 14. For the Greek present in the sense of an *intention* see 1 Cor. xvi. 5.

In the mouth of two or three witnesses shall every word be established] This is a quotation from Deut. xix. 15, and is an intimation of St Paul's intention to enter upon a full investigation of the condition of the Corinthian Church, if such a step be rendered necessary by their conduct. He will assume nothing, take nothing for granted of what he has heard, but will carry on his investigation on the principles alike of the Old Testament and of the New (St Matt. xviii. 16).

2. *I told you before, and foretell you*] Literally, I have spoken beforehand, and I say beforehand (*I seide bifor and scie bifor*, Wiclif. Similarly Tyndale and Cranmer). The repetition is for the sake of emphasis. Cf. Gal. i. 9. See also 1 Cor. iv. 21.

as if I were present the second time] Some, supposing that St Paul

I write to them which heretofore have sinned, and to all
3 other, that, if I come again, I will not spare: since ye seek
a proof of Christ speaking in me, which to you-ward is not
4 weak, but is mighty in you. For though he was crucified
through weakness, yet he liveth by the power of God. For

had already visited Corinth twice, would render '*when* present the second
time.' But the rendering in the text is more literal.

and being absent now] The word *now* belongs to *being absent*, not,
as in the A. V., to what follows. The meaning is that though now
absent (cf. 1 Cor. v. 3), the Apostle speaks as he will find it necessary to
speak when present, with decision and sternness, unless (ch. xii. 21) the
offending persons repent.

them which heretofore have sinned] The same words as were translated
have sinned already in ch. xii. 21.

and to all other] Literally, **to all the rest**, inasmuch as some of the
Corinthians derided the idea that St Paul would act with firmness, and
the whole Church needed some assurance to that effect. See note on
ch. i. 23.

3. *since ye seek*] They had demanded a proof of his power, and he
would not fail to give it.

a proof of Christ speaking in me] Literally, **of the in-me-speaking
Christ.** The delicate shade of meaning here can hardly be rendered into
English. Perhaps 'of a Christ who speaks in me' would be the nearest
approach to it. Our version hardly conveys a sufficient idea of the
perpetual indwelling of Christ in His members and of the inspiring
influence which He constantly exerted on one so devoted to Him as St
Paul. See St Matt. x. 20. For *proof* see ch. ii. 9, viii. 2. The connection of this verse with what precedes and what follows is to be found
in the fact that everything St Paul did, whether in the exercise of his
Apostolic power, or in any other way, was done to produce in their lives
a conformity to that of Christ. Cf. ch. vi.

which to you-ward is not weak] Rather, **Who** to you-ward. St Paul
continually (see ch. iv. 10, 11, and ch. xi., xii.) identifies himself with
Christ, in his weakness as well as his strength. He is going (see next
verse) to point to the weakness of Christ as united with his own. But
he prefaces this remarkable statement with the observation (cf. 1 Cor. iv.
11) that at present the Corinthians knew little of communion with Christ
in His weakness, much of His power to change the heart and life. Cf.
1 Cor. i. 18, 24, ii. 5. Also ch. x. 4.

4. *For though he was crucified through weakness*] Chrysostom observes that these words were a great difficulty to the weaker sort. But
he explains them by St John xi. 3, 4; Phil. ii. 27; 1 Tim. v. 23, where
the word in the original is the same as, or cognate to, that employed
here. There is another reading here, which by omitting 'though,' or
rather 'if,' in the original, strengthens the Apostle's statement. There
need be no difficulty. Our Lord assumed our human nature with all its
infirmities (Heb. ii. 10—18, iv. 15, v. 2, 3; see also ch. viii. 9, and

we also are weak in him, but we shall live with him by the
power of God toward you. Examine yourselves, whether ye 5
be in the faith; prove your own selves. Know ye not your
own selves, how that Jesus Christ is in you, except ye

Phil. ii. 7, 8), although they were the result of sin. He bore all
those infirmities, death itself included. And then He shook them all
off for ever when He rose again 'by the power of God.' Cf. Rom.
i. 4; 1 Cor. i. 24.

For we also are weak in him] In this present life the Apostles of
Christ were like their Master. Upborne by the power of God within,
they had nevertheless to bear the load of human infirmity, to 'take up
their Cross and follow Him.' See notes on ch. iv. 10—12, and cf. Gal.
vi. 17. And not only so, but the words 'in Him' shew that it was a
necessary part of their union with Him that they should be partakers of
His tribulation, before they were translated into the fulness of His glory.
See 2 Thess. i. 4—7; 1 Pet. i. 5—7, v. 10.

we shall live with him] Not, as the following words shew, hereafter,
but in the Apostle's ministry to the Corinthians. Cf. *v*. 3. Also
Rom. i. 16; John xiv. 19; 1 Cor. i. 18, and ch. x. 4—6, and note on
ch. iv. 14. The Gospel was a *power* which enabled men to change their
lives, in that it was a ministering to them of the Spirit of Jesus Christ.
Compare ch. iii. 3, 6, 8, 9 with Rom. viii. 9, 10 and Phil. i. 19.

5. *Examine yourselves, whether ye be in the faith; prove your own
selves*] The words rendered (1) *examine* and (2) *prove* have the sense
(1) of *testing* (the word is often translated *tempt*) and (2) subjecting to a
process the result of which is satisfactory. See for (2) 1 Cor. xi. 28.
The words *yourselves* are in each case emphatic. The connection with
what has gone before would seem to be as follows. The Apostle had
been among the Corinthians in weakness (1 Cor. ii. 3; cf. ch. x. 1, 10). He
had boasted of nothing but his infirmity (ch. xi. 30, xii. 5, 9). So that
many of them had come to regard him with contempt. But the Gospel,
he says, is a power. He appeals to the testimony of their own Christian
experience on the point, as in ch. iv. 2, v. 11, vi. 4. 'Is it *not* a power?'
he says. 'Look at yourselves. Do you not feel it to be so in your own
hearts? Does not Jesus Christ dwell in you, at least in all who are not
finally cast off by Him, and does He not make manifest His power in
the subjugation of the natural man within you? Could this have taken
place unless the Gospel were a real power of God? And then to whom,
humanly speaking, do you owe this power? Is it not to him of whom
you are ready to believe that he is no true Apostle of Christ?'

whether ye be in the faith] i.e. whether "Christ be present and actively
working within you, the certain result of all true faith." Meyer. Cf.
St John xv. 1—7, xvii. 21—23; Rom. vi. 23 (in the Greek), viii. 1, 10;
Gal. ii. 20, iv. 19; Eph. iii. 16—19; Col. i. 27, iii. 1—4, &c.

except ye be reprobates] Rather, **unless indeed ye be rejected.** The
word translated *reprobates* (see note on ch. ii. 9, and *v*. 3) signifies those
who have been *tried and found wanting*. See also Rom. i. 28; 1 Cor. ix.
27; 2 Tim. iii. 8; Tit. i. 16; and Heb. vi. 8, where the word again occurs.

6 be reprobates? But I trust that ye shall know that we are
7 not reprobates. Now I pray to God that ye do no evil;
not that we should appear approved, but that ye should
8 do *that which is* honest, though we be as reprobates. For
9 we can do nothing against the truth, but for the truth. For
we are glad, when we are weak, and ye are strong: and

6. *But I trust that ye shall know that we are not reprobates*] i.e. I trust that you will find that we have not lost this Divine power of Christ dwelling within us, but that you will find it as mighty to confront and to subdue the obstinate resistance of evil, as it was to implant the first strivings after good.

7. *Now I pray to God that ye do no evil*] St Paul's whole heart is set upon the desire that the power of Christ which dwells in the Christian body should be displayed in the victory of his converts over evil, and this not for any personal ends of his own—not even in order that he might manifest the high estimation in which God holds him—but simply for the sake of Him Whose minister he is, and for their sakes to whom he ministers Him.

approved] The opposite to *reprobate*, or rather *rejected*. See also ch. x. 18.

honest] Rather, what is **noble, right.**

though we be as reprobates] St Paul carries his self-denial a step further. Even if he were regarded as rejected himself, his object would be attained, and he would be quite satisfied, if the Corinthians did what was right in the sight of God. It was for what they did, not for what they thought of him, that he laboured.

8. *For we can do nothing against the truth*] The original carries on the idea of *power* of which St Paul has been speaking above. If we are endued with any power from on high, it is not that we may exercise it on our own behalf, and against the truth of God. We can but use it for the purpose for which it was given us, namely for the glory of God and the increase of His kingdom.

but for the truth] More literally, **on behalf of** the truth.

9. *For we are glad, when we are weak, and ye are strong*] This passage is very similar to 1 Cor. iv. 8—10. At present none of the burdens, but many of the blessings of the Gospel, have fallen on the Corinthians. St Paul rejoices that their immature faith is not subjected to the severe strain of persecution and affliction, while as respects himself, he rejoices in sorrows (ch. xii. 10), regarding them as proofs of the ascendency of the life of the Spirit over that of the flesh. Cf. ch. iv. 10—16. The word translated *am glad* is somewhat stronger in the original—*rejoice*. And the word translated *strong* is cognate with that translated *mighty* in v. 3. See also ch. x. 4. It refers to the inner strength of spirit with which the believer in Christ is endued. It is also to be observed—and the Greek here displays it more clearly than the English—that St Paul does not say that the Corinthians *are* strong, but that he rejoices *when* they are so.

this also we wish, *even* your perfection. Therefore I write
these *things* being absent, lest being present I should use
sharpness, according to the power which the Lord hath
given me to edification, and not to destruction.

11—14. *Conclusion.*

Finally, brethren, farewell. Be perfect, be of good comfort, be of one mind, live in peace; and the God of love

and this also we wish] More literally, **pray**. St Paul rejoices when
the Corinthians are strong, but whether they are so or not, he does not
cease to pray for their advancement in holiness.
perfection] The word is not that usually rendered *perfection* in our
translation, i.e. the fulfilment by any creature of the *end* for which it
was designed. It rather signifies the *fitting together* of a number of souls
as the pieces in a mosaic. Cf. 1 Cor. i. 10, where the cognate word
(see *v.* 11) is used of unity of mind and judgment; Heb. x. 5, where it
is used of preparing a body for Christ; Mark i. 19, where it is used of
mending nets; Gal. vi. 1, where it is used of restoring a sinner. The
first and last of these meanings are probably combined here.
10. *lest being present I should use sharpness*] See ch. i. 23, and
v. 2.
power] Rather, **authority**, as in ch. x. 8.
to edification] See note on 1 Cor. viii. 1. Also ch. xii. 19, and
especially x. 8, the words in which St Paul here repeats.

11—14. CONCLUSION.

11. *farewell*] Or perhaps **rejoice** (*ioie ye*, Wiclif; *gaudete*, Vulgate).
Cf. Phil. iv. 4; 1 Thess. v. 16. *Joy* (Gal. v. 22) was one of the foremost fruits of the Spirit, and ought to be the natural result of the sense
of our favour with God through Christ. See John xv. 11; Acts xiii. 52;
Rom. xiv. 17; Heb. xiii. 17; James i. 2; 1 Pet. i. 8, iv. 13; 1 John i. 4,
&c. Our translation follows Tyndale here.
Be perfect] See note on *perfection* in *v.* 9, where the Greek word is
a derivative of the word used here.
be of good comfort] The word is the same as in ch. i. 4. Our translation here follows Tyndale. Wiclif, following the Vulgate, renders *ex-
cite ye.*
be of one mind] Cf. 1 Cor. i. 10, and observe the close connection of
ideas there between unity of spirit and the word translated *be perfect*
above. The literal rendering is **think the same thing**. See also Rom.
xii. 16.
the God of love] It would have been impossible even in the 16th
century to render here 'the God of *charity*.' The Vulgate here has
dilectionis, not *caritatis*. *Caritas* and *charity* seem to have been used
for the human reflection of God's love, to the grievous obscuration of the
great Christian fact that all love is His love, whether manifested *by* Him
or *in* man. It may be asked whether in order to think the same thing

₁₂ and peace shall be with you. Greet one another with a ₁₃ holy kiss. All the saints salute you. The grace of the Lord ¹⁴ Jesus Christ, and the love of God, and the communion of the Holy Ghost, *be* with you all. Amen.

and be at peace, we do not first need the God of love and peace to be with us. Undoubtedly, but if we do not follow His promptings while with us, we drive Him away. Therefore if we wish Him to abide continually with us, we must walk according to the Spirit which He hath given us.

12. *Greet one another with a holy kiss*] See note on 1 Cor. xvi. 20.

14. *The grace of the Lord*] This is the fullest form of any of the benedictions given by St Paul, and it comes fitly at the end of the harshest of his Epistles. It must be regarded as the overflowing of a loving heart, conscious of the severity of the language the Apostle has been compelled to use, yet deeply penetrated with a sense of its necessity for the well-being of the flock. The benediction is invoked upon all, the slanderers and gainsayers, the seekers after worldly wisdom, the hearkeners to false doctrine, as well as the faithful and obedient disciples. In regard to its form, we may remark that it was the *grace* or *favour* of Jesus Christ in condescending to visit us, through which we received the revelation of the love of God, and that it was through that love that we received the gift of the Holy Spirit, to dwell in our hearts by faith, and thus to knit us into one body in Christ. For *communion* or *fellowship* (a rendering familiar to us through the Prayer Book, being that of Tyndale and Cranmer) see note on 1 Cor. i. 9. The form of this benediction has always been regarded as a proof of the essential unity and equality of Father, Son and Holy Ghost.

INDEX I.

Abib, 91
Abraham, 118
Achaia, 25, 96, 113
Acts of the Apostles, coincidences between, and the Epistles to the Corinthians, 11—13
Afghanistan, 120
Alfred the Great, 16
Ambassadors for Christ, 72
Andrew, 44
Aretas, 123
Aristotle's *Ethics*, 92
Asia, 28
Authorized Version, 18

Barbarossa, 120
Barnabas, 17, 93
Bartholomew, 44
Bedouins, 120
Belial, 78
Betrothal, 110

Caractacus, 44
Christ, the image of God, 58; made to be sin for us, 73; for our sakes became poor, 90
Claudius, 44
Clement, 15
Clementine Recognitions, 9 note; Homilies, ib.
Corinthian Church, given to faction, 9
Cranmer's Translation, 18

Damascenes, 123
Damascus, 123
Douay Bible, 18

Earthen vessels, 59
Ebionitish writings, 9
Elymas the sorcerer, 17
English Versions of the New Testament, 18
Epistle of Clement, 9
Epistle, Second, to the Corinthians, date of, 7; whence written, 7, 8; character and contents of, 8—10; genuineness of, 10, 11; analysis of, 19—23
Epistle to Diognetus, 11

Epistle to Laodicea, 25
Erastus, 7
Eve, 110

Forty stripes save one, 119
Frederick Barbarossa, 120

Geneva Bible, 18
Greece, condition of, 88

Herod Antipas, 123
Herodias, 123

Ignatius, 11, 15
Incense burnt in ancient triumphs, 43
Ink, 47
Irenaeus, 11, 15

Jerusalem, collection for the poor saints at, 87
Justin Martyr, 15

Latrocinium, 117
Letter and spirit, 49
Luke, St, 93
Luther, 16

Macedonia, 32, 43, 82, 96, 97, 113; churches of, 87
Mahomet, 126
Ministration of death, 49
Moses, 50; the vail over his face, 52

New testament, 48
Nisan, 91

Paley's *Horae Paulinae*, 11
Paul, St, his trouble in Asia, 28; his defence of himself, 109; his labours and sufferings, 116—123; his escape from Damascus, 123; his visions, 125; thorn in the flesh, 13—18, 127
Perils of waters, 120
Plainness of speech, 51
Play upon words, 31, 59, 106

Rhemish Version, 18
Robbers, 120

INDEX I.

Robber-Synod, 117
Rods, beating with, 119

Salutation, 25
Satan, power of, 14
Scourging, 119
Seal, 35
Show of hands, voting by, 94
Silas, 33, 93
Silvanus, 33
Stake in the flesh. *See* Thorn

Tables of stone, 47
Tertullian, 11, 15
Thomas, St, 44
Thorn in the flesh, 13—18, 127
Timotheus, 7, 33
Timothy, 25

Tisri, 91
Titus, 7, 42, 89, 92, 93, 95, 131
Troas, 41
Trophimus, 94
Tychicus, 94
Tyndale, 18

Undesigned coincidences, 11—13

Valentinian heretics, 125
Veil on Moses' face, 52; on the heart of the Jews, 53
Versions of the New Testament in English, 18
Voting by show of hands, 94

Wiclif's translation, 18
William III., 16

INDEX II.

WORDS AND PHRASES EXPLAINED.

Abound, 27
Abundance, 92
Accepted time, 74
Anguish, 38

Base, 102
βῆμα, 67

Call for a record, 36
Causeth to triumph, 43
Comfort, 26
Commend, 57
Constrain, 68
Conversation, 30
Corrupt, 45
Craftiness, 56

Debate, 132
Deep, 88
Despaired, 29
Devices, 41
Dishonesty, 56
Done away, 50
Door = opportunity, 42

Earnest, 35
Edification, 105
Epistles of commendation, 46
Excellency, 59

Expedient, 90

Father of mercies, 26
Fleshy, 48

Gospel, 42
Governor, 123
Grace, 30, 89
γυμνός, 64

Hebrew, 118

Image, 58
Imputed, 72
Israelite, 118

Judgment seat, 67

λειτουργοί, 100
Liturgy, 100

Make you sorry, 37
Messengers, 93
Minister, 96
Ministry, 96

Narcissus, 113
Narcotic, 113
νάρκη, 113

Offence, 74
Out of measure, 29

Paradise, 125, 126
παραπτώματα, 71
Person, 30, 41
Poor, 90
Preached, 33
Pressed, 28
Proof, 40
Provoke, 97
Punishment, 39

Rejoicing, 31
Repentance, 84
Revelations, 124
Rule, 107

Savour, 43
Sentence, 29
Sight, 66

Signs and wonders, 129
Simplicity, 110
Sincerity, 30, 90
Stablisheth, 35
Straitened, 77

ταπεινος, 82
Thanks, 92
Third heaven, 125
Transgress, 71
Trespasses, 71
Tribulation, 26

Visions, 124

Wilderness, 121
Willing mind, 91
Wit, 87
Wonders, 129
Workers, 114

THE CAMBRIDGE BIBLE FOR SCHOOLS AND COLLEGES.
GENERAL EDITOR, J. J. S. PEROWNE,
BISHOP OF WORCESTER.

Opinions of the Press.

"*It is difficult to commend too highly this excellent series.*"—Guardian.

"*The modesty of the general title of this series has, we believe, led many to misunderstand its character and underrate its value. The books are well suited for study in the upper forms of our best schools, but not the less are they adapted to the wants of all Bible students who are not specialists. We doubt, indeed, whether any of the numerous popular commentaries recently issued in this country will be found more serviceable for general use.*"—Academy.

"*One of the most popular and useful literary enterprises of the nineteenth century.*"—Baptist Magazine.

"*Of great value. The whole series of comments for schools is highly esteemed by students capable of forming a judgment. The books are scholarly without being pretentious: and information is so given as to be easily understood.*"—Sword and Trowel.

"*The value of the work as an aid to Biblical study, not merely in schools but among people of all classes who are desirous to have intelligent knowledge of the Scriptures, cannot easily be over-estimated.*"—The Scotsman.

The Book of Judges. J. J. LIAS, M.A. "His introduction is clear and concise, full of the information which young students require, and indicating the lines on which the various problems suggested by the Book of Judges may be solved."—*Baptist Magazine.*

1 Samuel, by A. F. KIRKPATRICK. "Remembering the interest with which we read the *Books of the Kingdom* when they were appointed as a subject for school work in our boyhood, we have looked with some eagerness into Mr Kirkpatrick's volume, which contains the first instalment of them. We are struck with the great improvement in character, and variety in the materials, with which schools are now supplied. A clear map inserted in each volume, notes suiting the convenience of the scholar and the difficulty of the passage, and not merely dictated by the fancy of the commentator, were luxuries which a quarter of a century ago the Biblical student could not buy."—*Church Quarterly Review.*

"To the valuable series of Scriptural expositions and elementary commentaries which is being issued at the Cambridge University Press, under the title 'The Cambridge Bible for Schools,' has been added **The First Book of Samuel** by the Rev. A. F. KIRKPATRICK. Like other volumes of the series, it contains a carefully written historical and critical introduction, while the text is profusely illustrated and explained by notes."—*The Scotsman.*

II. Samuel. A. F. KIRKPATRICK, M.A. "Small as this work is in mere dimensions, it is every way the best on its subject and for its purpose that we know of. The opening sections at once prove the thorough competence of the writer for dealing with questions of criticism in an earnest, faithful and devout spirit; and the appendices discuss a few special difficulties with a full knowledge of the data, and a judicial reserve, which contrast most favourably with the superficial dogmatism which has too often made the exegesis of the Old Testament a field for the play of unlimited paradox and the ostentation of personal infallibility. The notes are always clear and suggestive; never trifling or irrelevant; and they everywhere demonstrate the great difference in value between the work of a commentator who is also a Hebraist, and that of one who has to depend for his Hebrew upon secondhand sources."—*Academy*.

"The Rev. A. F. KIRKPATRICK has now completed his commentary on the two books of Samuel. This second volume, like the first, is furnished with a scholarly and carefully prepared critical and historical introduction, and the notes supply everything necessary to enable the merely English scholar—so far as is possible for one ignorant of the original language—to gather up the precise meaning of the text. Even Hebrew scholars may consult this small volume with profit."—*Scotsman*.

I. Kings and Ephesians. "With great heartiness we commend these most valuable little commentaries. We had rather purchase these than nine out of ten of the big blown up expositions. Quality is far better than quantity, and we have it here."—*Sword and Trowel*.

I. Kings. "This is really admirably well done, and from first to last there is nothing but commendation to give to such honest work."—*Bookseller*.

II. Kings. "The Introduction is scholarly and wholly admirable, while the notes must be of incalculable value to students."—*Glasgow Herald*.

"It is equipped with a valuable introduction and commentary, and makes an admirable text book for Bible-classes."—*Scotsman*.

"It would be difficult to find a commentary better suited for general use."—*Academy*.

The Book of Job. "Able and scholarly as the Introduction is, it is far surpassed by the detailed exegesis of the book. In this Dr DAVIDSON's strength is at its greatest. His linguistic knowledge, his artistic habit, his scientific insight, and his literary power have full scope when he comes to exegesis.... The book is worthy of the reputation of Dr Davidson; it represents the results of many years of labour, and it will greatly help to the right understanding of one of the greatest works in the literature of the world."—*The Spectator*.

"In the course of a long introduction, Dr DAVIDSON has presented us with a very able and very interesting criticism of this wonderful book. Its contents the nature of its composition, its idea and purpose, its integrity, and its age are all exhaustively treated of.... We have not space to examine fully the text and notes before us, but we can, and do heartily, recommend the book, not only for the upper forms in schools, but to Bible students and teachers generally. As we wrote of a previous volume in the same series, this one leaves nothing to be desired. The notes are full and suggestive, without being too long, and, in itself, the introduction forms a valuable addition to modern Bible literature."—*The Educational Times.*

"Already we have frequently called attention to this exceedingly valuable work as its volumes have successively appeared. But we have never done so with greater pleasure, very seldom with so great pleasure, as we now refer to the last published volume, that on the **Book of Job**, by Dr DAVIDSON, of Edinburgh.... We cordially commend the volume to all our readers. The least instructed will understand and enjoy it; and mature scholars will learn from it."—*Methodist Recorder.*

Job—Hosea. "It is difficult to commend too highly this excellent series, the volumes of which are now becoming numerous. The two books before us, small as they are in size, comprise almost everything that the young student can reasonably expect to find in the way of helps towards such general knowledge of their subjects as may be gained without an attempt to grapple with the Hebrew; and even the learned scholar can hardly read without interest and benefit the very able introductory matter which both these commentators have prefixed to their volumes. It is not too much to say that these works have brought within the reach of the ordinary reader resources which were until lately quite unknown for understanding some of the most difficult and obscure portions of Old Testament literature."—*Guardian.*

Ecclesiastes; or, the Preacher.—"Of the Notes, it is sufficient to say that they are in every respect worthy of Dr PLUMPTRE'S high reputation as a scholar and a critic, being at once learned, sensible, and practical.... An appendix, in which it is clearly proved that the author of *Ecclesiastes* anticipated Shakspeare and Tennyson in some of their finest thoughts and reflections, will be read with interest by students both of Hebrew and of English literature. Commentaries are seldom attractive reading. This little volume is a notable exception."—*The Scotsman.*

"In short, this little book is of far greater value than most of the larger and more elaborate commentaries on this Scripture. Indispensable to the scholar, it will render real and large help to all who have to expound the dramatic utterances of **The Preacher** whether in the Church or in the School."—*The Expositor.*

"The '*ideal* biography' of the author is one of the most exquisite and fascinating pieces of writing we have met with, and, granting its starting-point, throws wonderful light on many problems connected with the book. The notes illustrating the text are full of delicate criticism, fine glowing insight, and apt historical allusion. An abler volume than Professor PLUMPTRE'S we could not desire."—*Baptist Magazine.*

Jeremiah, by A. W. STREANE. "The arrangement of the book is well treated on pp. xxx., 396, and the question of Baruch's relations with its composition on pp. xxvii., xxxiv., 317. The illustrations from English literature, history, monuments, works on botany, topography, etc., are good and plentiful, as indeed they are in other volumes of this series."—*Church Quarterly Review*, April, 1881.

"Mr STREANE's **Jeremiah** consists of a series of admirable and wellnigh exhaustive notes on the text, with introduction and appendices, drawing the life, times, and character of the prophet, the style, contents, and arrangement of his prophecies, the traditions relating to Jeremiah,

meant as a type of Christ (a most remarkable chapter), and other prophecies relating to Jeremiah."—*The English Churchman and Clerical Journal.*

Obadiah and Jonah. "This number of the admirable series of Scriptural expositions issued by the Syndics of the Cambridge University Press is well up to the mark. The numerous notes are excellent. No difficulty is shirked, and much light is thrown on the contents both of Obadiah and Jonah. Scholars and students of to-day are to be congratulated on having so large an amount of information on Biblical subjects, so clearly and ably put together, placed within their reach in such small bulk. To all Biblical students the series will be acceptable, and for the use of Sabbath-school teachers will prove invaluable."—*North British Daily Mail.*

"It is a very useful and sensible exposition of these two Minor Prophets, and deals very thoroughly and honestly with the immense difficulties of the later-named of the two, from the orthodox point of view."—*Expositor.*

Haggai and Zechariah. This interesting little volume is of great value. It is one of the best books in that well-known series of scholarly and popular commentaries, 'the Cambridge Bible for Schools and Colleges' of which Dean Perowne is the General Editor. In the expositions of Archdeacon Perowne we are always sure to notice learning, ability, judgment and reverence.... The notes are terse and pointed, but full and reliable."—*Churchman.*

Malachi. "Archdeacon Perowne has already edited Jonah and Zechariah for this series. Malachi presents comparatively few difficulties and the Editor's treatment leaves nothing to be desired. His introduction is clear and scholarly and his commentary sufficient. We may instance the notes on ii. 15 and iv. 2 as examples of careful arrangement, clear exposition and graceful expression."—*Academy*, Aug. 2, 1890.

"**The Gospel according to St Matthew**, by the Rev. A. CARR. The introduction is able, scholarly, and eminently practical, as it bears on the authorship and contents of the Gospel, and the original form in which it is supposed to have been written. It is well illustrated by two excellent maps of the Holy Land and of the Sea of Galilee."—*English Churchman.*

"**St Matthew**, edited by A. CARR, M.A. **The Book of Joshua**, edited by G. F. MACLEAR, D.D. **The General Epistle of St James**, edited by E. H. PLUMPTRE, D.D. The introductions and notes are scholarly, and generally such as young readers need and can appreciate. The maps in both Joshua and Matthew are very good, and all matters of editing are faultless. Professor Plumptre's notes on 'The Epistle of St James' are models of terse, exact, and elegant renderings of the original, which is too often obscured in the authorised version."—*Nonconformist.*

"**St Mark**, with Notes by the Rev. G. F. MACLEAR, D.D. Into this small volume Dr Maclear, besides a clear and able Introduction to the Gospel, and the text of St Mark, has compressed many hundreds of valuable and helpful notes. In short, he has given us a capital manual of the kind required—containing all that is needed to illustrate the text, i.e. all that can be drawn from the history, geography, customs, and manners of the time. But as a handbook, giving in a clear and succinct form the information which a lad requires in order to stand an examination in the Gospel, it is admirable......I can very heartily commend it, not only to the senior boys and girls in our High Schools, but also to Sunday-school teachers, who may get from it the very kind of knowledge they often find it hardest to get."—*Expositor.*

"With the help of a book like this, an intelligent teacher may make 'Divinity' as interesting a lesson as any in the school course. The notes are of a kind that will be, for the most part, intelligible to boys of the lower forms of our public schools; but they may be read with greater profit by the fifth and sixth, in conjunction with the original text."—*The Academy.*

"**St Luke.** Canon FARRAR has supplied students of the Gospel with an admirable manual in this volume. It has all that copious variety of illustration, ingenuity of suggestion, and general soundness of interpretation which readers are accustomed to expect from the learned and eloquent editor. Any one who has been accustomed to associate the idea of 'dryness' with a commentary, should go to Canon Farrar's **St Luke** for a more correct impression. He will find that a commentary may be made interesting in the highest degree, and that without losing anything of its solid value. . . . But, so to speak, it is *too good* for some of the readers for whom it is intended."—*The Spectator.*

"Canon FARRAR'S contribution to The Cambridge School Bible is one of the most valuable yet made. His annotations on **The Gospel according to St Luke**, while they display a scholarship at least as sound, and an erudition at least as wide and varied as those of the editors of St Matthew and St Mark, are rendered telling and attractive by a more lively imagination, a keener intellectual and spiritual insight, a more incisive and picturesque style. His *St Luke* is worthy to be ranked with Professor Plumptre's *St James*, than which no higher commendation can well be given."—*The Expositor.*

"**St Luke.** Edited by Canon FARRAR, D.D. We have received with pleasure this edition of the Gospel by St Luke, by Canon Farrar. It is another instalment of the best school commentary of the Bible we possess. Of the expository part of the work we cannot speak too highly. It is admirable in every way, and contains just the sort of information needed for Students of the English text unable to make use of the original Greek for themselves."—*The Nonconformist and Independent.*

"As a handbook to the third gospel, this small work is invaluable. The author has compressed into little space a vast mass of scholarly information. . . The notes are pithy, vigorous, and suggestive, abounding in pertinent illustrations from general literature, and aiding the youngest reader to an intelligent appreciation of the text. A finer contribution to 'The Cambridge Bible for Schools' has not yet been made."—*Baptist Magazine.*

"We were quite prepared to find in Canon FARRAR'S **St Luke** a masterpiece of Biblical criticism and comment, and we are not disappointed by our examination of the volume before us. It reflects very faithfully the learning and critical insight of the Canon's greatest works, his 'Life of Christ' and his 'Life of St Paul', but differs widely from both in the terseness and condensation of its style. What Canon Farrar has evidently aimed at is to place before students as much information as possible within the limits of the smallest possible space, and in this aim he has hit the mark to perfection."—*The Examiner*.

The Gospel according to St John. "Of the notes we can say with confidence that they are useful, necessary, learned, and brief. To Divinity students, to teachers, and for private use, this compact Commentary will be found a valuable aid to the better understanding of the Sacred Text."—*School Guardian*.

"The new volume of the 'Cambridge Bible for Schools'—the **Gospel according to St John**, by the Rev. A. PLUMMER—shows as careful and thorough work as either of its predecessors. The introduction concisely yet fully describes the life of St John, the authenticity of the Gospel, its characteristics, its relation to the Synoptic Gospels, and to the Apostle's First Epistle, and the usual subjects referred to in an 'introduction'."—*The Christian Church*.

"The notes are extremely scholarly and valuable, and in most cases exhaustive, bringing to the elucidation of the text all that is best in commentaries, ancient and modern."—*The English Churchman and Clerical Journal*.

"(1) **The Acts of the Apostles.** By J. RAWSON LUMBY, D.D. (2) **The Second Epistle of the Corinthians**, edited by Professor LIAS. The introduction is pithy, and contains a mass of carefully-selected information on the authorship of the Acts, its designs, and its sources. ......The Second Epistle of the Corinthians is a manual beyond all praise, for the excellence of its pithy and pointed annotations, its analysis of the contents, and the fulness and value of its introduction."—*Examiner*.

"The concluding portion of the **Acts of the Apostles**, under the very competent editorship of Dr LUMBY, is a valuable addition to our school-books on that subject. Detailed criticism is impossible within the space at our command, but we may say that the ample notes touch with much exactness the very points on which most readers of the text desire information. Due reference is made, where necessary, to the Revised Version; the maps are excellent; and we do not know of any other volume where so much help is given to the complete understanding of one of the most important and, in many respects, difficult books of the New Testament."—*School Guardian*.

"The Rev. H. C. G. MOULE, M.A., has made a valuable addition to THE CAMBRIDGE BIBLE FOR SCHOOLS in his brief commentary on the **Epistle to the Romans**. The 'Notes' are very good, and lean, as the notes of a School Bible should, to the most commonly accepted and orthodox view of the inspired author's meaning; while the Introduction, and especially the Sketch of the Life of St Paul, is a model of condensation. It is as lively and pleasant to read as if two or three facts had not been crowded into well-nigh every sentence."—*Expositor*.

"**The Epistle to the Romans.** It is seldom we have met with a work so remarkable for the compression and condensation of all that is valuable in the smallest possible space as in the volume before us. Within its limited pages we have 'a sketch of the Life of St Paul,' we have further a critical account of the date of the Epistle to the Romans, of its language, and of its genuineness. The notes are numerous, full of matter, to the point, and leave no real difficulty or obscurity unexplained."—*The Examiner*.

OPINIONS OF THE PRESS.

"**The First Epistle to the Corinthians.** Edited by Professor LIAS. Every fresh instalment of this annotated edition of the Bible for Schools confirms the favourable opinion we formed of its value from the examination of its first number. The origin and plan of the Epistle are discussed with its character and genuineness."—*The Nonconformist.*

"**The Second Epistle to the Corinthians.** By Professor LIAS. **The General Epistles of St Peter and St Jude.** By E. H. PLUMPTRE, D.D. We welcome these additions to the valuable series of the Cambridge Bible. We have nothing to add to the commendation which we have from the first publication given to this edition of the Bible. It is enough to say that Professor Lias has completed his work on the two Epistles to the Corinthians in the same admirable manner as at first. Dr Plumptre has also completed the Catholic Epistles."—*Nonconformist.*

The Epistle to the Ephesians. By Rev. H. C. G. MOULE, M.A. "It seems to us the model of a School and College Commentary—comprehensive, but not cumbersome; scholarly, but not pedantic."—*Baptist Magazine.*

The Epistle to the Philippians. "There are few series more valued by theological students than 'The Cambridge Bible for Schools and Colleges,' and there will be no number of it more esteemed than that by Mr H. C. G. MOULE on the *Epistle to the Philippians*."—*Record.*

"Another capital volume of 'The Cambridge Bible for Schools and Colleges.' The notes are a model of scholarly, lucid, and compact criticism."—*Baptist Magazine.*

Hebrews. "Like his (Canon Farrar's) commentary on Luke it possesses all the best characteristics of his writing. It is a work not only of an accomplished scholar, but of a skilled teacher."—*Baptist Magazine.*

"We heartily commend this volume of this excellent work."—*Sunday School Chronicle.*

"**The General Epistle of St James,** by Professor PLUMPTRE, D.D. Nevertheless it is, so far as I know, by far the best exposition of the Epistle of St James in the English language. Not Schoolboys or Students going in for an examination alone, but Ministers and Preachers of the Word, may get more real help from it than from the most costly and elaborate commentaries."—*Expositor.*

The Epistles of St John. By the Rev. A. PLUMMER, M.A., D.D. "This forms an admirable companion to the 'Commentary on the Gospel according to St John,' which was reviewed in *The Churchman* as soon as it appeared. Dr Plummer has some of the highest qualifications for such a task; and these two volumes, their size being considered, will bear comparison with the best Commentaries of the time."—*The Churchman.*

"Dr PLUMMER's edition of **the Epistles of St John** is worthy of its companions in the 'Cambridge Bible for Schools' Series. The subject, though not apparently extensive, is really one not easy to treat, and requiring to be treated at length, owing to the constant reference to obscure heresies in the Johannine writings. Dr Plummer has done his exegetical task well."—*The Saturday Review.*

THE CAMBRIDGE GREEK TESTAMENT
FOR SCHOOLS AND COLLEGES

with a Revised Text, based on the most recent critical authorities, and English Notes, prepared under the direction of the General Editor,

THE BISHOP OF WORCESTER.

"*Has achieved an excellence which puts it above criticism.*"—Expositor.

St Matthew. "Copious illustrations, gathered from a great variety of sources, make his notes a very valuable aid to the student. They are indeed remarkably interesting, while all explanations on meanings, applications, and the like are distinguished by their lucidity and good sense."—*Pall Mall Gazette.*

St Mark. "The Cambridge Greek Testament of which Dr MACLEAR'S edition of the Gospel according to St Mark is a volume, certainly supplies a want. Without pretending to compete with the leading commentaries, or to embody very much original research, it forms a most satisfactory introduction to the study of the New Testament in the original....Dr Maclear's introduction contains all that is known of St Mark's life; an account of the circumstances in which the Gospel was composed, with an estimate of the influence of St Peter's teaching upon St Mark; an excellent sketch of the special characteristics of this Gospel; an analysis, and a chapter on the text of the New Testament generally."—*Saturday Review.*

St Luke. "Of this second series we have a new volume by Archdeacon FARRAR on *St Luke*, completing the four Gospels....It gives us in clear and beautiful language the best results of modern scholarship. We have a most attractive *Introduction*. Then follows a sort of composite Greek text, representing fairly and in very beautiful type the consensus of modern textual critics. At the beginning of the exposition of each chapter of the Gospel are a few short critical notes giving the manuscript evidence for such various readings as seem to deserve mention. The expository notes are short, but clear and helpful. For young students and those who are not disposed to buy or to study the much more costly work of Godet, this seems to us to be the best book on the Greek Text of the Third Gospel."—*Methodist Recorder.*

St John. "We take this opportunity of recommending to ministers on probation, the very excellent volume of the same series on this part of the New Testament. We hope that most or all of our young ministers will prefer to study the volume in the *Cambridge Greek Testament for Schools.*"—*Methodist Recorder.*

The Acts of the Apostles. "Professor LUMBY has performed his laborious task well, and supplied us with a commentary the fulness and freshness of which Bible students will not be slow to appreciate. The volume is enriched with the usual copious indexes and four coloured maps."—*Glasgow Herald.*

I. Corinthians. "Mr LIAS is no novice in New Testament exposition, and the present series of essays and notes is an able and helpful addition to the existing books."—*Guardian.*

The Epistles of St John. "In the very useful and well annotated series of the Cambridge Greek Testament the volume on the Epistles of St John must hold a high position... The notes are brief, well informed and intelligent."—*Scotsman.*

CAMBRIDGE: PRINTED BY C. J. CLAY, M.A. AND SONS, AT THE UNIVERSITY PRESS.

CAMBRIDGE UNIVERSITY PRESS.

THE PITT PRESS SERIES.

⁎ *Many of the books in this list can be had in two volumes, Text and Notes separately.*

I. GREEK.

Aristophanes. Aves—Plutus—Ranæ. By W. C. GREEN, M.A., late Assistant Master at Rugby School. 3s. 6d. each.
Aristotle. Outlines of the Philosophy of. By EDWIN WALLACE, M.A., LL.D. Third Edition, Enlarged. 4s. 6d.
Euripides. Heracleidae. By E. A. BECK, M.A. 3s. 6d.
—— **Hercules Furens.** By A. GRAY, M.A., and J. T. HUTCHINSON, M.A. New Edit. 2s.
—— **Hippolytus.** By W. S. HADLEY, M.A. 2s.
—— **Iphigeneia in Aulis.** By C. E. S. HEADLAM, B.A. 2s. 6d.
Herodotus, Book V. By E. S. SHUCKBURGH, M.A. 3s.
—— **Book VI.** By the same Editor. 4s.
—— **Books VIII., IX.** By the same Editor. 4s. each.
—— **Book VIII. Ch. 1—90. Book IX. Ch. 1—89.** By the same Editor. 3s. 6d. each.
Homer. Odyssey, Books IX., X. By G. M. EDWARDS, M.A. 2s. 6d. each. BOOK XXI. By the same Editor. 2s.
—— **Iliad. Book XXII.** By the same Editor. 2s.
—— —— **Book XXIII.** By the same Editor. [*Nearly ready*.
Lucian. Somnium Charon Piscator et De Luctu. By W. E. HEITLAND, M.A., Fellow of St John's College, Cambridge. 3s. 6d.
—— **Menippus and Timon.** By E. C. MACKIE, M.A. [*Nearly ready*.
Platonis Apologia Socratis. By J. ADAM, M.A. 3s. 6d.
—— **Crito.** By the same Editor. 2s. 6d.
—— **Euthyphro.** By the same Editor. 2s. 6d.
Plutarch. Lives of the Gracchi. By Rev. H. A. HOLDEN, M.A., LL.D. 6s.
—— **Life of Nicias.** By the same Editor. 5s.
—— **Life of Sulla.** By the same Editor. 6s.
—— **Life of Timoleon.** By the same Editor. 6s.
Sophocles. Oedipus Tyrannus. School Edition. By R. C. JEBB, Litt.D., LL.D. 4s. 6d.
Thucydides. Book VII. By Rev. H. A. HOLDEN, M.A., LL.D. [*Nearly ready*.
Xenophon. Agesilaus. By H. HAILSTONE, M.A. 2s. 6d.
—— **Anabasis.** By A. PRETOR, M.A. Two vols. 7s. 6d.
—— **Books I. III. IV. and V.** By the same. 2s. each.
—— **Books II. VI. and VII.** By the same. 2s. 6d. each.
Xenophon. Cyropaedeia. Books I. II. By Rev. H. A. HOLDEN, M.A., LL.D. 2 vols. 6s.
—— —— **Books III. IV. and V.** By the same Editor. 5s.
—— —— **Books VI. VII. VIII.** By the same Editor. 5s.

London: Cambridge Warehouse, Ave Maria Lane.
50/12/90

II. LATIN.

Beda's Ecclesiastical History, Books III., IV. By J. E. B. MAYOR, M.A., and J. R. LUMBY, D.D. Revised Edition. 7s. 6d.

—— **Books I. II.** By the same Editors. *[In the Press.*

Caesar. De Bello Gallico, Comment. I. By A. G. PESKETT, M.A., Fellow of Magdalene College, Cambridge. 1s. 6d. COMMENT. II. III. 2s. COMMENT. I. II. III. 3s. COMMENT. IV. and V. 1s. 6d. COMMENT. VII. 2s. COMMENT. VI. and COMMENT. VIII. 1s. 6d. each.

—— **De Bello Civili, Comment. I.** By the same Editor. 3s.

Cicero. De Amicitia.—De Senectute. By J. S. REID, Litt.D., Fellow of Gonville and Caius College. 3s. 6d. each.

—— **In Gaium Verrem Actio Prima.** By H. COWIE, M.A. 1s. 6d.

—— **In Q. Caecilium Divinatio et in C. Verrem Actio.** By W. E. HEITLAND, M.A., and H. COWIE, M.A. 3s.

—— **Philippica Secunda.** By A. G. PESKETT, M.A. 3s. 6d.

—— **Oratio pro Archia Poeta.** By J. S. REID, Litt.D. 2s.

—— **Pro L. Cornelio Balbo Oratio.** By the same. 1s. 6d.

—— **Oratio pro Tito Annio Milone.** By JOHN SMYTH PURTON, B.D. 2s. 6d.

—— **Oratio pro L. Murena.** By W. E. HEITLAND, M.A. 3s.

—— **Pro Cn. Plancio Oratio,** by H. A. HOLDEN, LL.D. 4s. 6d.

—— **Pro P. Cornelio Sulla.** By J. S. REID, Litt.D. 3s. 6d.

—— **Somnium Scipionis.** By W. D. PEARMAN, M.A. 2s.

Horace. Epistles, Book I. By E. S. SHUCKBURGH, M.A., late Fellow of Emmanuel College. 2s. 6d.

Livy. Book IV. By H. M. STEPHENSON, M.A. 2s. 6d.

—— **Book V.** By L. WHIBLEY, M.A. 2s. 6d.

—— **Books XXI., XXII.** By M. S. DIMSDALE, M.A., Fellow of King's College. 2s. 6d. each.

—— **Book XXVII.** By Rev. H. M. STEPHENSON, M.A. 2s. 6d.

Lucan. Pharsaliae Liber Primus. By W. E. HEITLAND, M.A., and C. E. HASKINS, M.A. 1s. 6d.

Lucretius, Book V. By J. D. DUFF, M.A. 2s.

Ovidii Nasonis Fastorum Liber VI. By A. SIDGWICK, M.A., Tutor of Corpus Christi College, Oxford. 1s. 6d.

Quintus Curtius. A Portion of the History (Alexander in India). By W. E. HEITLAND, M.A., and T. E. RAVEN, B.A. With Two Maps. 3s. 6d.

Vergili Maronis Aeneidos Libri I.—XII. By A. SIDGWICK, M.A. 1s. 6d. each.

—— **Bucolica.** By the same Editor. 1s. 6d.

—— **Georgicon Libri I. II.** By the same Editor. 2s.

—— —— **Libri III. IV.** By the same Editor. 2s.

—— **The Complete Works.** By the same Editor. Two vols. Vol. I. containing the Introduction and Text. 3s. 6d. Vol. II. The Notes. 4s. 6d.

London: Cambridge Warehouse, Ave Maria Lane.

III. FRENCH.

Corneille. La Suite du Menteur. A Comedy in Five Acts.
By the late G. MASSON, B.A. 2s.

De Bonnechose. Lazare Hoche. By C. COLBECK, M.A.
Revised Edition. Four Maps. 2s.

D'Harleville. Le Vieux Célibataire. By G. MASSON, B.A. 2s.

De Lamartine. Jeanne D'Arc. By Rev. A. C. CLAPIN,
M.A. New edition revised, by A. R. ROPES, M.A. 1s. 6d.

De Vigny. La Canne de Jonc. By Rev. H. A. BULL,
M.A., late Master at Wellington College. 2s.

Erckmann-Chatrian. La Guerre. By Rev. A. C. CLAPIN,
M.A. 3s.

La Baronne de Staël-Holstein. Le Directoire. (Considérations sur la Révolution Française. Troisième et quatrième parties.) Revised and enlarged. By G. MASSON, B.A., and G. W. PROTHERO, M.A. 2s.

—— —— **Dix Années d'Exil. Livre II. Chapitres 1—8.**
By the same Editors. New Edition, enlarged. 2s.

Lemercier. Fredegonde et Brunehaut. A Tragedy in Five
Acts. By GUSTAVE MASSON, B.A. 2s.

Molière. Le Bourgeois Gentilhomme, Comédie-Ballet en
Cinq Actes. (1670.) By Rev. A. C. CLAPIN, M.A. Revised Edition. 1s. 6d.

—— **L'Ecole des Femmes.** By G. SAINTSBURY, M.A. 2s. 6d.

—— **Les Précieuses Ridicules.** By E. G. W. BRAUNHOLTZ,
M.A., Ph.D. 2s.

—— —— **Abridged Edition.** 1s.

Piron. La Métromanie. A Comedy. By G. MASSON, B.A. 2s.

Racine. Les Plaideurs. By E. G. W. BRAUNHOLTZ, M.A. 2s.

—— —— **Abridged Edition.** 1s.

Sainte-Beuve. M. Daru (Causeries du Lundi, Vol. IX.).
By G. MASSON, B.A. 2s.

Saintine. Picciola. By Rev. A. C. CLAPIN, M.A. 2s.

Scribe and Legouvé. Bataille de Dames. By Rev. H. A.
BULL, M.A. 2s.

Scribe. Le Verre d'Eau. By C. COLBECK, M.A. 2s.

Sédaine. Le Philosophe sans le savoir. By Rev. H. A.
BULL, M.A. 2s.

Thierry. Lettres sur l'histoire de France (XIII.—XXIV.).
By G. MASSON, B.A., and G. W. PROTHERO, M.A. 2s. 6d.

—— **Récits des Temps Mérovingiens I.—III.** By GUSTAVE
MASSON, B.A. Univ. Gallic., and A. R. ROPES, M.A. With Map. 3s.

Villemain. Lascaris ou Les Grecs du XVe Siècle, Nouvelle
Historique. By G. MASSON, B.A. 2s.

Voltaire. Histoire du Siècle de Louis XIV. Chaps. I.—
XIII. By G. MASSON, B.A., and G. W. PROTHERO, M.A. 2s. 6d. PART II.
CHAPS. XIV.—XXIV. 2s. 6d. PART III. CHAPS. XXV. to end. 2s. 6d.

Xavier de Maistre. La Jeune Sibérienne. Le Lépreux de
la Cité D'Aoste. By G. MASSON, B.A. 1s. 6d.

London: Cambridge Warehouse, Ave Maria Lane.

IV. GERMAN.

Ballads on German History. By W. WAGNER, Ph.D. 2s.

Benedix. Doctor Wespe. Lustspiel in fünf Aufzügen. By KARL HERMANN BREUL, M.A., Ph.D. 3s.

Freytag. Der Staat Friedrichs des Grossen. By WILHELM WAGNER, Ph.D. 2s.

German Dactylic Poetry. By WILHELM WAGNER, Ph.D. 3s.

Goethe's Knabenjahre. (1749—1759.) By W. WAGNER, Ph.D. New edition revised and enlarged, by J. W. CARTMELL, M.A. 2s.

—— **Hermann und Dorothea.** By WILHELM WAGNER, Ph.D. New edition revised, by J. W. CARTMELL, M.A. 3s. 6d.

Gutzkow. Zopf und Schwert. Lustspiel in fünf Aufzügen. By H. J. WOLSTENHOLME, B.A. (Lond.). 3s. 6d.

Hauff. Das Bild des Kaisers. By KARL HERMANN BREUL, M.A., Ph.D., University Lecturer in German. 3s.

—— **Das Wirthshaus im Spessart.** By A. SCHLOTTMANN, Ph.D. 3s. 6d.

—— **Die Karavane.** By A. SCHLOTTMANN, Ph.D. 3s. 6d.

Immermann. Der Oberhof. A Tale of Westphalian Life, by WILHELM WAGNER, Ph.D. 3s.

Kohlrausch. Das Jahr 1813. By WILHELM WAGNER, Ph.D. 2s.

Lessing and Gellert. Selected Fables. By KARL HERMANN BREUL, M.A., Ph.D. 3s.

Mendelssohn's Letters. Selections from. By J. SIME, M.A. 3s.

Raumer. Der erste Kreuzzug (1095—1099). By WILHELM WAGNER, Ph.D. 2s.

Riehl. Culturgeschichtliche Novellen. By H. J. WOLSTENHOLME, B.A. (Lond.). 3s. 6d.

Schiller. Wilhelm Tell. By KARL HERMANN BREUL, M.A., Ph.D. 2s. 6d.

—— —— **Abridged Edition.** 1s. 6d.

Uhland. Ernst, Herzog von Schwaben. By H. J. WOLSTENHOLME, B.A. 3s. 6d.

V. ENGLISH.

Ancient Philosophy from Thales to Cicero, A Sketch of. By JOSEPH B. MAYOR, M.A. 3s. 6d.

An Apologie for Poetrie by Sir PHILIP SIDNEY. By E. S. SHUCKBURGH, M.A. The Text is a revision of that of the first edition of 1595. 3s.

Bacon's History of the Reign of King Henry VII. By the Rev. Professor LUMBY, D.D. 3s.

Cowley's Essays. By the Rev. Professor LUMBY, D.D. 4s.

London: Cambridge Warehouse, Ave Maria Lane.

Milton's Comus and Arcades. By A. W. VERITY, M.A.,
sometime Scholar of Trinity College. 3s.

More's History of King Richard III. By J. RAWSON LUMBY,
D.D. 3s. 6d.

More's Utopia. By Rev. Prof. LUMBY, D.D. 3s. 6d.

The Two Noble Kinsmen. By the Rev. Professor SKEAT,
Litt.D. 3s. 6d.

VI. EDUCATIONAL SCIENCE.

Comenius, John Amos, Bishop of the Moravians. His Life
and Educational Works, by S. S. LAURIE, A.M., F.R.S.E. 3s. 6d.

Education, Three Lectures on the Practice of. I. On Marking, by H. W. EVE, M.A. II. On Stimulus, by A. SIDGWICK, M.A. III. On the Teaching of Latin Verse Composition, by E. A. ABBOTT, D.D. 2s.

Stimulus. A Lecture delivered for the Teachers' Training
Syndicate, May, 1882, by A. SIDGWICK, M.A. 1s.

Locke on Education. By the Rev. R. H. QUICK, M.A. 3s. 6d.

Milton's Tractate on Education. A facsimile reprint from
the Edition of 1673. By O. BROWNING, M.A. 2s.

Modern Languages, Lectures on the Teaching of. By C.
COLBECK, M.A. 2s.

Teacher, General Aims of the, and Form Management. Two
Lectures delivered in the University of Cambridge in the Lent Term, 1883, by
F. W. FARRAR, D.D., and R. B. POOLE, B.D. 1s. 6d.

Teaching, Theory and Practice of. By the Rev. E. THRING,
M.A., late Head Master of Uppingham School. New Edition. 4s. 6d.

British India, a Short History of. By E. S. CARLOS, M.A.,
late Head Master of Exeter Grammar School. 1s.

Geography, Elementary Commercial. A Sketch of the Commodities and the Countries of the World. By H. R. MILL, D.Sc., F.R.S.E. 1s.

Geography, an Atlas of Commercial. (A Companion to the
above.) By J. G. BARTHOLOMEW, F.R.G.S. With an Introduction by HUGH
ROBERT MILL, D.Sc. 3s.

VII. MATHEMATICS.

Euclid's Elements of Geometry. Books I. and II. By H. M.
TAYLOR, M.A., Fellow and late Tutor of Trinity College, Cambridge. 1s. 6d.

——— ——— Books III. and IV. By the same Editor. 1s. 6d.

——— ——— Books I.—IV., in one Volume. 3s.

Elementary Algebra (with Answers to the Examples). By
W. W. ROUSE BALL, M.A. 4s. 6d.

Elements of Statics. By S. L. LONEY, M.A. 5s.

Elements of Dynamics. By the same Editor. [*Nearly ready.*
Other Volumes are in preparation.

London: Cambridge Warehouse, Ave Maria Lane.

The Cambridge Bible for Schools and Colleges.

GENERAL EDITOR: J. J. S. PEROWNE, D.D.,
BISHOP OF WORCESTER.

"It is difficult to commend too highly this excellent series.—Guardian.

"The modesty of the general title of this series has, we believe, led many to misunderstand its character and underrate its value. The books are well suited for study in the upper forms of our best schools, but not the less are they adapted to the wants of all Bible students who are not specialists. We doubt, indeed, whether any of the numerous popular commentaries recently issued in this country will be found more serviceable for general use."—Academy.

Now Ready. Cloth, Extra Fcap. 8vo. With Maps.

Book of Joshua. By Rev. G. F. MACLEAR, D.D. 2s. 6d.
Book of Judges. By Rev. J. J. LIAS, M.A. 3s. 6d.
First Book of Samuel. By Rev. Prof. KIRKPATRICK, B.D. 3s. 6d.
Second Book of Samuel. By the same Editor. 3s. 6d.
First Book of Kings. By Rev. Prof. LUMBY, D.D. 3s. 6d.
Second Book of Kings. By Rev. Prof. LUMBY, D.D. 3s. 6d.
Book of Job. By Rev. A. B. DAVIDSON, D.D. 5s.
Book of Ecclesiastes. By Very Rev. E. H. PLUMPTRE, D.D. 5s.
Book of Jeremiah. By Rev. A. W. STREANE, M.A. 4s. 6d.
Book of Hosea. By Rev. T. K. CHEYNE, M.A., D.D. 3s.
Books of Obadiah & Jonah. By Archdeacon PEROWNE. 2s. 6d.
Book of Micah. By Rev. T. K. CHEYNE, M.A., D.D. 1s. 6d.
Haggai, Zechariah & Malachi. By Arch. PEROWNE. 3s. 6d.
Book of Malachi. By Archdeacon PEROWNE. 1s.
Gospel according to St Matthew. By Rev. A. CARR, M.A. 2s. 6d.
Gospel according to St Mark. By Rev. G. F. MACLEAR, D.D. 2s. 6d.
Gospel according to St Luke. By Arch. FARRAR, D.D. 4s. 6d.
Gospel according to St John. By Rev. A. PLUMMER, D.D. 4s. 6d.
Acts of the Apostles. By Rev. Prof. LUMBY, D.D. 4s. 6d.
Epistle to the Romans. By Rev. H. C. G. MOULE, M.A. 3s. 6d.
First Corinthians. By Rev. J. J. LIAS, M.A. With Map. 2s.
Second Corinthians. By Rev. J. J. LIAS, M.A. With Map. 2s.
Epistle to the Galatians. By Rev. E. H. PEROWNE, D.D. 1s. 6d.

London: Cambridge Warehouse, Ave Maria Lane.

Epistle to the Ephesians. By Rev. H. C. G. MOULE, M.A. 2s. 6d.
Epistle to the Philippians. By the same Editor. 2s. 6d.
Epistles to the Thessalonians. By Rev. G. G. FINDLAY, M.A. 2s.
Epistle to the Hebrews. By Arch. FARRAR, D.D. 3s. 6d.
General Epistle of St James. By Very Rev. E. H. PLUMPTRE, D.D. 1s. 6d.
Epistles of St Peter and St Jude. By Very Rev. E. H. PLUMPTRE, D.D. 2s. 6d.
Epistles of St John. By Rev. A. PLUMMER, M.A., D.D. 3s. 6d.
Book of Revelation. By Rev. W. H. SIMCOX, M.A. 3s.

Preparing.

Book of Genesis. By the BISHOP OF WORCESTER.
Books of Exodus, Numbers and Deuteronomy. By Rev. C. D. GINSBURG, LL.D.
Books of Ezra and Nehemiah. By Rev. Prof. RYLE, M.A.
Book of Psalms. Part I. By Rev. Prof. KIRKPATRICK, B.D.
Book of Isaiah. By Prof. W. ROBERTSON SMITH, M.A.
Book of Ezekiel. By Rev. A. B. DAVIDSON, D.D.
Epistles to the Colossians and Philemon. By Rev. H. C. G. MOULE, M.A.
Epistles to Timothy & Titus. By Rev. A. E. HUMPHREYS, M.A.

The Smaller Cambridge Bible for Schools.

The Smaller Cambridge Bible for Schools *will form an entirely new series of commentaries on some selected books of the Bible. It is expected that they will be prepared for the most part by the Editors of the larger series (The Cambridge Bible for Schools and Colleges). The volumes will be issued at a low price, and will be suitable to the requirements of preparatory and elementary schools.*

Now ready.

First and Second Books of Samuel. By Rev. Prof. KIRKPATRICK, B.D. 1s. each.
First Book of Kings. By Rev. Prof. LUMBY, D.D. 1s.
Gospel according to St Matthew. By Rev. A. CARR, M.A. 1s.
Gospel according to St Mark. By Rev. G. F. MACLEAR, D.D. 1s.
Gospel according to St Luke. By Archdeacon FARRAR. 1s.
Acts of the Apostles. By Rev. Prof. LUMBY, D.D. 1s.

Nearly ready.

Second Book of Kings. By Rev. Prof. LUMBY, D.D.
Gospel according to St John. By Rev. A. PLUMMER, D.D.

London: Cambridge Warehouse, Ave Maria Lane.

The Cambridge Greek Testament for Schools and Colleges,

with a Revised Text, based on the most recent critical authorities, and English Notes, prepared under the direction of the

GENERAL EDITOR, J. J. S. PEROWNE, D.D.,
BISHOP OF WORCESTER.

Gospel according to St Matthew. By Rev. A. CARR, M.A.
With 4 Maps. 4s. 6d.

Gospel according to St Mark. By Rev. G. F. MACLEAR, D.D.
With 3 Maps. 4s. 6d.

Gospel according to St Luke. By Archdeacon FARRAR.
With 4 Maps. 6s.

Gospel according to St John. By Rev. A. PLUMMER, D.D.
With 4 Maps. 6s.

Acts of the Apostles. By Rev. Professor LUMBY, D.D.
With 4 Maps. 6s.

First Epistle to the Corinthians. By Rev. J. J. LIAS, M.A. 3s.

Second Epistle to the Corinthians. By Rev. J. J. LIAS, M.A.
[*In the Press.*]

Epistle to the Hebrews. By Archdeacon FARRAR, D.D. 3s. 6d.

Epistle of St James. By Very Rev. E. H. PLUMPTRE, D.D.
[*Preparing.*]

Epistles of St John. By Rev. A. PLUMMER, M.A., D.D. 4s.

London: C. J. CLAY AND SONS,
CAMBRIDGE WAREHOUSE, AVE MARIA LANE.
Glasgow: 263, ARGYLE STREET.
Cambridge: DEIGHTON, BELL AND CO.
Leipzig: F. A. BROCKHAUS.
New York: MACMILLAN AND CO.

www.ingramcontent.com/pod-product-compliance
Lightning Source LLC
Chambersburg PA
CBHW030306170426
43202CB00009B/885